Arrow Rock

Crossroads of the Missouri Frontier

Arrow Rock

Crossroads of the Missouri Frontier

by Michael Dickey

Published by
The Friends of Arrow Rock, Inc.
Arrow Rock, Missouri

Published by The Friends of Arrow Rock, Inc.,
Arrow Rock, Missouri.

First Edition

Library of Congress Control Number: 2004103966

ISBN 0-9753577-0-0

Front cover: *The County Election*, 1852, George Caleb Bingham, American, 1811–1879;
oil on canvas; The Saint Louis Art Museum.

Back cover, left to right: George Caleb Bingham, the excursion boat *Idlewild*, John Sappington
Marmaduke. Photos: Missouri Department of Natural Resources & State Historical Society
of Missouri.

Printed in the United States by
United Graphics, Inc., Mattoon, Illinois.

Dedication

This history is dedicated to the memory of Jean Tyree Hamilton, who wrote *Arrow Rock: Where Wheels Started West* for the Friends of Arrow Rock in 1963 and who was instrumental in efforts to preserve this historic community.

Contents

Publisher's Preface

THE FRIENDS OF ARROW ROCK ARE PLEASED TO PUBLISH THIS NEW HISTORY of the town of Arrow Rock and its vicinity, as part of the 45th anniversary celebration of our organization. During the tenure of the late Sue Stubbs, president of the Friends from May 2001 to January 2004, the FAR commissioned Michael Dickey to write a new and updated history of Arrow Rock to carry on the tradition so ably begun by Jean Tyree Hamilton. The Friends published Mrs. Hamilton's popular illustrated history, *Arrow Rock: Where Wheels Started West*, in 1963. After several revisions, it is now out of print. In author Michael Dickey, Arrow Rock has found a very capable new historian, and the Friends are most grateful to Mr. Dickey for his thorough research, skillful writing, and careful attention to this project.

For a town whose current population is only 79, Arrow Rock has a fascinating and important history that has been recorded by a series of talented historians, with Michael Dickey as a worthy new member of that group. From the first recorded visit to the site of Arrow Rock on April 20, 1714, by the French explorer, Etienne de Véniard, sieur de Bourgmont, preserved in his 1714 report, "The Route to Be Taken to Ascend the Missouri River," to the description of the site of Arrow Rock by Meriwether Lewis and William Clark when their expedition passed by the future site of the town on June 9, 1804, and up to the present, Arrow Rock has not lacked for narrators of its colorful history.

John Beauchamp Jones' 1854 *Life and Adventures of a Country Merchant* gives an account of his life as a storekeeper in Arrow Rock, as does T. C. Rainey's 1914 publication, *Along the Old Trail: Pioneer Sketches of Arrow Rock and Vicinity*. William B. Napton, Jr. both lived and recorded dramatic history along the Santa Fe Trail from Arrow Rock. The anonymous author of the 1881 *History of Saline County, Missouri* ably preserved the terrible history of the Civil War in the Arrow Rock neighborhood.

More recent historians have included Charles van Ravenswaay, Director of the Missouri Historical Society and author of the April, 1959 article "Arrow Rock: The Story of a Town, Its People and Its Tavern." This article may be regarded as the impetus for the formation of the Friends of Arrow Rock at a meeting of the Old Tavern Board of the Missouri State Society of the Daughters of the American Revolution at the Tavern on June 14 of that year. Other recent Arrow Rock historians, in addition to Jean Tyree Hamilton, have been John Percy Huston, Sr., Paul Biggs, F. C. Barnhill, Thomas B. Hall, Jr., Pauline Sappington Elsea, John R. Hall, Jr., Richard R. Forry, Virginia Lee Fisher, Lynn Morrow, Catherine Waters Kennedy, Gary R. Kremer, and Timothy E. Baumann, all equally dedicated to telling aspects of the story of this one small town on the Missouri River. Now Michael Dickey has written the most comprehensive history of Arrow Rock to date, with information from numerous sources, giving us the context of life in this region from the time of the native Indian inhabitants to the 21st century.

The Friends of Arrow Rock wish to express our gratitude to the State Historical Society of Missouri and its Executive Director, James W. Goodrich, for providing a Brownlee Grant, which partially funded the publication of this book. The Friends invite you to join us in our work of preserving Arrow Rock and telling its story. We feel that a renewed emphasis on teaching American history in our schools is especially important at this time, and the Friends are committed to using our restored buildings and collections in Arrow Rock to further this effort. We hope you will join us in this endeavor.

Thomas B. Hall III, M.D.
President, Friends of Arrow Rock, Inc.
P.O. Box 124
Arrow Rock, Missouri 65320
(660) 837-3231
www.Friendsar.org
office@friendsar.org

June 14, 2004

Acknowledgments

MANY INDIVIDUALS CONTRIBUTED TO THE DEVELOPMENT OF THIS PUBLICATION, directly and indirectly. A great debt is owed them for research, transcription of documents, reviewing text, and providing the encouragement that made this book possible.

Special thanks to my mentor Richard R. Forry, Ph.D., for pointing out all the resources and notes over the years; to Louis F. Burns, Hulah Kiheka (Eagle Chief) of the Osage Mottled Eagle Clan, for reviewing the sections on Native American history; to Catherine Waters Kennedy and William Lay, for researching original documents and compiling them for easy use.

Many members of the Friends of Arrow Rock contributed to the editing of the book. Thanks to Sue Stubbs, Margaret Lyddon, and Bill Lovin for reading the initial manuscript and offering suggestions; to Mary Burge, David Finke, Day Kerr, and Sarah Riddick for proofreading; and to Executive Director Kathy Borgman and Education Director Pam Parsons who served as project managers doing a multitude of tasks to keep the process moving along. Thanks also to Dr. Tom Hall who paid attention to countless details from the beginning to the end of the editing process.

I would like to thank my daughter, Ruth, who put her new graphic arts degree to work scanning and "tweaking" the photographs and developing maps, and my wife, Diana, for putting up with all the late hours on the computer.

Foreword

AS ENUMERATED BY DR. HALL IN THE PUBLISHER'S PREFACE, NUMEROUS individuals have been recording and compiling Arrow Rock's history. However, this information has never been used to write a comprehensive general history book for the public. The goal of this publication is to help fill that gap. This publication emphasizes the period from 1732, when the name "Arrow Rock" was first published, to 1901, when the town was devastated by fire and nearly passed into oblivion.

There are no new major revelations here. This book relies primarily on secondary materials and existing research. It is merely an attempt to compile that information into one format. Every effort is made to credit each source of information properly, and any failure to do so is purely accidental. I apologize in advance for the inevitable mistakes that occur when trying to write a complex document. Spelling in period quotations adheres to the documents cited. Therefore, do not be surprised when you see "woods" spelled as "wods."

Period quotations and phraseology are used whenever practical to convey the perceptions and attitudes of the times. Some of these may offend modern sensibilities, but it is important to convey "the good, the bad and the ugly" of history. Different sources may offer conflicting information and dates for the same incident. Information from the 1880s county histories is used even though they must be read with a critical eye. Though notorious for errors, these histories do contain nuggets of truth and convey past perceptions of historical events. In some cases, they are the only surviving source of information about a particular event.

Subjects relating to women and minorities were especially difficult to write. Women impacted society in the 18th and 19th centuries but were seldom in the forefront of leadership. African Americans were disenfranchised and frequently illiterate and thus unable to record and transmit much information. American Indians had no written language, so we rely largely upon the interpretations of traders or government officials for their stories. Oral traditions of these groups become important in conveying their perceptions of events. It is the intent of the author to examine these facets as much as possible.

This volume should not be regarded as the definitive book on Arrow Rock history. This author has discovered much primary research remains to be done. For example, probate and county court records remain largely untapped. A large volume could be researched and written on almost any topic mentioned in this book. It is my hope this book will spur more research and publications on the history of Arrow Rock and central Missouri.

Introduction

APPROXIMATELY 200,000 PEOPLE ANNUALLY VISIT ARROW ROCK, Missouri. Some merely take a "windshield tour," while others linger a day or more. A small town with a population of only 79, historic Arrow Rock represents a microcosm of the frontier experience in Missouri. Established in 1829, the town of Arrow Rock is located in the central Missouri region known historically as the "Boonslick Country."

Located at the intersection of the Missouri River and the Santa Fe Trail, Arrow Rock became one of the busiest trade centers between Kansas City and St. Louis. Immigrants and commercial traffic following the two major thoroughfares made Arrow Rock a crossroads of the Missouri frontier. Long before there was a town, the Arrow Rock bluff was a landmark for Native American tribes and early European explorers.

The 1881 *History of Saline County* correctly states:

> *The history of this township would fill a large volume. Its early settlement, its prominence for so long in the history of the county, the number of its citizens prominent and leading in state and national affairs, its vast resources and natural wealth, added to the substantial development made of them — all place it among the very first townships, not only in Saline county, but in the state of Missouri.*[1]

Recognition of this prominent role led some early historians to proclaim Arrow Rock and its 1834 Tavern as "the most historic spot in Missouri."[2] Preservation of the Arrow Rock Tavern led to its establishment as Missouri's oldest state historic site. In many respects, Arrow Rock can truly be considered the birthplace of modern historic preservation efforts in Missouri.

In 1963, Arrow Rock was designated a National Historic Landmark by the Department of the Interior, National Park Service. This is the highest designation a historic property can have. The National Park Service has also certified sites within the community as part of the Santa Fe National Historic Trail and the Lewis and Clark National Historic Trail. Arrow Rock residents take seriously their community's role in history and the ambiance of the town. They seek to maintain it as a crossroads for the traveler today.

ARROW ROCK

LOCATED IN ARROW ROCK TWP.

Scale 300 ft. to one inch.

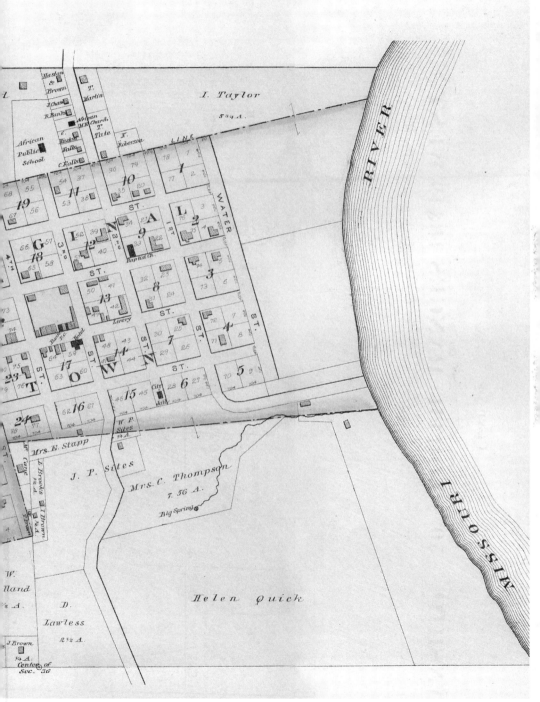

Plat map of Arrow Rock in 1896. Thirty-six years earlier, the number of buildings in town was probably almost double what this map showed. *Friends of Arrow Rock, Inc.*

10

Arrow Rock and Vicinity, Key to Historic Landmarks

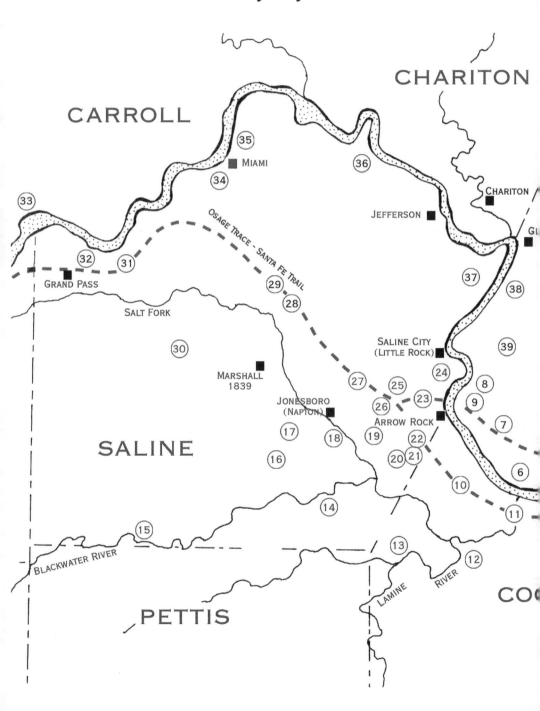

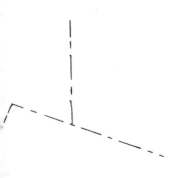

HOWARD

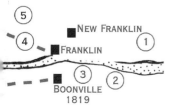

(*Locations are approximations*)

1. Head's Fort, ca. 1812–1816
2. Stephen Cole's Fort, ca. 1812–1816
3. Hannah Cole's Fort, ca. 1812–1816
4. Kincaid's Fort, ca. 1812–1816
5. Fort Hempstead, ca. 1812–1816
6. John Hardeman's Gardens and Ferry
7. Home of Ezekiel Williams
8. Boone's Lick Salt Works
9. Cooper's Fort, ca. 1812–1816
10. Jones, Turley, and McMahan Settlement: Reid's Fort and McMahan's Fort, ca. 1812–1814 (both burned)
11. Lamine Ferry Crossing
12. Chouteau Springs Salt Works
13. George Heath's Salt Works
14. "Elk Hill," home of William B. Napton, Sr. and Jr.
15. Edward Reavis' Blackwater Settlement
16. Pennytown
17. "Experiment," home of General Thomas A. Smith
18. "Oak Grove," plantation of George Murrell
19. Home of Meredith Miles Marmaduke
20. "Pilot Hickory," home of Dr. John Sappington, renamed "Fox Castle" by Claiborne Fox Jackson
21. Sappington Cemetery and Sappington Negro Cemetery
22. "Prairie Park," home of William B. Sappington
23. Sibley's Osage Trading House, 1813–1814
24. Cox's Bottoms: Cox's Fort, ca. 1812–1816
25. "Chestnut Hill," home of Philip W. Thompson
26. "Lo Mismo," home of John Locke Hardeman and Dr. Glen O. Hardeman
27. Neff Tavern, Smokehouse and Cemetery
28. Maupin Tavern
29. Harvey Springs
30. Big Salt Spring, Salt Works of Col. John Smith T
31. Little Osage Indian Village, ca. 1719–1780
32. Missouri Indian Village, ca. 1725–1790
33. Fort Orleans, ca. 1723–1728
34. Missouri Indian Village, ca. 600 AD to 1725 (Van Meter State Park)
35. Piankashaw Miami Indian Village, ca. 1812–1814
36. Edmondson Bottoms, (early settlement area)
37. Big Bottoms, (early settlement area)
38. Home of Dr. John Sappington, 1817–1819
39. Lindsay Carson Farm, (Boyhood Home of Frontiersman Kit Carson)
40. Claiborne Fox Jackson residence, ca. 1837–1856
41. Home of Judge Abiel Leonard

Origins

Native Americans, Coureurs des Bois and Frenchmen

The great muddy Pekitanoui River was first recorded on a map in 1673 by French explorers, Marquette and Joliet, as they followed the upper Mississippi River. Later, on April 9, 1682, Robert Sieur de la Salle claimed the vast territory drained by the Mississippi and its tributaries for France naming it "Louisiana" in honor of King Louis xiv.[3] Itinerant French-Canadian hunters known as "coureurs des bois" or woods runners were even then wandering into Louisiana seeking the pelts of beaver, deer, bear and otter and trading with the native peoples.

Some unnamed coureurs des bois followed the Pekitanoui upstream and reached the principal village of the Oumessourit native nation located in what is now Van Meter State Park. Oumessourit was corrupted into "Missouri." The river became identified with this Indian nation of 5,000 people living on the high bluffs known as the Pinnacles. Thus, the Pekitanoui River eventually became the Missouri River. The name Oumessourit was from the neighboring Peoria tribe and means "he (or people) of big canoe,"[4] a reference to the 30-foot long wooden dugout canoes these people used on the river. They called themselves "Niutachi," meaning something like "people at the river mouth."[5]

The coureurs des bois had passed a prominent flint-bearing limestone bluff located about 40 miles downriver or 20 miles by land from the Missouri village. This bluff became such a significant landmark to the French in 1732 that cartographer d'Anville identified it on his map, "Carte de la Louisiane" as "Pierre à Fleche," literally meaning "Rock of Arrows."[6] Eighty-seven years later, American explorer Major Stephen Long explained the origin of the name: "Arrow Rock is so-called from its having been formerly resorted to by neighboring Indians, for the stone used to point their arrows."[7]

Long's explanation for the Arrow Rock name was reiterated April 14, 1833, by Maximilian, Prince of the German state of Wied. "We lay for the night at Arrow Rock, a chain in which flint is found of which the Indians formerly made heads of their arrows,"[8] he wrote. He was touring the American West to study the native cultures, and in his employ was Swiss artist, Karl Bodmer. As a result of this trip, Bodmer went on to produce a series of some of the most striking and detailed images of Northern Plains Indians ever rendered. This series included one of only two illustrations known to exist of a Missouri Indian. His sketchbook also had a pencil rendering of the bluff line at the Arrow Rock.

Concentrations of charred flint nodules, tools and points in various stages of manufacture clearly show Arrow Rock was a manufacturing site. Some of the implements point to native cultures inhabiting the area as far back as 12,000 years. Thomas C. Rainey, an early chronicler of Arrow Rock, speculated in 1914, "...that the region ...was neutral territory, visited alike by the tribes of the upper river and the surrounding territory."[9] Rainey based his theory on the red pipestone quarries of Minnesota, which were sacred and therefore neutral ground for all native peoples. Western artist George Catlin documented this fact in 1832 from various Indian nations themselves. However, there is no direct evidence supporting this theory for Arrow Rock. Rainey was correct, though, in stating, "One of the reasons Arrow Rock was chosen as a place to make arrowheads is, doubtless, because there is not any where up the river and near to it, any other considerable outcropping of flint."[10]

Several colorful but apocryphal tales about the origin of the name Arrow Rock appeared in the late 19th century and were published through the 1950s. One said a group of "Indian braves" camped on the opposite side of the river entered an archery contest for the right to marry a "...beautiful daughter of the chief." The chief would give her "...to the one who could stand on the bank of the river and strike with an arrow shot from a bow, the white rock bluff on the western bank ...one after another they saw their arrows fall short of the mark and splash in the waters of the Big Muddy. The last Indian to shoot was the one the maiden loved...the arrow sped out over the waters of the Big Muddy and on and on and on until it landed on the white bluff on the western shore. The happy Indian maiden cried out to her father in broken English, 'Arrow Rock.'"[11]

Another story says the site was the scene of a massive battle between Indian tribes, one situated on top of the bluff and the other below it. "Afterwards the site was found to abound in these arrowheads, which all pointed one way as they lay on the earth, and the first whites that landed at the bluff gave it the name it now bears."[12] Finally, in the frontier dialect of southern origin, the word "arrow" was sometimes actually pronounced as "airy." But, in the phraseology of the Victorian period, "airy" meant "cool or breezy." Thus, there was a point on the bluff where Indians gathered on hot days to feel the cool breeze rising from the river. "The name of this point was 'windy rock' or 'airy rock,' the latter designation being more commonly used. Airy rock was eventually corrupted into 'Arrow Rock.'"[13] These stories are merely interesting pieces of local folklore.

First Nations: The Missouri and the Osage

The Missouri were the dominant Indian nation in the Arrow Rock area, descendants of the Oneota culture, which had occupied the Pinnacles site for over 600 years. Several miles to the west were the high river bottoms known as the "Petite Osage" or "Petitsaw" plains. Two to three thousand Little Osage people were living there by 1719, although they may have been contemporaries of the Oneota. "Little" was a misnomer, for the Osage were not small of stature, especially compared to Europeans of the time. In 1811, John Bradbury wrote this description: "The Osage are so tall and robust as almost to warrant the application of the term gigantic; few of them appear to be under six feet tall, and many above it. Their shoulders and visages are broad, which tends to strengthen the idea of their being giants."[14]

The Little Osage were the U-Dse-Ta or the "Down Below People" because they traditionally lived below a hill or bluff. The French apparently misunderstood Osage sign language for "down below" as meaning "little." The other Osage bands lived on higher ground and were thus called the Big Osage. The name "Osage" was a French corruption of Wah-sha-she, the name of one particular band. They actually called themselves Ni-U-Ko'n-Ska, "Children of the Middle Waters," a reference to the great river systems of their homeland.[15] They called the Frenchmen I'n-Shta-Heh, meaning "Heavy Eyebrows," contrasting the abundant facial hair of the French to the lack of their own.[16]

A substantial amount of information exists about the Osage lifestyle and material culture. Little information survives about the culture of the Missouri tribe. They ceased to be an independent nation long before Euro-Americans began making anthropological records. As early as 1804, William Clark wrote of their decline: "This nation once the most numerous nation in this part of the continent now reduced to about 80 fies [families] and that few under the protection of the Otos on the River Platt who are themselves declining."[17] Some assumptions are made about Missouri culture based on archaeological evidence and the known habits of neighboring tribes. Cultural elements of the woodland tribes to the east and the plains tribes to the west met and mixed in the prairie homeland of the Little Osage and Missouri tribes.

Both tribes spoke dialects of the Siouan language; the Osage dialect, called Dheigan and the Missouri, known as Chiwere. Their lodges were round or oval in shape, 15 to 30 feet in diameter, and consisted of woven mats of cattails or reeds overlaid on a framework of saplings. In the spring and again in the fall, almost the entire tribe would pack up and hunt buffalo on the Great Plains. Every aspect of their activities was regulated by highly sophisticated and complex ceremonies rooted in hundreds of years of tradition. Through these, they maintained social order and a perspective on their relationship to the universe.[18]

Many explorers and pioneers claimed that Indian men were idle and lazy while women were treated like chattel. This perception is incorrect. The Osage women planted fields of corn, squash and beans in the spring and gathered roots, nuts and berries in their season. They owned the fields, lodges and the property they contained. They organized and built the villages and hunting camps. The men were engaged in highly dangerous occupations: hunting to secure meat and hides and warfare to protect their family and tribal territory. A truly lazy or worthless man could find his meager possessions thrown out of the lodge, and he would be without a home. Each gender had its separate but equally vital role to play in the survival of the tribe.[19]

The Osage and Missouri primarily hunted large game like bison, elk, white-tailed deer, black bears and turkey. On the Great Plains they also hunted on foot mi-tzo, the grizzly bear, whose claws were made into the sacred necklace few were privileged to wear.[20] After trade with Europeans commenced, they started hunting and trapping smaller fur-bearing animals such as beaver, otter, raccoon and muskrat for their winter pelts. With the introduction of horses around 1680, parties of Osage ranged as far north as the Des Moines River, east to the Cumberland River, south to the Arkansas and Red Rivers, and west to the foothills of the Rocky Mountains.

The Arrow Rock bluff was an important crossroads and landmark to the native inhabitants. An ancient Indian trail followed the Missouri River from the Mississippi, and at the Arrow Rock, it divided into two branches. The southwest branch led to the Big Osage villages along the Osage River. The other branch angled northwest to the Missouri and Little Osage villages then headed west towards the Great Plains. This trail was known as the "Osage Trace." European explorers and later American settlers followed the trace, gradually improving it. Eventually it became the eastern section of the Santa Fe Trail and Missouri Highway 24.

The Arrow Rock was about 25 miles from the Indian villages, a short trip for native peoples who could easily travel 80 or more miles a day. Mo'n-ce, or metal obtained through trade with the Heavy Eyebrows, quickly made trips to the Arrow Rock for flint unnecessary. While trade goods made life easier for the Indians, the desire for such goods created a dependency the Europeans could manipulate. The introduction of guns and horses shifted the balance of power among Indian nations, leading to competition for trade and the best hunting grounds. The Little Osage and Missouri were allied against increasing incursions into the Missouri valley by other Indian nations, especially the Sauk, Fox and Ioway.

The Mines

Several miles southwest of Arrow Rock, members of Long's 1819 Yellowstone Expedition noted: "...the diggings so often mentioned in this region as objects of curiosity. These are irregular but very numerous excavations of little depth, but evidently the united labours of many persons, who were possessed of instruments of iron and steel...These excavations occur frequently in the extent of two or three miles...."[21] Early settlers in the area were unaware of the origin of the diggings. "Intrigued by the ancient excavations found along the Lamine and Blackwater, Charles Lockhart searched in vain for precious metals in 1819 and 1820, sometimes using as many as 30 laborers."[22] The river nearest to this site was originally called the Vermillion. By Lewis and Clark's time, it was known as "Le

Mine" (The Mine), later contracted to Lamine.

Thomas Rainey and other early historians attributed the diggings to Philippe Renault, who conducted mining activities throughout southeast Missouri in the 1720s. It seems doubtful Renault's mining company came this far west. If so, this would have been the first time people of African descent were in the region. Renault's mining company brought the first slaves into Missouri.[23] French explorer Etienne de Véniard, sieur de Bourgmont gave a simple explanation of the origin of the diggings as he passed the mouth of the Lamine in April of 1714, "...there are some prairies and a little low land, above where the Indians mine lead [Mine River]."[24] Galena (lead ore) was mined for ornamental and trade purposes and has been found at prehistoric as well as Osage village sites.[25] Rainey observed these diggings were still visible in 1914, though overgrown by large trees.[26]

Native cultures were indeed capable of excavation without using "instruments of iron and steel." Numerous burial and ceremonial mounds in the area, dating as far back as A.D. 300, attest to that ability. By the time of Bourgmont's 1714 exploration, the Little Osage were acquiring wahdon-skas or guns in trade and may have been mining the lead to make bullets. Osage-made metal molds in the Arrow Rock State Historic Site collection show they had learned simple metallurgical processes by that time.

The French Presence: Bourgmont and Fort Orleans

Spain laid claim to the lands between New Mexico and the Missouri River. Officials in New Mexico were alarmed by French activity on the Missouri River. Captain Pedro de Villasur led a small army from Santa Fe in 1720 to ascertain French strength in the Missouri valley. An account appearing in the late 19th century claimed Villasur reached the Missouri Indian village and mistook them as Little Osage. He proposed an alliance for the purpose of exterminating the Missouri tribe, and they played along until they could wipe out the Spaniards. The account is apocryphal, as the Pawnee and Otoe Indians, allies of France, had wiped out the expedition before it reached the Missouri River.[27] French officials decided, "This enterprise of the Spaniards shows the necessity of establishing a post on the Missouri."[28]

France's Royal Company of the Indies commissioned Bourgmont to establish this post. He had lived with the Missouri Indians from 1714 to

1719 and had mapped the Missouri River from its mouth to the Platte River in Nebraska. In November of 1723, fifteen French soldiers under Bourgmont's command built Fort Orleans across the river from the Missouri and Little Osage villages in present-day Carroll County. Bourgmont sought to strengthen French ties with the Missouri, Osage, Kansa, Otoe, Pawnee and Padouca (Comanche) nations.

Bourgmont took Missouri, Osage, Otoe and Illinois chiefs and his Missouri mistress to France in 1725. The Indians hunted deer in the King's forest preserve, to the delight of the nobility. French courtiers showered the Indians with gifts, and the Osage chief recalled "that the French ladies smelled like alligators"[29] owing to their musky perfume. Despite this interchange, Fort Orleans was abandoned by the Indies Company in 1728, as it "caused considerable expense to the company."[30] But the alliances formed by Bourgmont remained important to France.

The French and Indian War, 1754–1763

In the late 1740s, British traders penetrated the Ohio valley and upper Louisiana Territory in an attempt to undermine Indian loyalty to the French and to dominate the fur trade. Competition between France and Britain turned into war for control of the North American continent in 1754. Although the Arrow Rock area was far removed from the scene of fighting, French agents recruited over 200 local Osage, Missouri and Kansa warriors to aid in the fight. They traveled over 800 miles up the Wah-Ba-She, the Ohio River, in 1755, to help rout a British army under the command of General Edward Braddock at Fort Duquesne near present-day Pittsburgh, Pennsylvania.

The prairie Indians were unaccustomed to the damp towering forests of the East. It was difficult for them to fight from behind trees and brush like the woodland Indians. A chieftain of the Little Osage became bored of fighting in this manner. He adjusted his sacred red shield and war amulets and stepped into the open prancing like a bull elk and singing his war challenge. The Osage said he was the only Indian the "Long Knives"[31] could see, "...and their guns roared, and he fell, with his song fluttering in his throat."[32]

According to Osage oral tradition, their warriors tried in vain to kill one tall "Long Knife" officer who rode close by them. Members of the Eagle Clan shot two horses out from under him, but all their arrows seemed to curve around the man himself. They said this was Wah-Kon, or "Mystery," and they left him alone, fearing the medicine that made their arrows miss.[33] Present at this major battle was a tall, young colonel of the Virginia Militia, George Washington. Four bullets passed through his coat, one through his hat, and two horses were shot out from under him. Of the 61 officers present, Washington was one of the few not killed or wounded. The Osage, of course, knew nothing of Washington until much later in history, but he then became identified with this story passed down by the Eagles.[34]

Despite early French victories, British blockades cut the French supply line to North America. French trading outposts were closed, leaving Indians without the trade goods they now were dependent upon. A small-pox epidemic late in the war struck many tribes, further hampering their ability to fight. Finally in 1763, French Canada and the territory east of the Mississippi River were surrendered to Great Britain. The Louisiana Territory was ceded to Spain to keep it out of English hands. When Spain formally assumed control of the territory in 1767, only a few hundred Europeans were living along the Mississippi and lower Missouri River in what would become the present state of Missouri.

The Spanish and Osage Conflict, 1767–1796

The Spanish did not get along well with the Osage. The French had conformed their policies to the reality of Osage power, whereas the Spanish did not. The Osage sought to dominate trade by blocking traders from reaching other tribes. The French often allowed the Osage to act as their middlemen with other tribes. In contrast, Spain withheld trade goods to punish the Osage. In retaliation, the Osage would raid settlements in the Mississippi Valley.

Minimal blood was shed in this conflict, but the fear of the Osage was such that a single death caused the Europeans to retreat to the safety of larger settlements. Although a warrior society, the Osage did not dispense death wantonly. Traders caught going to other Indian nations were usually relieved of their goods, whipped and sent back to the settlements. Trappers or hunters usually fared worse since they were killing game on Osage land, in effect, stealing from them. Spain encouraged other Indian nations to attack the recalcitrant Osage and Missouri. In 1787, Spanish officials invited Shawnee and Delaware Indians to settle in Missouri to form a buffer between themselves and the mighty Osage.[35]

Commandant Perez of St. Louis outlined to Governor Miro in New Orleans a proposal for diplomacy in March of 1790: "The Osages are the worst two tribes that we have on the Missouri and at the same time the strongest. For this reason it is necessary to temporize with them to some extent, handle them as tactfully as possible in order to restrain their excess, as the few forces in the country do not permit anything else."[36] But despite their lack of military muscle, Spanish officials remained stubborn and continued to try to bend the will of the Osage. They relied on other Indian nations to act as their surrogate army with some effect.

Henry Marie Brackenridge passed the Saline County village site in 1811 and wrote, "There was formerly a village of the Little Osage here, but from the frequent attacks of the Ayuwas they were compelled to move...."[37] By 1780, the Little Osage were gone, and the Missouri fled a few years later. William Clark wrote about the fate of the Little Osage and Missouri between June 13 and June 15, 1804: "... behind a small willow island in the bend is a Prairie in which the Missouries once lived and a spot where 300 of them fell sacrifice to the fury of the Saukees."[38] Two days later at the Pettitsaw Plain he wrote, "On the river in this low Prairie the Missouries lived after They were reduced by the Saukees at Their Town Some Dist[ance] Below...."[39] "The Missouries Nation resided under the protection of the Osarges, ...the War was so hot & both nations becom So reduced that the Little Osage & a fiew of the Missoures moved & built a village 5 ms. Near the Grand Osage, the rest of the Missouries went and took protection under the Otteaus on Platt river."[40]

European diseases such as smallpox, cholera and measles had also reduced the Little Osage and especially the Missouri. There were probably only a thousand Missouri left by the time they took refuge near the Little Osage around 1725. The Otoe and Missouri merged into one tribe, the Otoe-Missouria by 1829. The combined Little Osage and Missouri continued to make excursions into the Missouri valley. The presence of the Sauk, Ioway and Fox nations increased in the area as well.

The Chouteau family of St. Louis long had influence with the Osage nation. In fact, the Osage called St. Louis "Sho-to-T'won" meaning "Chouteau's town."[41] Spanish officials granted brothers Pierre and Auguste Chouteau exclusive rights to trade with the Osage in 1794, and they in turn persuaded the Osage to stop their war with Spain. The fur trade with the Osage amounted to 40% of the market in the Louisiana Territory. The Osage gave Pierre title to 30,000 arpents (22,550 acres) along the Lamine River.[42] The Spanish government confirmed the land grant in 1799. This was one of the few land grants made by an Indian nation to an individual to be recognized by a colonial government. The Arrow Rock bluff marked the northernmost corner of Chouteau's holdings. However, the U.S. government later challenged the legality of the grant.

Louisiana Changes Hands, 1797 – 1803

Spain often rewarded its subjects with land grants for services performed on behalf of the government. One significant Spanish grant of 400 arpents (340 acres) was located across the river from Arrow Rock in present-day Howard County.[43] It was given to James Mackay, a Scotsman turned Spanish subject. Mackay surveyed and mapped the Missouri River in 1797 as far north as the Mandan villages in present day North Dakota. He built a Spanish post, Fort Charles, on the Missouri River at the Omaha village, and he evicted British traders who had established a trading post in a Mandan village.[44]

The Louisiana Territory became increasingly more costly for Spain to maintain, and in 1800, the Spanish deeded the territory back to France. At that time President Thomas Jefferson sought to purchase the port of New Orleans to assure an outlet for American goods and produce shipped down the Ohio and Mississippi Rivers. Napoleon Bonaparte, strapped for cash to finance his military campaigns in Europe, offered to sell all of Louisiana Territory to the United States for $15 million or about three cents an acre.

On April 30, 1803, the Louisiana Territory became a United States possession, doubling the size of the country overnight. Once again, the native nations of the region were not consulted by any of the colonial powers. They were merely informed they had new "fathers" to watch over and trade with them. Within the next decade, the Arrow Rock would come to play a significant role in the advancing frontier.

American Exploration & Occupation

The Lewis & Clark Expedition

Neither the French nor the Spanish had fully explored and mapped the 838,000 square miles of the territory from which Missouri and twelve other states were later carved. President Jefferson gained Congressional approval to explore Louisiana. He commissioned his long-time friend and personal aide, Meriwether Lewis, to explore the territory and locate a water route to the Pacific Ocean. Jefferson charged Lewis to record details of everything they saw, including, "landmarks of a permanent kind."[45] On May 14, 1804, the expedition led by Captain Lewis and his co-commander Lt. William Clark began their epic journey and entered the mouth of the Missouri River.

On June 8th, the expedition passed the mouth of the Lamine River, and Clark reported, "the french inform that Lead Ore is found in defferrent parts of this river."[46] They camped for the night on the "Island of mills" about four miles below Arrow Rock. They discovered there "...Kanteens, Axs, Pumey Stone & peltry hid and buried" by a party of hunters, which they left alone.[47] A few years later this island was renamed "Arrow Rock Island." The following day Clark reported seeing, "Several small Chanels running out of the River below a [Bluff] & Prarie (Called the Prariee of Arrows) where the river is confined within a width of [300] yds. Passed a Creek of 8 yds. Wide called Creek of Arrows...."[48] In the first official publication of the Lewis & Clark journals in 1814, editor Nicholas Biddle identified this bluff as "...a cliff called the Arrow Rock."[49]

The Expedition did not stop at the bluff nor did they make any noteworthy observations about it. The keelboat and two pirogues stayed close to the opposite bank to avoid the swift current. About three miles beyond at the mouth of Blackbird (now Richland) Creek, they experienced a near disaster: "June 9 1804 — Current exceeding strong...struck her bow and turn the boat against some drift and snags which [were] below with a great fierce; this was a disagreeable and dangerous situation, particularly as immense large trees were drifting down and we lay immediately in their course, — some of our men being prepared for all situations, leaped into the water, swam ashore with a rope, and fixed themselves in such situations, that the boat was off in a few minutes. I can say with confidence that our party is not inferior to any that was ever on the waters of the Missoppie (Mississippi)."[50] Passage through the lower Missouri had trained and welded the members of the Expedition into a well-coordinated team.

Salt and the Boone's Lick

Lewis and Clark reported an abundance of brackish creeks and salt-water springs or "licks" in the Arrow Rock region now comprised of Howard, Cooper and Saline counties. These springs, also known as "salines," were commonly called licks because deer, bison and elk would congregate around them to lick the salt from the ground. This concentration of game made licks favored hunting spots for both Indians and whites alike. The largest was located on the James Mackay Spanish land grant. Biddle identified it in 1814 as "... a large lick and salt spring of great strength" about four miles southeast of Arrow Rock.[51]

Salt was indispensable for preserving food on the frontier. In tanning hides to make leather, it took one-third the weight of a hide in salt to complete the process. Salt sold for as much as $2.50 a bushel in St. Louis, a hefty sum at the time. In 1805, Nathan and Daniel Morgan Boone, sons of the famous pioneer Daniel Boone, began manufacturing salt at Mackey's Lick in partnership with James and Jesse Morrison of St. Charles. They boiled the briny water in iron kettles until all that was left was the salty sludge. This was dried, packed in barrels called "hogsheads," and sent downriver to St. Louis on a keelboat owned by the Morrisons. About every two weeks, the keelboat would return laden with supplies and would pick up another load of salt.[52]

As the Boone brothers worked at Mackay's Lick, it soon became identified with their more famous family name, becoming known as the Boone's Lick. Commercial salt making continued there until 1833. After that period, production appears to have been intermittent and mainly for local consumption. In 1869, a 1,001-foot shaft was sunk in a failed attempt to revive the salt industry. "The Oyster Plan," an attempt to breed saltwater fish and oysters in the briny springs in 1901, also failed. The site of the Boone's Lick salt works is now preserved as Boone's Lick State Historic Site.[53]

The abundant supply of salt springs was an inducement for settlers to come to the region. As settlement increased, dozens of salt works were established. Most of these were small operations producing for local consumption although others shipped their product downriver. Besides Boone's Lick, one of the larger salines was Chouteau's Spring south of the Lamine River in Cooper County. In addition to making salt, water from this spring was sold in crock jugs for its "healthful qualities" well into the latter half of the 19th century.[54]

At Arrow Rock, members of the 1819 Yellowstone Expedition "...turned off from the Osage trace, in which they had been traveling, and went eight miles to visit the salt works, and some remarkable diggings on the saline fork of the Le Mine. Here at one establishment, one hundred bushels of salt are manufactured per week; eight men are employed, and one hundred and eighty gallons of water are evaporated to produce a bushel of salt."[55] These works were operated by Charles Lockhart, who had more luck making salt than looking for precious minerals at the site.

Jesse Lankford either took over the works from Lockhart or had another operation nearby from the mid-1820s through the 1830s. Dr. John Sappington, the first physician in the area, had investments in Lankford's operation. Another important salt works was at the Big Salt Spring located just west of present day Marshall. Colonel John Smith T, brother of Brigadier General Thomas A. Smith, moved there from Arrow Rock Township soon after 1830. He expanded and improved the salt-making operation. Smith was described as "a bachelor and in every other particular an odd character ... By his own command, Col. Smith was called 'Jack [John] Smith T.' His commands were always obeyed, or there was a funeral if they were not."[56] John Smith T apparently used this designation to distinguish himself from every other John Smith. He was well educated, but credited with killing fifteen men in duels, a common practice at the time for responding to insults or other personal affronts.[57]

The Boonville *Western Emigrant* newspaper reported in 1839: "The extraordinary number of salt springs found in the Boon's Lick country & the quantities of pure salt water they discharge, forms a marvel to the curious, and must at some future day, prove a source of great profit. In Saline county, in particular, they are very numerous, and form large streams of salt water."[58] The names in the area reflect this abundance: Salt Fork, Salt Creek, and Big Saline and Little Saline Creek, etc. General Thomas Smith and Benjamin Chambers designed the first Saline County seal around 1830.[59] It represents two men boiling saltwater in a vat over a furnace. It is the only known period illustration depicting this early but important pioneer industry. For a time, it was thought salt manufacturing would become the predominant business of the county.[60]

The name "Boone's Lick" was passed on to describe the neighboring countryside. Boone's Lick is also variously spelled as "Boon's Lick," "Booneslick" or "Boonslick" in 19th century documents and newspapers, the last appearing to be the most common variant. Naturalist John Bradbury was perhaps the first person to describe the geographical extent of the Boone's Lick Country as he traveled up the Missouri River in 1810: "…We encamped this night a little above the mouth of the Bonne Femme, a small river on the north side, where the tract of land called Boone's Lick settlement commences, supposed to be the best tract of land in Western America for so great an area: it extends about 150 miles up the Missouri and is near fifty miles in breadth."[61] Subsequent descriptions appearing in the Franklin *Missouri Intelligencer* in 1819 confirm the extent of the Boonslick Country.

The first American settlers came to the Boonslick in the spring of 1808; "…four brothers, Benjamin & Sarshal Cooper, with two younger brothers, all with large families, came from Kentucky where they had been associated with Boone and Kenton, & took therein in the Morrisons Keel-boat — a noble set of border men. They settled on the Missouri river on the northern bank, about a mile below Arrow Rock (a flint rock on the Southern bank, such as the Indians made arrows of) within three or four miles of Boone's Lick…."[62] The region was still Indian Territory that had not yet been ceded to the United States. Permanent settlement was therefore illegal; so Meriwether Lewis, now the governor of Upper Louisiana Territory, eventually ordered the Coopers to leave.

Fort Osage and the Treaty of 1808

In August of 1808, William Clark, now the Superintendent of Indian Affairs and General of the Militia for Upper Louisiana, led a military expedition up the Missouri River. The goal was to build a military and trading post in Osage country and acquire a large tract of Indian land for white settlement. Regular army troops of the First U.S. Infantry traveled upriver by keelboat with the supplies while militiamen from St. Charles under Clark went overland.[63] Nathan Boone, acting as scout for the expedition, led them over a trail he possibly blazed in 1805 from St. Charles to the Boone's Lick salt spring. This path was developed into the Boone's Lick Trail and connected to the Osage Trace. The Boone's Lick Trail became an important route of westward migration after 1815.

Clark had instructed Captain Eli Clemson of the U.S. Army, as the keelboat passed Arrow Rock, to leave a pirogue [dugout canoe] on the riverbank to facilitate crossing the river by the militiamen. The militia reached the Arrow Rock on August 31, and Clark wrote, "Made 23 miles to day — From St. Charles to this place Arrow Rock S. Side is 155 M[iles] estimated by land river 200 yds wide. Thursday 1 [September 1808] Commenced Crossing early & formed a Camp on top of the Hill which is about 90 feet above the water, a fine landing on a Rocky Shore under the Clift and a gentle assent. I had markd On the Clift a Hickory tree GI. W C 155 Miles, ordered all the party to fire off their guns and Clean them & load them … all crossed at half passed 11 a.m. after putting their guns in perfect order drawing up the perogue, and taking Breakfast, we proceded on at one oClock."[64]

From Arrow Rock they headed west on the Osage Trace and on September 5th, reached the "Fire Prairie" east of present-day Independence. Fire Prairie took its name from the fact Osage and Kansa hunters burned the area periodically to drive up game. Clark led the troops to a prominent river bluff he had seen on the Corps of Discovery journey. "This Situation I had examined in the year 1804 and was delighted with it and am equally so now…."[65] Soldiers began construction of Fort Osage, which is also sometimes identified as Fort Clark. Nathan Boone was sent to bring the Big and Little Osage tribes to the fort site for treaty negotiations.

Leaders of the Big and Little Osage tribes signed a treaty on September 14, 1808, ceding their land east of a line running from the fort south to the Arkansas River. A buffer zone was included in the treaty. "To prevent any misunderstanding in future Between the Osage Indians, a line Shall be Run from the Arrow Rock a South course to the Arkansas & no White man Shall be permitted to hunt west of that line without the permission of the United States."[66] In return for surrendering 30 million acres of land, the Big Osage received $800 worth of gifts and an annuity payment of $1,000, and the Little Osage got $400 worth of gifts and an annuity of $500. The treaty promised "... a Blacksmith and Tools to mend their Arms & utensils of Husbandry, and to build them a Horse or Water Mill."[67] A "factory," or fur trading post, at the fort was to be operated by U.S. agent George Champlin Sibley. The Osage, now dependent on these tools and trade items, had no way of gaining them other than by signing the treaty.

The Osage tribe was also given the "protection" of the U.S. government, which consisted of the government not encouraging their enemies to attack them. The Osage had been at war with most of their neighbors at one time or another, and there were many old scores to settle. Prior to the treaty negotiations, the Secretary of War had threatened to send a war party of 800 Shawnee, Delaware, Potawatomie, Cherokee and Kickapoo against the Osage for being "bad Indians." The gathering tribes were disappointed when the government called off the planned attack.[68]

At the conclusion of treaty ceremonies, Clark headed down river to St. Louis. On September 18th he again passed the Arrow Rock and wrote another description: "passed the Little arrow Rock at Sunset which is about 6 miles above the Big arrow rock by water & 2 1/2 or 3 [miles] by land. This Spot is handsome for a fort being only a point projecting with a high rich bottom below, and Some prarie, back the Praries are near, above the bottom is high and rich, river narrow and opposite bottom a mile wide, this is also a handsome Spot for a town, we arrived after dark at the arrow rock where we Crossed going out... The River having fallen the place is better to Cross."[69]

Upon reaching St. Louis, Clark met 74 Osage men who were delivering up stolen horses to the government. Hearing of the treaty, they claimed it was invalid because they had not been present at the signing. Governor Meriwether Lewis quickly drew up a new treaty containing all the original provisions, but he added a new one: the Osage must surrender all claims to land north of the Missouri River, another 20 million acres. Lewis got Pierre Chouteau to persuade the Osage to sign the revised treaty, which was ratified by Congress on April 28, 1810. Clark later expressed regret over the Osage treaty saying, "...it was the hardest treaty on the Indians that he ever made, and that if he was damned hereafter, it would be for making that treaty."[70]

The way was now "officially" opened for the permanent settlement of the Boonslick Country. By the summer of 1810, the Cooper families returned to the cabins and cornfields they had vacated earlier. They trans-planted slavery to the region, bringing a small but substantial number of black people with them, as did the families that followed them in later years. By 1812, about 100 other families had joined them, and glowing descriptions of the natural wealth and rich resources of the Boonslick Country began trickling back east.

Descriptions of the Land and Its Resources

Numerous factors determined the settlement patterns of early pioneers: geography, fertility of the soil, accessibility by land or water, an abundance of wild game, timber for fuel and building, and prairies for pasture land. The Boonslick Country had all these features in seemingly unlimited abundance. The high concentration of salt licks and thus abundance of the mineral, merely enhanced the appeal of the Boonslick for settlement.

William Clark's expedition to build Fort Osage provided a detailed description of the countryside around the Boone's Lick spring and Arrow Rock. When he passed through the area, there was no human habitation save for the small Cooper settlement and the Boone salt works. He described a land rich in timber, prairies and salt licks: "... 5 miles from the Sulpher lick, passed thro a butifull small plain Makays about a mile wide and crossed a Cart Road leading from Boones lick ... found men working at the Lick, the water is Very Strong 250 gallons to a Bushell of Salt, Some Corn is raised on the river, proceded on after crossing the Road 2 Miles to the point opst. [opposite] Arrow Rock, wods thick ... The lands are fine on the N. Side in every Direction, and well timb[ere]d not well watered, an emense Number of Small licks in every direction on both Sides, the Strongest & most water on the Mine River, and some licks contain sufficient water to turn a Mill quite Salt. The water of this river Cant be drank for some distance up."[71]

The men working at the salt lick were probably some of the Coopers employed by the Boones and Morrisons. After crossing the river and climbing to the top of the Arrow Rock bluff, the landscape began chang-ing dramatically: "The Dreans (drains) We passed to day all run into Mine River which is to our left, the timber on that river is not very considerable, and may be Seen from our Rout about Six or 8 Miles ... 10Clock Set out passed through thick undergrowth and scattering timber 1 mile to the open plains and proceeded through those plains."[72]

Duke Paul of Wuerttemberg, Germany, toured the American West in 1823. He had training as a naturalist, and as a European, was awed by the vastness of the American wilderness. His narratives of the area are more descriptive and even poetic compared to Clark's "nuts and bolts" descriptions. Although settlement was rapidly expanding by 1823, the land still retained its wilderness character: "The road to Pierre de la Fleche (Arrow Rock) by way of the river, a distance of twelve English miles from Franklin, led through a sparsely inhabited region. For the first two miles the way was passable. The forests consisted of beautiful trees spaced apart and a dense composite undergrowth of herb-like plants. Magnificent groups of trees were created by the numerous sycamores mixed with luxuriant gledistia, locust, ashes and oaks …. A swamp hard by the road bordered the latter for more than an English mile. This stagnant water was covered with aquatic plants … A beautiful flowering Nymphaea (water lily) also delighted my eye. Countless water fowls took wing in fright and a huge flock of Anas sonsa (wood ducks) passed over my head. From a botanical and ornithological point of view this region seemed engrossing, and I regretted very much that I did not have the opportunity to remain a longer time."[73]

Like Clark, Duke Paul noticed the transition in the land from forest to prairie after crossing the river at the Arrow Rock: "We climbed a rather high, steep hill on which nut trees and sassafras grew. On the ridge of these hills the timber becomes thinner, Forest and prairie alternate with one another. The vegetation becomes more luxuriant, the dense underbrush give way to grass-covered spaces, and more and more the region takes on a lighter aspect clearly indicating the transition from the forest region to the prairie."[74] Today this same landscape contains considerably more timber, and the open, panoramic vistas seen by these early explorers scarcely exist.

For many moving west, the land back home was "played out" and no longer very productive. To them, the Boonslick Country was a land flowing with milk and honey. A report by Franklin merchant Augustus Storrs in 1820 listed some of the rich flora and fauna that attracted many early settlers to the area: "The spontaneous productions are plums of different kinds, blackberries, gooseberries, persimmons, pawpaw, red and black haws and strawberries and pecans. Bear, deer, and turkies are plentiful …Wild geese and duck in the spring and fall. Wild honey is so abundant that two hundred gallons have sometimes been obtained…There are prairie fires in November."[75]

The mix of forest and prairie created diverse habitats for multiple species, and the concentration of salt licks in the region attracted large herds of hoofed animals. At the "Sulpher Lick" on the Howard County side of the river, Clark reported in 1808 his hunters had "… killed a Buffalow Bear & 3 Deer."[76] Jesse Morrison recalled "buffalo plenty within a few miles of our salt works… and in one instance a buffalo came up with our oxen to the furnace, where one of the Frenchmen killed it while licking in the trough…."[77] A large herd of elk crossed the river above the Arrow Rock in 1816, pursued by hunters from Howard County. As word spread, hunters from the Saline County side joined in the chase. They pursued the herd south into Cooper County and back across the Missouri River.

Hunting, of course, provided an important source of food for the settlers. The hides were valuable for leather and for the fur trade. Although an abundance of wildlife was an inducement to settle in an area, it was viewed as a threat when agriculture became more developed. Wildlife ate or trampled field crops. In 1831, Reverend Timothy Flint wrote of wild turkeys, "In some places, they are so numerous, as to be easily killed, beyond the wants of the people. We have seen more than a hundred driven from one field."[78] Predators such as black bears frequently attacked livestock. "Bruin evidenced a decided fondness for pork and veal, and was a frequent but unwelcomed visitor in many a pig-pen and calf-lot. Bear-hunts were frequently organized, and quite a number of the animals were killed…."[79]

Timber or gray wolves were common, and one became a Saline County legend in 1837. This large wolf left part of his tail in a trap, earning him the nickname "Old Bob-tail." This wolf was credited with whipping every pack of dogs sent after it and accused of taking every calf, sheep or pig that turned up missing. A large hunting party drove him along the Blackwater River, and for two days, he was pursued before swimming across the Missouri River near Boonville. For the next two years, "Old Bob-tail" took up residence at the Grand Prairie in present-day Boone County and was finally poisoned by a hunter who collected a $100 bounty on the wolf.[80]

Cougars or "painters" (panthers) were another common predator. One interesting story from around 1825 comes from the Blackwater settlement, southwest of Arrow Rock. "Mrs. Miller started her two little daughters, aged eight and seven, to school a mile away... they saw a large panther crouched on the trunk of a leaning tree ...The older of the little girls said to her sister; 'O! There's the bad old wolf that kills our pigs and lambs. You stay here and watch it, and I'll go back and tell daddy....'"[81] The youngest girl agreed and sat at the foot of a tree to watch. She recalled in later years the animal was watching her and frequently paced back and forth on the trunk. Her sister reached the cabin and informed her mother about the "big old wolf." Paralyzed with fright, Mrs. Miller called her husband then fell on her knees to pray for her daughter's safety. Miller and a man named Plunkett ran to the scene with their rifles and found the cougar asleep in the tree, and "... but a few feet away, was the faithful but innocent and unsuspicious little sentinel ... still watching the bad old wolf."[82] Both men fired and killed the animal. "It is perhaps needless to say that the children did not attend school any more at the Blackwater school house."[83]

Whether for food or protection of property, wildlife of all types was usually shot whenever and wherever it was encountered. There was a general belief the supply of wildlife was inexhaustible. White-tailed deer were so abundant, even as late as 1850, three men named Gaines, White and Herndon killed a total of 246 deer in Saline County. Such harvests were unsustainable, and the largest animals were the first to be exterminated. Bison were gone from the area by 1816. The last herd of elk sighted in Saline County was in 1836; the last confirmed cougar was shot in 1838, and the last black bears were killed in 1840. Gray wolves, owing to their keen intelligence and adaptability, survived beyond the Civil War.[84] The bounty system, however, resulted in their total extermination, and the few stragglers were eliminated by 1880.

The February 7, 1868 edition of the *Saline County Progress* reported a steady decline of game animals and a sharp increase in the number of gray foxes. "Deer have become so scarce, and hunters and dogs so skilled in the chase, that we fear the time is not far distant when this kind of game, once so plenty on our prairies, will become extinct. As the deer, turkeys, and other game disappear amidst the tread and progress of civilization, so the fox follows westward in his march from the Allegheny Mountains the settlements of the white men. They were, until within the last few years, entirely unknown in these regions."[85]

The Missouri River

The Missouri River in this early period was totally unlike what we see today. The river was filled with islands, sand bars and shallow backwaters. The floodplain contained oxbow lakes and marshes. The natural Missouri ranged anywhere from 200 yards to nearly two miles wide. Some of the holes were fifty feet deep while other stretches of water were only knee-deep. In normal water flows, the average depth was around five feet. The river was filled with logjams, sunken trees and root wads, producing ideal habitat for countless numbers of fish. Buffalo and drum of 50 pounds, blue and flathead catfish of 100 pounds were common. One catfish taken at Arrow Rock in the 1840s was claimed to weigh 200 pounds.[86] Lake sturgeon and paddlefish of nearly 150 pounds were also taken. The quiet backwaters and sloughs teemed with largemouth bass, white bass, bluegill, crappie, gar, mooneye, shad, pickerel and walleye.

The river corridor attracted wading birds, ducks, geese, cranes and trumpeter swans by the hundreds of thousands. They were so common that hunting contests were sometimes carried on between neighboring communities. One such competition was conducted between Arrow Rock and Marshall in March of 1868. "The largest count made by any one of the winning side, was … by Jesse Baker. He killed 35 geese on a sand bar one mile below Arrow Rock. The highest count on the losing side was made by Mr. Yates of this place [Marshall] … having killed fifteen geese and two ducks."[87]

In the latter half of the 19th century, commercial fishing and waterfowl hunting on the Missouri River supplied markets both locally and farther east. Plumes from wading birds such as herons, egrets, and cranes became popular in ladies' hats. Individual market hunters numbered their daily kills in the hundreds, even during the breeding seasons. As was proven with deer and turkey, this type of harvesting was unsustainable. Even flocks of Carolina parakeets and passenger pigeons, which darkened the skies during Lewis and Clark's passage, were exterminated by the turn of the century.

During the first half of the 20th century, the U.S. Army Corps of Engineers undertook construction projects to improve river navigation and control flooding on the Missouri River. This activity destroyed much of the riverine habitat. Wetlands and marshes were drained, islands and sandbars were dredged, and river bends were shortened. The Missouri was reduced to a narrow drainage channel of uniform width and depth, largely devoid of islands, sandbars and shallow backwaters. Levees protected the bottomlands of which over 95% were then drained and placed in agricultural production. Dams were constructed in the Dakotas and Montana to regulate water flow. When the engineering project was completed, the cover of the August 22, 1955 edition of *Life* magazine proclaimed, "The Wild Missouri Tamed at Last." The huge flocks of waterfowl and the giant fish were largely relics of the past.

Modern game regulations and conservation education by the Missouri Department of Conservation have reversed the trend of over-harvesting of the past. Deer, turkeys, and smaller predators such as bobcats are once again common around Arrow Rock. Beaver and otters are now more abundant on the Missouri River and its tributaries than at any time in the 20th century. Mitigation projects by the Army Engineers have restored some of the fish and waterfowl habitat to the Missouri River. Hopefully, the agency will be able to manage the river to meet ecological as well as economic needs. Large blue, channel and flathead catfish are caught more frequently, and there is cautious hope of partially restoring the populations of the critically endangered lake and pallid sturgeon. In 1996, pallid sturgeon fingerlings were found in the river near Arrow Rock, the first evidence in nearly 30 years the fish were breeding in the wild.[88]

As a result of record flooding in 1993 and 1995, many bottomland farms were decimated. Congress authorized the United States Fish & Wildlife Service (USFWS) to purchase up to 60,000 acres of devastated bottomland from willing sellers between Kansas City and St. Louis for conversion to wetlands. The USFWS has acquired 1,800 acres of bottomland adjacent to Arrow Rock. As part of the Big Muddy National Fish & Wildlife Refuge, the Jameson Island Unit is being allowed to naturally reconnect to the Missouri River and regenerate itself as marsh and cottonwood forest. A hiking trail to the river with interpretive signage opened in 2004. Eventually, visitors to the refuge will be able to see a piece of the riverine habitat as Lewis and Clark saw it.

The Arrow Rock Bluff
The Arrow Rock was a landmark dating back to prehistoric Indian cultures. A frequent question of visitors to the area is, *"Exactly what is the Arrow Rock or where is it?"* The Burlington limestone bluffs that compose

the Arrow Rock were laid down in the Mississippian Period approximately 325 million years ago. About 400,000 years ago, the bluffs were exposed by runoff from melting glaciers that poured into the Missouri River.

The first person to record the Arrow Rock as he passed its location was Bourgmont. On April 20, 1714, he simply described it as "... outcrops of rocks to the west and at the end of these is an island of about 15 arpents."[89] This island was possibly what William Clark identified as "Island of Mills" (Arrow Rock Island). Its size and shape were undoubtedly changed multiple times by the river over the years.

Later journals are more specific in naming these "rocks," but William Clark, in 1808, provides a direct reference to both a "big Arrow Rock" and a "little Arrow Rock." Saline City, located about 5 miles north of Arrow Rock, was founded in 1858. Its post office was originally designated "Little Rock" but changed to Saline City as the name was already in use. The nearby Salem Church is sometimes still called the "Little Rock Church." According to the 1881 Saline County history, both Indians and pioneers alike had long referred to the site of the town as "Little Arrow Rock."[90] A few 19th century maps even showed the name of the town as Little Rock instead of Saline City.

Duke Paul described the appearance of the Arrow Rock on June 23, 1823: "The bank forming the Pierre de la Fleche (Arrow Rock) is high and composed of beautiful rocks. This chain of hills on the right bank of the Missouri is hardly twelve English miles long...."[91] In 1833, Maximilian, Prince of Wied, described the Arrow Rock as "... a chain in which flint is found...." He also noted passing "the Little Arrow Rock."[92] There is a series of rock bluffs which could be described as a "chain of hills or rocks" running from Saline City to about a mile south of the village of Arrow Rock. Arrow Rock Island, which no longer exists, began near where the south tip of the rock bluff ended.

Major Stephen Long, in 1819, described the prominence of the Arrow Rock bluff saying, "It is a beautiful situation, and rises to considerable elevation above the water. From its summit is a pleasing view of the river...."[93] In the early 19th century, this bluff must have been an impressive sight from the river. It seems reasonable to conclude from these descriptions that the "big" and "little" Arrow Rock were especially noticeable when compared to the other parts of the bluff.

Obviously, these two prominent features of the bluff were in close proximity to the communities that bore their name. Prince Maximilian noted a new town located in the ravine before "Arrow Rock hill."[94] The 1881 Saline County history states, "This name was given to the large rock or cliff at the town. Upon the formation of the town it was christened after the rock."[95]

This series of flint-bearing bluffs is geographically isolated from any similar bluffs along the Missouri River. This isolation of the bluff and the pluralistic terms used in the descriptions seem to indicate this entire stretch of stone bluffs was loosely termed "the Arrow Rock." When the area was wilderness, two people could have agreed to meet at "the Arrow Rock," and they would have gotten reasonably close enough to find each other.

The river itself has moved away from the bluff, and trees now grow in the intervening ground, obscuring the view. Brush and vines cover the bluff face much of the year. Thus, it is impossible to see the line of bluffs as the early river travelers would have. Furthermore, during the first quarter of the 20th century many sections of the bluff were dynamited and quarried for the rock used in river channelization projects. It is quite possible the bluff face seen by early explorers simply no longer exists. The remaining sections of bluff that appear to be natural are largely sheer rock walls, containing layers and nodules of chert (low grade flint).

Many visitors believe there is a large rock or particular ledge in the shape of an arrowhead. The Arrow Rock *Statesmen* in August, 1912, stated this was one possible explanation for the name. Some guides and early tourism literature have perpetuated that story. Nothing, however, has been found in any historical documents to support this notion. What the records do make clear is the name "Arrow Rock" was derived from the manufacturing of arrow points.

American Settlement and the Clash of Cultures

The United States government viewed the Osage Treaty of 1808 as extinguishing Indian title to the Boonslick Country. The Ioway, Sauk and Fox nations also claimed the area, but the government never consulted with them in the matter. Consequently, these Indian nations viewed the Boonslick settlers as trespassers on prime hunting ground. Resentment and clashes between them and the settlers began to occur with greater frequency. For example, Nathan Boone recalled his salt works "…would have been profitable but for the troubles and pilferings of the Indians at the works…

chiefly in stealing & killing the working & beef cattle."⁹⁶

The year 1811 was a tense one on the frontier. The Shawnee Chief, Tecumseh, and his brother, Tenskawata, had been exhorting Indian nations from the Great Lakes to the Gulf of Mexico to unite and halt the advance of white settlement. Sauk war leader, Black Hawk, expressed the sentiments of many Indian people: "Why did the Great Spirit ever send the whites to this island, to drive us from our homes and introduce among us poisonous liquors, diseases and death? They should have remained on the island where the Great Spirit first placed them."⁹⁷ The Americans simply blamed Great Britain for fomenting Indian unrest, overlooking the taking of Indian lands as the source of the problem.

British traders from Canada had operated in American territory since the end of the Revolutionary War. They did not want to give up the rich fur harvests provided by the Indians. A number of Indian tribes made trips to Canada to trade or consult with British officials. The English also wanted to maintain Indian tribes as allies in the event of any future war with the United States. There is no evidence they were directly encouraging attacks at this time.

British traders gave the Indians generous terms of credit for trade, which included firearms and gunpowder. U.S. government traders were obligated to follow a more restrictive policy, and sometimes trade goods were withheld to punish tribes for perceived misconduct. These policies tended to work in favor of Great Britain. In the words of Black Hawk, "I had not discovered one good trait in the character of the Americans that had come to the country. They made fair promises but never fulfilled them. Whilst the British made but few but we could always rely on their word."⁹⁸

In the fall of 1811, Tecumseh was recruiting among the Creek Indians. Needing more time for his confederacy to grow, he left strict orders to avoid any confrontation with Americans. On November 8, General William Henry Harrison marched his troops within sight of the main Indian village named Prophet's Town on Tippecanoe Creek in Indiana. This was enough to goad Tenskawata into ordering an attack the following morning. Harrison's troops repulsed the attack and then proceeded to burn Prophet's Town. The Indian confederacy was knocked off balance. War would now begin sooner than later. Isolated cabins from Ohio to Missouri began to go up in flames. These events eventually led to the main military campaign in the Boonslick Country over 400 miles away.

In January of 1812, John Johnson, the U.S. government factor to the Sauk and Fox at Fort Madison, Iowa, expressed the general feeling on the frontier: "Every hour, I look for a war party and God only knows when it will end." [99] The U.S. Army had only about 260 soldiers available for defense of the western frontier. In response to the crisis, Congress authorized the raising of companies of Rangers to defend the frontier. Known as the "minutemen of the frontier," the Rangers were backwoodsmen who provided their own arms, horses and provisions. The United States paid each man "seventy-five cents a day when serving on foot and one dollar for every day of mounted service." [100] On March 3, 1812, Nathan Boone was commissioned Captain of the Rangers. Boone then sold out his interest in the salt-making operation.

On June 18, 1812, the United States declared war on Great Britain, citing, among other reasons, the relationship of the British to the Indian nations in American territory. Although the loyalty of many tribes was in question, it seemed clear a large number were going to support Britain in the struggle. Once war was declared, the British commissioned Tecumseh and Black Hawk as generals and then actively encouraged Indian raids on frontier settlements.

The Boonslick settlement now contained about 400 people and was virtually an island, isolated from the closest line of settlement by a hundred miles. Territorial Governor Benjamin Howard advised the Boonslick settlers to move to the main settlements where they could be protected. Benjamin Cooper sent his reply: "We have maid our hoams here and all we have is here and it wud ruen us to leave now. We be all good Americans, not a Tory or one of his Pups among us, and we have 2 hunderd Man and Boys that will fight to the last and have 100 Wimen and Girls that will take there places with. Makes a good force So we can defend the settlemnt. With Gods Help we will do." [101]

The Boonslick settlers were scattered on both sides of the Missouri, from Big Moniteau Creek near present-day Rocheport to Arrow Creek north of Arrow Rock. They tended to live in enclaves that had recognized leaders. The closest settlements to Arrow Rock were as follows: the Cooper settlement was located in the river bottoms across the river from Arrow Rock. Benjamin, Sarshall and Braxton Cooper were leaders. Cox's settlement was located in the river bottoms about three miles north of

Arrow Rock. Jesse Cox and his son-in-law William Gregg were leaders. Jones' settlement was located about six miles south of Arrow Rock. David Jones, a veteran of the Yorktown campaign in the Revolutionary War, and his sons-in-law, Thomas McMahan and Stephen Turley, were leaders.

Despite fears for the worst, the Missouri frontier suffered only sporadic and isolated raids, such as horse stealing. Black Hawk wanted to lead his warriors against the Missouri settlements, but the British convinced him and other Indian leaders of the importance of first capturing Detroit and securing the Great Lakes. The lack of serious confrontation in the West led to a false sense of security on the Missouri frontier. American officials erroneously believed they were successfully placating the Indian tribes.

The Osage Trading House

By the summer of 1813, the United States had suffered severe setbacks in the war. Military posts in the Great Lakes region had been destroyed, captured or were under siege by the British and their Indian allies. Fort Osage was so far out on the frontier it was deemed useless as part of the line of defense and was vulnerable to having its supply line cut. Factor George C. Sibley removed all the trade goods from the fort's factory to St. Louis. The fort was officially closed in June, and the 63 soldiers of the 1st United States Infantry were sent to other assignments.[102]

The Osage disliked the British because of the firearms trade with their traditional enemies, the Sauk, Fox, Ioway and Winnebago. Also, unlike many agents in the U.S. Indian Service, Sibley showed some interest and tolerance of Osage culture and had been fair in his dealings with them. In fact, Fort Osage was the only government Indian factory of 22 built that had been profitable. The Little Osage chiefs offered to fight for the United States, but their offer was refused, which angered Sibley. Frontier military officials apparently distrusted any armed Indians, whether they were friends or not.[103]

It was important for the United States to maintain trade with the Osage because the British were trying to use trade goods to entice them into an alliance. While officials pondered where to place the new Osage Trading House, they also decided to construct a trading house on Little Moniteau Creek about forty miles downstream from Arrow Rock. A portion of the Sauk and Fox tribe that remained neutral was to be relocated on the site. William Clark hoped to keep them separate from their hostile kinsmen and their British benefactors.

Under orders from Clark, Sibley moved his trade goods by his keelboat, *The Osage Factor*, to the Arrow Rock bluffs in October of 1813. He paid several of the local settlers to construct a blockhouse of cottonwood logs and huts for trade goods. The fact the fort was built of cottonwood rather than oak indicated the post was to be temporary. Sibley wrote his brother, Samuel, that he expected to remain at Arrow Rock until June of 1814. During construction of the post, he and his servant boarded at the cabin of William Gregg in Cox's settlement. When the Osage chiefs arrived in early November, Sibley asked them where they wanted the factory placed on a permanent basis. He dutifully recorded the divided opinions of the Osage leaders for Clark:

> *Sans-nerf head warrior of the Big Osage and Father in law of the grand chief Said — You have heard what my chief has said relative to the removal of the Trading House. We all agree to his determination to abide by this Treaty. You asked me before if I thought this plan would suit and I told you yes — We do not like Ft. Clark for very good reason. The road between that place and our village is nearly as long as the one to this place, and it is very dangerous one to travel. Our enemies lay in wait for us when we go there to trade and have killed several of our people. I think we will be more secure coming here on account of the large settlement of Americans near this and I am in favor of this place also on account of our being able to procure provisions there from the Settlers when we need any. I wish the Trading House to be fixed somewhere as soon as possible and hope if it is not to be on the Osage River it may be here.*
>
> *Nee-zu-mo-nee — head chief of the Little Osages said — I never consented to have the trading town removed. I will never consent to its being altogether discontinued. Genl. Clark placed it at the Fire Prairie and the President solemnly promised to keep it there. I have their treaty now in my hand, look at it (handling the treaty) I express it was not their intention to trifle with it and cheat us out of our land. It is my wish and also that of all my people that the Trading Town be re-established as soon as possible at*

Ft. Clark (Osage). We do not like this place —

The Grey Bird uncle of the head chief B.P. and oldest brother of "White Hair" deceased Said — I like this place better than the old one on account of the Settlements of Americans near it which I think afford us more security when we come to trade — The bones of my oldest Brother "White Hair" are buried on the road between this place and my Village — The bones of several of my Nation lie unburied and bleaching on the prairie between my Village and Ft. Clark. They were murdered by our enemies who lay in ambush for them when they went to trade. I find it is hard for us to agree with the Little Osages on this subject. I and my nephew are willing that you shall decide the question. I hope you will fix on some place soon. I think you had better remain here.

The Big Soldier, a distinguished warrior and orator of the Little Osages Said — Whose fault is it that these two Villages are divided? The Big Red Head (Genl. Clark) built a Fort at the Fire Prairie — Old White Hair as well as my Chief agreed to settle there — We have kept our promises, they have not remembered theirs. After much difficulty we have fixed our village convenient to Fort Clark under the full expectation that the Trading House was fast. But just as we had settled ourselves, we see all broke up. I was lately on a visit to the Great American Chief. He told me that Ft. Clark should be made stronger than ever, that he would plant an iron post there that could not be pulled up and that would never decay. I fear he has forgotten that promise and instead of planting an iron post intends to let the old wooden one rot. The Trading House is not for nothing. We have given our Sons for it and I tell you plainly I think the President has done very wrong to remove it all, I have seen him and his Country and millions of his people and am very certain that he is able to protect the Trading House where ever he is bound by Contract to keep one. We do not like this place at all.[104]

Possibly, the Little Osage objected to the site because the terrain would not accommodate locating their camps "below the hill" as was their tradition. At this time, the Missouri River ran directly underneath the limestone bluffs, leaving only room on the bank for landing boats. Despite the objections of the Little Osage, trade at the Arrow Rock factory commenced, and by December 31st, the Osage brought in $2,016.02 worth of furs. This amount included 526 pounds of beaver skins, 640 dressed deerskins, 230 bearskins, 250 raccoon skins, five dressed elk skins, two buffalo robes and 6,044 pounds of shaved deerskin. In return the Osage received items like "point blankets," silk ribbons, bells, wampum beads, buttons, saws, files, awls, knives, tomahawks, gunpowder and rifles and even decks of playing cards. The small number of elk and buffalo skins traded may indicate the animals were already becoming relatively scarce in central Missouri.[105]

A trapper named Ezekiel Williams served on occasion as an interpreter for Sibley. Earlier in the year he had been trapping on the Kansas (Kaw) River and was robbed of his cache of furs by members of the Kansa nation. When a group of Kansa appeared at the Arrow Rock post to trade, Williams asked "Mr. Cibley"[106] for his assistance in recovering the stolen furs. Sibley informed the Kansa chief "he would not pay them their annuities unless they returned the furs properly belonging to Mr. Williams." The Kansa leaders "returned with four packages, which Captain Williams proved by the initials of his name, E. W. which were on them. The agent inquired if that was all. Captain Williams replied there were eight more."[107] Eventually the Kansa produced all but one bale of fur. "Here the matter ended, and in the end it resulted to the great advantage of Mr. Williams, as he got rid of the very difficult job of conveying his peltries to the Missouri River."[108]

Meanwhile, Black Hawk grew tired of fighting alongside the British. General Proctor blamed the Indians for his failure to capture Fort Meigs and Fort Stephenson in Ohio. Late in the fall, the frustrated warriors returned to their homes. Attacks on the Missouri frontier increased in the spring of 1814, and even the Osage became restive. They robbed a group of trappers on the Gasconade River and killed another on the White River. William Clark made the decision to abandon the Arrow Rock trading post before the situation got worse.[109] On April 14, 1814, soldiers from Fort Bellefontaine had to free Sibley's boat from a sandbar at the mouth of the Missouri River, bringing the story of the Arrow Rock trading house to its official end.[110]

The fate of the Osage Trading House remains unknown. Possibly, it fell into ruin, as the soft cottonwood logs would have decomposed rather quickly.

More likely, local settlers dismantled it and used the lumber. The exact location of the post is yet to be determined. Sibley's letters and ledgers simply give the location as "Arrow Rock, Missouri (Territory)." Oral tradition placed the trading house at the end of High Street in the town limits of Arrow Rock. This location is not supported by documentation or archaeological evidence. Documentary evidence suggests the factory location was a mile or so north of the town, lending further credence to the idea anywhere along the bluff was loosely defined as "the Arrow Rock."

The Indian War, 1814 – 1816

At the same time Sibley was establishing the operation at the Arrow Rock, nearly half of the Sauk and Fox were relocated to Little Moniteau Creek, about 40 miles downriver. Under Chief Quashquame, this faction of the allied tribes had professed neutrality in the war. A trading house was established there by factor John Johnson. The Sauk and Fox who remained on the Rock River in Illinois were deemed "hostile" by the U.S. government and subject to attack.

In the spring of 1814, a large group of Rock River Sauk appeared at the Little Moniteau factory to visit their relatives. They attempted to pillage the factory but were restrained by their kinsmen. The May 14, 1814 edition of the *Missouri Gazette* reported an incident that had occurred in the Sauk village: "...while in council with a band of Osages, to which Mr. Johnson was invited Nomwaite, the principal chief of the Sac nation raised the English flag at the door of the council house...."[111] This incident resulted in the evacuation of the Little Moniteau installation. The Sauk began conducting raids in the area, although it is not clear if it were the Rock River or Moniteau group. Possibly it was a combination of both.

The first death among the settlers occurred April 26, 1814, when Jonathan Todd and Thomas Smith were slain on the Boone's Lick Trail. The settlers "found both men dead, and Todd's head cut off and stuck on a pole...."[112] Judge Joseph Thorp, who lived in Cooper's Fort as a boy, recalled, "At a very early hour next morning the men in our settlement were called together, guns in hand, ready for self-defense...they immediately set to work to build forts for protection, each settlement having its own fortifications, and the result was there were five forts built."[113] As with many early events, there is some conflict in the reminiscences of the settlers. Joseph Cooper recollected the killing of Todd and Smith and the fort building as occurring in the spring of 1812.[114] Undoubtedly the men were killed in 1814, but it is possible some of the forts were built in 1812.

The Boonslick forts were not formal military installations. "The forts were simply strong log-houses, with a projecting upper story, and with loop-holes for musketry."[115] It is likely existing structures were simply modified and reinforced to meet the emergency. A stockade or palisade of logs surrounded some of the forts. Thorp evidently did not count every blockhouse or reinforced cabin as a fort. That would have brought the total Boonslick fortifications up to nine. There were no regular army troops available, so able-bodied men formed a militia for protection of the settlements.

Cooper's Fort was the largest of the forts in the area and seems to fit the vision most people hold of a frontier fort. Several cabins were enclosed in a stockade encompassing about one acre. It housed about 20 families and a number of unmarried young men. It was located "... about a mile and half below Arrow Rock, half a mile back from the river — on a beautiful prairie in the river bottom...."[116] A small blockhouse was constructed in Cox's settlement in the river bottoms three miles above Arrow Rock. There were two fortifications for the fifteen families in the Jones' settlement located six miles below Arrow Rock. McMahan's Fort was described as a "little stockade"[117] and was located on the bluff. William Reid built a smaller blockhouse or fortified cabin that was probably in the river bottoms. McMahan's Fort was also sometimes known as Anderson's Fort.[118]

Fields nearest to the stockade or forts could be cultivated in relative safety. However, not enough corn could be grown in these locations to satisfy all needs of the settlers. "Parties were detailed to cultivate fields more distant. These were divided into plowmen and sentinels. The one party followed the plows and the other with rifles loaded and ready, scouted around the field on every side...."[119] "Spies" or scouts were sent out to the surrounding countryside to watch for signs of an approaching war party. "About one half of the men would usually go on these scouts, severally mounted and the others would remain for the protection of the forts and families...."[120]

In July of 1814, a large party of the Sauk and Fox swept through the Boonslick Country. They first struck at Cole's Settlement, at present-day Boonville. They then proceeded upriver toward David Jones' settlement. "They all abandoned their homes, hearing of the suspicious approach of the Indians, crossed the river in boats & repaired to Cooper's Fort & had hardly got the last load of goods into their boats when the Indians crept up & fired McMahan's Fort. That night the Indians stole all the canoes on the north side of the river, & got all the horses belonging to the McMahan settlement, sixty six in number. The Indians made their encampment near McMahan's' Fort for some two weeks — destroying the cattle and sheep, & green corn, burnt John McMahan's house, 3 miles from the Fort which was filled with flax & which they probably fired to witness the conflagration...."[121] The inhabitants of Cox's settlement also fled to Cooper's Fort, and their cabins were ransacked at the same time.

The August 13, 1814 edition of the *Missouri Gazette* offered this assessment: "A few days ago, a barge belonging to Messrs. M. Lisa & Co. which was ascending the Missouri to their trading establishment, were induced to stop at Mackay's Saline, (commonly called Boon's Lick) as the country was overrun by the Indians and all the inhabitants were in Forts. The crew which arrived here on Saturday night, last ... reports that on the south side of the Missouri, the Indians had taken all the horses and were killing the cattle for food; that on their arrival at the Saline, the people of Coles' fort were interring a man just shot by the Indians. On the north side near Kincaid's fort a man was killed in a flax field."[122] The man killed in the flax field was a potter named Campbell Bolen. Being the only person with that trade in the Boonslick, his loss was seriously felt and would influence a military campaign about to unfold.

The Sauk passed through a village of Miami Indians as they left the area. The Piankashaw band of the tribe "...were sent west by Gov. Harrison, in order to detach them from the prophets [Tenskawata] band. They came to the Mississippi, and from thence wandered to the Missouri...."[123] They settled near the site of the present town of Miami. The Sauk sold or traded them some of the plunder they had taken during the raid. Many settlers assumed the Miami had a hand in the raid. The Boonslick settlers appealed to Governor William Clark in St. Louis for assistance. Colonel Henry Dodge was dispatched from St. Genevieve with 200 mounted Missouri Rangers. Acting as scouts for the Rangers were about 50 Shawnee allies led by "Captain Pap-piqua, Wa-pe-pil-le, Na-kom-me and Kish-kal-wa."[124] Ironically, only 25 years earlier in Kentucky, these men had been in war parties against the Boonslick men they were now helping.

Dodge's Rangers rendezvoused at Cooper's Fort in early September where about 90 men of the Boone's Lick militia under Colonel Benjamin Cooper reinforced them. "The force crossed the Missouri from the northern to the southern bank at the Arrow Rock by swimming the stream ... and following the horses in canoes...When about half way over, they struck the strong eddy, which soon wafted them over to the southern bank in safety. The friendly Shawnees found & reported the locality of the hostile Miamis, who had thrown up a small fort. Dodge's men pushed forward several miles up the river, & in the night neared the enemy in what is now known as Miami Bend, in Saline county...Ascertaining this fact, the Miamis knew it would be folly to resist such odds, proposed through the Shawnees to surrender themselves as prisoners."[125]

Dodge held a council with his officers, and they agreed to accept the Miami as prisoners and pledged to spare their lives. "The Indians now formally surrendered — 31 warriors, and about one hundred and twenty-two women and children about 153 in all."[126]

"The next morning, while Capt. Cooper & many others were scouting around to make discoveries of hidden property, the Captain found the well-known rifle of the poor potter slain in the Boone's Lick region...."[127] This angered Cooper who threatened to kill the Indians. His men "...as if by common consent, cocked their rifles and assumed a shooting attitude."[128] Dodge confronted Cooper, reminding him of the pledge to preserve the Indians' lives. The two leaders argued with each other. One account claims Dodge placed the point of his sword at Cooper's chest, and the Rangers and militia prepared to fire on each other. Yet another account says Cooper threatened Dodge's head "...would fly off his shoulders like hot popcorn off a shovel."[129] Regardless of the circumstances, Cooper yielded, but his men confiscated all the horses and property found with the Miami. Both the Miami and Shawnee scouts showed Colonel Dodge "marked expressions of joy & gratitude."[130] Kish-kal-wa visited Henry Dodge at Fort Leavenworth, Kansas, in 1835, where they reminisced about saving the Piankashaw Miami from the vengeful Boonslick militiamen.

The expedition reached the Arrow Rock, and the Boonslick men were mustered out of military service. The Miami were escorted to the Mississippi River and sent back east. The Rangers continued patrolling the Missouri wilderness but failed to encounter any other Indians. They had, in fact, failed to bring relief to the Boonslick settlements. Shortly after Dodge's departure, the attacks resumed in greater intensity. Braxton Cooper, named for his uncle, was killed while he was cutting logs for a new cabin near Bonne Femme Creek early in October. The Piankashaw Miami were clearly vindicated of wrongdoing, but too late to prevent being uprooted.

Governor Clark wrote to Secretary of War Armstrong on September 18, 1814, the British were "...making great exertions to gain over the Osage, Kanzis, Ottoes & Seioux of the Missouri which I am trying to prevent. Apearancies seems to be favorable to an opinion that the Object of the British is to destroy & drive off the American population in this territory, by the aid of their Indian Allies."[131] Colonel William Russell in St. Louis correctly surmised it was the Sauk from the Rock River who were the main foe of the Boonslick settlers.

By October of 1814, the inhabitants of Cox's settlement returned to their homes. Jesse McMahan, who lived in McMahan's Fort as a boy, related on Christmas Eve of 1814, Indians killed William Gregg as he was rounding up some calves or feeding hogs. Another account says Gregg was retrieving a bear he had shot the previous day. McMahan said the warriors then went into a cabin and found Gregg's teenage daughter, Patsy, whom they took prisoner. Jesse Cox discovered what happened and immediately went to the fort to sound the alarm. A short time later a rescue party set off after Patsy.

The Indians crossed the Missouri River and started up the Chariton River north of present day Glasgow. Patsy was seated behind a warrior on horseback and was tied to him by one hand. "The horse being ridden by the Indian with Miss Gregg captive being overloaded, fell behind the train...When the pursuers came in sight. Miss Gregg with rare daring and presence of mind, snatched the Indian's knife from the scabbard, cut the cord which bound her other hand, and slid safely off the horse...."[132] Before the startled warrior could react, the rescue party opened fire sending the war party into a full gallop. "Miss Gregg was soon in the hands of friends, and speedily carried back to the fort, where she was joyously received by the inmates...."[133]

Thomas Rainey largely concurred with the previous version but said the abducted woman was Gregg's sister-in-law, Patsy Cox.[134] An account by Joseph Cooper said Gregg was shot at his cabin door and dragged inside by the women, where he died. Cooper said the abduction of Patsy actually occurred at Looking Glass Prairie, Illinois, a few years earlier and Patsy was Jesse Cox's daughter. She was tomahawked in the head and hip but recovered and married Gregg, who was part of the rescue party. The whole family then moved to Missouri.[135] This episode shows the difficulty of trying to reconstruct events based on the recollections of old pioneers taken down forty or fifty years after the fact. The truth of the incident will probably never be known.

On the same day Gregg was killed, Samuel McMahan was killed near the mouth of the Lamine River while chopping down a "bee tree" for its honey. Another account says he had crossed the river to gather his livestock; however, both agree as to the date of his death. The single most disastrous death for the Boonslick settlers was that of leader Sarshall Cooper. His son Joseph recalled, "It was April 14, 1815, that Capt. Cooper was killed in his 52nd year. Indians dug through the daubing [of the cabin] — fired through the crevice, on a very stormy night, & instantly killed. He and others had just closed a council to determine on what to do ...It produced a shock like to have broken up the settlement — a good many did leave."[136] Judge Joseph Thorp said an Ioway warrior had killed Cooper. "I often saw him after the war. He was a good-looking buck and took great pride in his name. If you got into a chat with him he would soon let you know, "Me Captain Cooper."[137]

Great Britain and the United States made peace on December 24, 1814, in Ghent, Belgium. The news was slow to reach America and brought no relief to the Boonslick. To frontier settlers, the War of 1812 was known as the Indian War since their foes were native warriors, not British soldiers. A separate peace treaty had to be made with the Indian tribes.[138] Missouri governor William Clark, Illinois governor Ninian Edwards, and Indian trader Auguste Chouteau were appointed on April 15, 1815, to make peace with the Indians. By late July, they had gathered two thousand Indians from 19 different tribes at Portage des Sioux, just north of St. Louis. On September 14, the peace ceremonies were concluded, and only the Rock River Sauk under Black Hawk had failed to sign the treaty.

After the peace treaty was concluded, William Reid reported: "... David Jones, Stephen Turley, Thomas McMahan, James McMahan and this deponent, who had removed to Cooper's Fort during the war, believing that their property would be safe, brought their horses across the river into the bottom, below the Arrow Rock."[139] Horses belonging to Henry Ferrill and Braxton Cooper (elder) were stolen from the fort. They followed the trail of the Indians to the river and "heard them shooting in the bottoms where the horses had been put, viz. below the Arrow Rock."[140]

The next morning a party from the fort crossed the river at the Arrow Rock and found "pens or pounds in the bottom which the Indians had made and driven the horses into, for the purpose of catching them."[141] They followed the Indians' trail to the Chariton River. The Ioway chiefs returning from Portage des Sioux promised to return the stolen horses to the settlers. The settlers went to the Ioway village on the Chariton, but only two of their horses were returned. As they left, a party of young men rushed them, recapturing one horse. Braxton Cooper drove off the second horse to keep it from being recaptured. The settlers filed a claim with the federal government for their loss.

On May 16, 1816, Black Hawk and his co-leaders signed the peace treaty officially ending the Indian War. One more hostile incident occurred in the Boonslick. On the 28th of May, two slaves named Harry and Nat, belonging to Robert and John Heath, disappeared from the Boone's Lick salt works where they had been cutting wood. An abandoned Indian camp was found nearby, and Benjamin Cooper led about fifty men in pursuit. Joseph Cooper gave the following deposition: "I was at the Indian camp, in company of William Becknall and others, where the Indians caught the negroes, where there was left some hog meat and a cane fife; that the party pursued on to the Chareton Creek, some sixty or eighty miles, where we found the Indians discovered us, and had dispersed and taken off the negroes, one of which we discovered by his tracks to have been taken down by the creek or branch, after which we were able to trace them no further. We found at this camp of the Indians the chopping axes of the negroes, and water jug."[142] Martin Dorian, an employee of Indian trader Denis Julien, identified the cane fife as the type made by the Ioway. Harry and Nat were never found and were presumed murdered; it is possible, however, they found freedom courtesy of the Ioways.

Despite the hardships and privations of the war, only about a dozen and a half Boonslick settlers were killed. The number of Indian casualties was probably about the same. A similar number were wounded on both sides. Lindsay Carson, father of the famous western scout Kit Carson, had both thumbs shot off in one skirmish. The settlers were as prone to scalp and butcher slain warriors as the Indians were the settlers. A large force from Cooper's Fort and Fort Hempstead surrounded and wiped out a party of Sauk warriors in 1814. The settlers "cut razor straps" from the backs of the Indians. A wheelwright in the settlement bleached some of their bones to make handles for his tools. Such was the savage nature of frontier warfare on both sides.

The greatest amount of losses occurred with livestock. So many horses were stolen plowing had to be done "…in some cases with their milk cows."[143] John Mason Peck, a Baptist missionary, wrote of the Boonslick settlers: "With all their vigilance during the war, about three hundred horses were stolen; many cattle and nearly all their hogs were killed. Bear-meat and raccoon-bacon became a substitute…."[144] Deerskin clothing became the daily attire, as neither cotton nor flax could be grown to manufacture cloth.

Fort Osage had been reopened in the fall of 1815. The Ioways moved their village from Missouri shortly after the abduction of Harry and Nat. By the summer of 1816, the settlers finally accepted that hostilities had ceased, and they moved out of their forts. The native presence in the Boonslick Country waned rapidly, save for the occasional group passing through. The Franklin *Missouri Intelligencer* reported on June 18, 1825: "A party of the Kansas [Kansa] tribe of Indians, consisting of about fifty, passed through this place on Wednesday last, from St. Louis, where they had been for the purpose of concluding the treaty with Gen. Clark…They exhibited a novel spectacle to our citizens, being nearly in a state of nakedness…."[145] Ten years earlier, their appearance would have generated fear and consternation instead of curiosity.

Taking Up the Land

The Great Migration of 1816 – 1820

During the War of 1812, immigration to Missouri stopped due to the Indian threat. In many outlying settlements, the population had actually decreased as citizens fled to the safety of larger towns. News of the Portage des Sioux peace treaty seemed to release the pent up urge to migrate. John Mason Peck, a Baptist Missionary in St. Charles, made this observation: "Some families came in the spring of 1815; but in the winter, spring, summer and autumn of 1816, they came like an avalanche. It seemed as though Kentucky and Tennessee were breaking up and moving to the Far West. Caravan after caravan passed over the prairies of Illinois all bound to the Boone's Lick. The stream of immigration had not lessened in 1817."[146]

Timothy Flint, another minister in St. Charles, recalled the composition of a typical immigrant caravan: "Between the second and third years of my residence in the country [1816–1817] the immigration from the western and southern states to this country poured in a flood...I have seen in this extent nine wagons harnessed with from four to six horses. We may allow a hundred cattle, besides hogs, horses and sheep, to each wagon; and from three or four to twenty slaves. The whole appearance of the train, the cattle with their hundred bells; the Negroes with delight in their countenances, for their labours are suspended and their imaginations excited; the waggons, often carrying two or three tons, so loaded that the mistress and children are strolling carelessly along in a gait which enables them to keep up with the slow traveling carriages; — the whole group occupies three quarters of a mile."[147]

Descriptions of the Boonslick Country, such as its situation on the Missouri River, fertile bottomland soil, timber and abundance of salt springs, all made it the destination for many settlers even before they arrived in Missouri. The association with the Boone name, made famous by the exploits of Daniel Boone in Kentucky, perhaps added to the attraction. Flint described this attraction: "...the whole current of immigration set towards this country, Boon's Lick...Boon's Lick was the common center of hopes, and the common union for the people. Ask one of them whither he was moving and the answer was, To Boon's Lick, to be sure."[148]

Towns sprang up in the wilderness literally overnight. In 1816, the territorial legislature created Howard County, and shortly thereafter, Franklin was laid off and became the seat of county government. It was located about 12 miles downstream from Arrow Rock. Growth was phenomenal as merchants, traders and land speculators flocked to what was described as the "gateway to the Boonslick El Dorado."[149] In 1819, Edwin James noted Franklin "...contained about one hundred and twenty log houses of one story, several framed dwellings of two stories, and two of brick, thirteen shops for the sale of merchandise, four taverns, two smiths' shops, two large steam-mills, two billiard rooms, court house, a log prison of two stories, a post-office and a printing press issuing a weekly paper."[150] This weekly paper was the *Missouri Intelligencer and Boon's Lick Advertiser*, and it circulated as far west as the Indian boundary.

Howard County encompassed almost the entire western third of Missouri Territory. A United States Land Office was set up in Franklin, specifically to handle the filing of all the land claims in the region. Retired General Thomas A. Smith, for whom Ft. Smith, Arkansas, is named, was appointed agent of the land office. Although many settlers arrived on keelboat as the Coopers had done in 1808, most followed the Boone's Lick Trail from St. Charles because overland travel was far cheaper. As late as 1819, the trail was really little more than a trace.

Although the river crossing at Arrow Rock was the scene of much emigrant traffic and activity, no large settlement took place there. Joseph Huston and Burton Lawless, who would later play important roles in the founding of the town, had settled near the Arrow Rock by 1819. As late as 1823, Duke Paul recorded seeing only one small cabin, about a mile beyond the Arrow Rock. Arrow Rock was destined to remain only a crossroads for several more years.

Since the site of Arrow Rock was mostly prairie, immigrants crossing the river there headed toward the river bottoms to the north or turned southwest toward the Lamine and Blackwater Rivers. Timber was found only along the rivers, and the settlers believed crops could not grow on land that did not grow timber. Furthermore, wood for building and fuel would have to be hauled longer distances on the prairie. William B. Napton, Jr. added that clouds of biting flies plagued the prairies in the summer months, making them almost uninhabitable.[151] George Sibley recounted in his journal of 1825 that green flies on the Missouri prairies were so troublesome, his survey party on the Santa Fe Trail "... were obliged to travel a great deal in the Night."[152]

Many settlers who later became associated with the town of Arrow Rock settled first in Cox's Bottoms. In June of 1816, Daniel Thornton, Isaac Clark and William Clark arrived from Tennessee by poling and pulling their keelboat up the Mississippi and Missouri Rivers. By the end of the year, Henry Nave, Abraham Nave, Jacob Nave and William Collector reached the settlement in Cox's Bottoms. This group came from St. Charles over the Boone's Lick Trail. As yet, the trail was not very well developed. They got lost and were delayed by high water. Their provisions ran out, and hunting was difficult as game was scarce due to over-hunting near the trail.[153]

The arrival of wagons signified changes in transportation and freight hauling. It was a harbinger of developed settlements and the roads to connect them. Thomas Keeney passed by Arrow Rock in December, 1816, with the first wagon brought into present-day Saline County. Henry Nave brought the second wagon across the Missouri River several days later. On Christmas Day of 1816, Nave "... secured two canoes, lashed them together, uncoupled his wagon, took the hind wheels and axle over on one trip, the fore wheels and tongue in another; then in successive trips he ferried over the wagon bed and its contents."[154]

Nave's experience demonstrates the rigors experienced by early pioneers. He set about building a cabin from the inside out. A hard freeze set in before he could make mud mortar for "chinking," or daubing between the logs. The chimney was built out of wood and lined with stones but could not be used until it had been daubed with mortar. "He therefore built a fire in the middle of the cabin, by which means he thawed the earth underneath the fire ... he dug up the earth near his fire and made his mortar inside; daubed the cracks in the wall and lined the chimney with mortar working from the inside."[155] He finished up with log joists he laid down and covered with a puncheon floor he shaped and fitted together with his adze. Nave is credited with being the first permanent settler of Saline County as he was the first one to remain here until he died of old age.

Fred Hartgrove and James Sappington joined the settlement shortly thereafter. Jesse Cox, possibly feeling crowded, sold out by 1818 and moved on to Tabo Creek in present-day Lafayette County.[156] By September of 1820, Isaac Nave and several more Tennesseeans arrived in Cox's Bottoms. Henry and Isaac Nave's stepmother soon changed the family name to Neff, which is how the family is usually identified in later documents. The Neff family owned substantial farms around Arrow Rock, and their descendants remain in the area today.

Another area of settlement north of Cox's Bottoms was the "Big Bottom." This area stretched along the south bank of the Missouri River opposite present-day Glasgow. For a brief period of time, this area would be the focal point of activities in Saline County. James Wilhite and William Hayes were the first to settle at the lower end of the bottom in the fall of 1816. Charles Lucas, Peter Lausson and George Tennille followed them in early 1817. These men and many others settled on "New Madrid certificates" in the Big Bottom.[157]

In the winter of 1811–12, one of the worst earthquakes in the history of the United States occurred near New Madrid, Missouri. There is no mention of the earthquake by Boonslick settlers, but shock waves rang church bells in Philadelphia, Pennsylvania. The Mississippi River changed course and even ran backwards in some places. New lakes formed as the waters from the Mississippi rushed in to fill sunken ground. Geysers of sand and water sprayed into the air in some areas. Landmarks disappeared, cabins and barns collapsed, and fields were either under water or under mountains of sand. Only the light population and minimal development prevented a catastrophic death toll.

All the landmarks that had been used for surveying property lines were gone. Rather than try to resurvey old boundaries, the U.S. government simply compensated landowners for their loss by issuing New Madrid certificates to exchange for land elsewhere in Missouri. Many of the certificates were issued for land in the Boonslick. One New Madrid certificate was issued to Luc Bellefeuille on the Arrow Rock bluff just north of the town site.[158] There is no record Bellefeuille actually took up residence here. He probably sold his certificate to land speculators without ever visiting the tract.

By the fall of 1817, nearly 300 people lived in the Big Bottom when

Jacob Ish arrived there with his family. Ish drove his wagon into the tall, dry prairie grass, made his camp and turned out his horses to graze. That night they strayed away, and he and his son set off to search for them in the morning. According to the 1881 Saline County history, "He had not long been gone when suddenly six painted Indians appeared at the wagon and began talking wildly and gesticulating alarmingly to and at Mrs. Ish. The poor woman was frightened and did not know what they meant. Directly she saw a volume of black smoke rising in and approaching from the west …. Then the Indians caught up fire-brands, and setting fire to the grass soon had quite an area burned over. Into this cleared place they rolled Ish's wagon, and removed all his other property and his family. Hardly was this done when the conflagration was upon them; but the fire passed them by on either side …."[159]

The grateful Ish gave the Indians all the tobacco he had. It is said these Indians, who were probably Osage, periodically visited Ish in the following years, and each time he would purchase for them "a whole caddy of tobacco of which they were very fond."[160] In March of 1819, Jacob Ish was appointed Justice of the Peace in Arrow Rock Township. The Cooper County Court in Boonville, which then had administrative oversight of the township, approved his appointment.

Small settlements also grew up along the Lamine and Blackwater Rivers. As early as 1817, Edward Reavis ascended the Lamine and Blackwater rivers in a flatboat, settling near present-day Sweet Springs. "His party numbered fourteen souls, one-half being his own family and the other half, his negro servants…."[161] Reavis engaged in salt manufacturing and supplied many of the settlers in that quarter for nearly 15 years. The Saline County seal used in the 1830s, which showed two men making salt, was purportedly based on Reavis' salt works. Arthur Hunt, a North Carolinian, formed another settlement on the Blackwater River near present-day Napton in 1818.

As the population of the Boonslick Country grew, so did its boundaries. The August 27, 1819 edition of the *Missouri Intelligencer* newspaper defined the boundary as "… extending on both sides the Missouri from the mouth of the Osage to the western Indian boundary, a distance of about 200 miles."[162] By the end of the territorial period in 1820, there were 21,300 people, including 3,216 slaves, living in this region. Over 1,000 people lived in Franklin alone, second only in size to St. Louis among

Missouri's towns. Chariton, another boomtown, was laid out by Duff Green in 1817, about 20 miles upriver from the Arrow Rock. Boonville was established about 15 miles downriver from Arrow Rock in 1819.

Land speculators generally purchased a quantity of property and then divided it into lots for a "new town." Prominent men were often solicited to become part of the deal, and newspaper ads extolled the virtues of owning a lot in the newly-platted town site. After the War of 1812, purchasers eager to make a profit envisioned their property increasing in value rapidly over the next few years. Timothy Flint wrote, "Art and ingenuity have been exhausted in devising new ways of alluring purchasers, to take lots and build in the new town. There are fine rivers, the healthy hills, the mineral springs, the clear running water, the eligible mill-seats, the valuable forests, the quarries of building-stone, the fine steam boat navigation, the vast country adjacent, the central position, the great connecting point between the great towns, the admirable soil, and last of all the cheerful and undoubting predictions of what the town must one day be."[163]

This land speculation in the Boonslick Country was nothing new in the American frontier experience. However, the explosive rate of growth and development was unprecedented in American history. Unfortunately, practices often associated with land speculation bordered on the unethical, if not illegal. Some speculators bought up New Madrid certificates for pennies on the dollar and then sold the land. Tradesmen and ministers were offered lots for free to attract interest, and then the remaining lots were sold at extravagant prices. A Mr. A. Fuller from Franklin wrote to a friend in 1819, "I went over the river last summer to attend the first sale of lots, intending to purchase some to build on, but they were run up to a fabulous price, away beyond my reach."[164] While fortunes were made by many, they were often as quickly lost. Many of the boomtowns simply failed to live up to their promises.

Banks throughout the western territories and states were caught up in the frenzy of speculation. People bought land on credit, hoping to sell it for a profit before making payments on the notes. Thus, banks were making loans on personal security and property of inflated values. This activity resulted in a financial depression known as the "panic of 1819."[165] After the spring of 1820, the flood of immigration that had fueled high prices and growth of the Missouri Territory halted. By 1821, land was no longer marketable, agricultural products had no outlets, and merchants who had purchased their stock on credit had no buyers.[166] The banking system completely disappeared from Missouri, as did many of the boomtowns, which were reclaimed by the prairies and forests from which they had been carved.

The Ferry Crossing

The Missouri River is today a great barrier that divides counties and the towns that dot its valley. But in the 19th century, the Missouri was the great water highway of the American West, linking farms, settlements and towns to form a strong regional identity. For example, at present, to reach the Boone's Lick salt spring in Boone's Lick State Historic Site from Arrow Rock requires a drive of 30 miles, using the bridges at either Glasgow or Boonville. In the 19th century, the trip was only three miles when crossing the river.

Fording the Missouri River could be a difficult and even treacherous proposition. The banks could be extremely muddy, steep or choked with brush. The wider stretches of river had an accumulation of snags, root wads, and debris making it impossible to wade or float through. A seemingly solid sandbar could disappear into the river within minutes. Conversely, it could reappear within minutes farther downstream. Conditions at the Arrow Rock, however, favored river crossing. The river was narrow, and a rocky landing provided a stable, solid bank. William Clark's descriptions indicated the locale was a good place to cross the river. Native Americans had used the river crossing at the Arrow Rock for untold generations.

Late in the 19th century, John Patterson, an old pioneer, stated the Arrow Rock ferry began operation in 1811.[167] Another date given by old settlers in some accounts was 1813. It is not unusual for these reminiscences to be off by a few years, and it seems unlikely the ferry was in operation at that time. The problem with the earliest dates is a ferry had few people to convey and no real destination. Very few settlers were living on the Saline County side of the river, and they simply used dugout canoes and would swim their livestock across.

The first documented record of the ferry being in operation is April of 1817. Judiah Osman was licensed as a ferryman by the Howard County circuit court. He may have been operating the ferry as early as the summer of 1815 when the first wave of immigrants began arriving in the Boone's Lick Country. The 1881 history says the first ferryman at Arrow Rock was Fred Hartgrove or Jerry Lecky, and they maintained a small cabin near the Arrow Rock.[168] Since these men were identified as living in Cox's Bottoms, they may have operated a ferry at the "little Arrow Rock." It is possible the old pioneer reminiscences are confused, as court records show "Benjamin Hartgrove appeared and prayed the court for a license to keep a ferry at the Missouri River at the Big Arrow Rock for seven months from the 9th of July [1830] which the court ordered to be granted by his paying $5.86 1/4 and it is ordered that the clerk certify the same to the auditor of P. A. [Public Accounts]."[169] Clearly, there was a succession of ferry owners and operators at Arrow Rock. Documentation regarding the operation is rather sporadic and incomplete. Further examination of Saline and Howard County court records may provide more details of who operated the ferries and when.

Another well-known and widely-used ferry was Hardeman's near the mouth of the Lamine River. This ferry was established by Thomas Hardeman around 1820 and was licensed to his son, John. It linked their experimental farm, "Fruitage Farm," with the south bank of the river. Hardeman's ferry was used as a crossing for some of the early Santa Fe caravans.[170] Because they were only a few miles apart, it is possible that some activity attributed to the Arrow Rock ferry may have actually occurred at Hardeman's ferry and vice versa.

On September 9, 1817, Judiah Osman, acting as administrator for the estate of John Busby,[171] deeded a tract of land to John Ferrill "in Boone's Lick Bottom and opposite the arrow rock of 150 acres ... and more or less to include the improvements and ferry established there."[172] The Howard County Circuit Court Minute Book recorded Ferrill was operating both the bar and the ferry. A young attorney named David Todd purchased the ferry from Ferrill, and in the October 1, 1819 edition of the Franklin *Missouri Intelligencer* he advertised to lease the "Arrow Rock ferry and farm, where Mr. Ferrill now lives, for one year ... Its notoriety and situation for a ferry and tavern, renders description unnecessary." Todd retained ownership of landings on both banks on the river "below the Arrow Rock" until at least 1833.[173] The stream immediately north of Arrow Rock was known as Todd's Branch.[174] Todd was the uncle of a Kentucky girl named Mary Todd who would become Mrs. Abraham Lincoln.

Members of Stephen Long's "Expedition to the Far West" wrote a detailed description of the Arrow Rock ferry in 1819: "The ferry boat used at Arrow Rock is one peculiarly adapted to the navigation of a rapid stream. It consists of two canoes, on which rests a platform, with a slight railing to prevent cattle from falling off."[175] Long also offered some comments that demonstrate how the river has changed over the years: "From its summit (Arrow Rock) is a pleasing view of the river, and near the base is a remarkable eddy, which as they were crossing, whirled their ferry boat entirely around."[176] Today the river is nearly a mile away from the bluff and is difficult to see. The cottonwood forest will obscure the view as the trees mature. Channelization of the river has eliminated most of the natural eddies as well.

When Duke Paul Wilhelm passed through the area in 1823, Hugh McCafferty was probably leasing the ferry and riverside tavern from Todd. Duke Paul described his stopover and dinner at the little tavern:

> *We made seven more miles through swampy primeval forests… About four o'clock in the afternoon we reached an isolated house on the Missouri opposite Pierre de la Fleche. Here lived the owner of the ferry on which one crosses the river. The inhabitants of the wretched hut were poor but good-hearted people, and we stayed an hour to rest … In this great heat, drinking water unmixed with some kind of spirituous drink is very harmful and may produce fever. In the house we could get nothing at all to eat except some old milk which had almost turned to cheese and some dried-out cornbread. This constituted dinner.*[177]

His description of the ferry operation revealed some details not given by Long:

> *Nothing remarkable occurred during my crossing of the river on a raft. Requiring almost an entire hour to get across, the raft had to be pulled half an English mile up the stream. The current in the neighborhood of the rocks called Pierre de la Fleche is extremely swift and it was most difficult to make the raft fast on the right bank.*[178]

Colonel John Glover of Kentucky, on the other hand, found the Spartan accommodations of the Arrow Rock ferry and tavern reasonably agreeable. He was scouting Missouri for new land to settle and on

October 19, 1826, he recorded in his diary, "came on to the Airy Rock
Ferry at Mr. Becknal where I tarried all night. Becknals house stands on
the north bank of the Missouria on a Bank of sand 2 small cabbands
bad appearance but good fair bill Ferriage and all 87 1/2 cents."[179] Some
sources indicate the ferryman was Henry Becknell, brother to Santa Fe
entrepreneur, William Becknell.[180] Other sources indicate it was William
Becknell himself who operated the ferry. William B. Napton noted 1827
was an especially busy year for the Arrow Rock ferry as the population of
the county itself swelled that year.[181]

By the fall of 1819 the volume of traffic had outgrown the old Osage
Trace leading to the ferry landing. The Howard County court appointed
Ezekiel Williams, William Thorp, Thomas Hardeman and Stephen Jack-
son to select a new road from Cooper's Fort to the ferry. At the second
session of the Saline County court on July 16, 1821, Littleberry Estes,
Daniel McDowell, and William White, Jr. were appointed commission-
ers to view and mark out a road leading from the Arrow Rock to Grand
Pass at the western boundary of the county. This was the first road in Saline
County; it followed much of the old Osage Trace.[182]

Abiel Leonard, the lawyer from Fayette who went on to become a
Missouri Supreme Court judge, kept an account with William Park who
was operating the Arrow Rock ferry in 1852 and 1853. Leonard's account is
the only record of the ferriage rates at Arrow Rock:

1852		*Abiel Leonard & Charles Leland to Wm. Park Dr.*	
		To fering Boy a foot twice	20
June	2	*to fering Boy & horse & 4 cows*	65
	19	*to fering Boy horse*	25
	21	*to fering Boy & horse & too yoak catel*	75
July	3	*to fering Leland & horse & Litel boy & horse*	50
	5	*to fering Leland & horse & Litel boy & horse*	50
Oct.	7	*to fering Boy & horse & too yoak of oxens*	75
	10	*to fering Boy & horse*	25
Dec.	25	*to fering Leland & horse & Boy twice*	95
		to fering cart & oxens & boy and horse	1.00
1853	Jan. 8	*to fering Leland & horse & Boy & yoak catel*	50
	12	*to fering Leland & horse*	25
	18	*to fering Boy a foot twice*	20

6.75

1852   July 5 credited by cash By Leland   1.00
1853   May 14 credited By cash by By Leonard   1.40

                                                          2.40

                              Due   5.35

Received Payment in full this the 23 July 1853

                              (Signed) Wm. Park [183]

Henry Cooper, a descendant of the famous pioneer family of Howard County, was operating the ferry in 1865.[184] The 1876 plat map of the town identified the waterfront along the Missouri as "Cooper's Ferry privilege." It is not known what type of craft Cooper was operating. The platform on canoes described by Long in 1819 undoubtedly underwent some revision. Unfortunately, no descriptions of the Arrow Rock ferry after 1823 have been located. We can only speculate on the ferry's development based on the experience of neighboring communities.

Steam technology was coming into wide use by the 1830s. A steam-powered ferry was operating in St. Louis in 1832. On April 25, 1849, the Glasgow *Weekly Times* reported a compact steam ferryboat had passed by on the river, bound for Lexington. This inspired Glasgow merchants to form the "Glasgow Steam-Ferry Company" which contracted $3,000 in January of 1850 for a ferryboat to be built at Louisville, Kentucky.[185] An 1872 handbill from Boonville illustrates a large sternwheeler steamer as the ferryboat.[186] At some point the Arrow Rock ferry converted to a steam-powered vessel as well. Arrow Rock certainly had the volume of traffic and level of prosperity to support such a venture. It may well have been that Abiel Leonard's ferry account was for a steamboat. Further research is needed to determine when such a transition occurred.

Around the turn of the century there was a succession of sternwheeler ferryboats. The *Hope* operated at the crossing around 1900. The *Dorothy* was in operation by 1916. The *Santa Fe* made its last run across the river at Arrow Rock in 1927. Daniel and Earl Kuhn were the operators, and they charged $1.00 per car for the crossing.[187] By that time the rural population of Saline and Howard County was decreasing, and modernization of the highway system had bypassed the ferry crossing. Furthermore, the ever-changing channel of the Missouri River had moved away from town. When highway bridges were opened over the Missouri River at Boonville and Glasgow, the Arrow Rock ferry was rendered obsolete.

The Santa Fe Trail

The Arrow Rock ferry was a crossroads and the scene of events of great importance in the development of Howard and Saline Counties. This was one factor that eventually led to the establishment of Arrow Rock at its locale. The ferry crossing's most famous association is with the Santa Fe Trail. Three sites in Arrow Rock have been certified by the National Park Service as part of the Santa Fe National Historic Trail: the old ferry landing (currently undeveloped), the Big Spring and the Huston Tavern.

The Panic of 1819 left Missouri in an economic depression. Money was in short supply, and only gold or silver coins (specie) were accepted as legal tender. Paper notes were deemed worthless, and as a result, Missouri had no banking system until 1837. Merchandise sat unsold in the stores of Franklin and other towns. Farmers had no market for their surplus produce. Times were desperate, and people faced prosecution for debts they could not afford to pay. One of those facing such prosecution was William Becknell. He owed Henry V. Bingham $495.70, and Bingham formally filed suit in November of 1821.[188]

Becknell had been a manager at the Boone's Lick salt works and a Ranger in the War of 1812. Seeking a way out of debt, he placed the following ad in the June 25, 1821 issue of the *Missouri Intelligencer*: "An article for the government of a company of men destined to the westward for the purpose of trading for Horses and Mules and catching Wild Animals of every description."[189] A meeting of all those who wished to go was held August 4 at the home of Ezekiel Williams, about midway between Arrow Rock and Franklin.

Becknell and four other men outfitted packhorses, each brought a rifle and ammunition, and each invested ten dollars in merchandise. "Our company crossed the Missouri near the Arrow Rock ferry on the first day of September 1821, and encamped six miles from the old ferry."[190] The party followed the road marked by the Saline County commissioners on the Osage Trace a few months before. They stopped at Fort Osage to write letters, purchase medicines and make other last minute preparations before heading southwest toward New Mexico.

Spain controlled vast lands in the southwest and viewed foreigners entering New Mexico with suspicion. Parties of American traders and trappers, who previously entered New Mexico, had their properties confiscated and were jailed. However, Becknell's expedition happened to coincide with the establishment of Mexico as an independent republic. On November 16, Becknell's party "…arrived at Santa Fe and were received with apparent pleasure and joy."[191] They returned to Franklin late in January of 1822.

Although the amount of goods Becknell carried was meager, the trip must have been extremely profitable. H. H. Harris recalled, "My father saw them unload when they returned, and when their rawhide packages of silver dollars were dumped on the sidewalk one of the men cut the thongs and the money spilled out clinking on the stone pavement and rolled into the gutter."[192] Some accounts claim this event occurred in Arrow Rock. This is false, as the town of Arrow Rock did not yet exist.

Becknell wasted no time in planning a return trip to Santa Fe: "Having made arrangements to return, on the 22nd day of May, 1822, I crossed the Arrow Rock ferry, and on the third day our company, consisting of 21 men, with three waggons concentrated."[193] This was the first use of wagons on the trail. Becknell was free of debt and earned the appellation "Father of the Santa Fe Trail." He appears to have operated the Arrow Rock ferry in 1826. By 1827, William Becknell became a resident of Saline County and was justice of the peace of Arrow Rock Township. He also filled other minor county positions before moving to the Red River country of Texas in 1835.

Spain had consumed the resources of New Mexico while returning little to the people in the way of finished goods. Now they were free to utilize their resources for their benefit, creating a market for economically depressed Missouri. It was only about 800 miles from Missouri to Santa Fe, whereas it was over 1,800 miles from Santa Fe to Vera Cruz, Mexico's official port of entry. Soon caravans were outfitting in Franklin and crossing the Arrow Rock ferry to cash in on the trade boom. Trade items included "Cotton goods, consisting of coarse and fine cambrics, calicos, domestic, shawls, handkerchiefs, steam-loom shirtings, and cotton hose. A few woolen goods, consisting of super blues, stroudings, pelisse cloths, and shawl, crapes, bombazettes, some light articles of cutlery, silk shawls, and looking glasses. In addition to these, many articles, necessary for the purpose of an assortment."[194]

The *Missouri Intelligencer* heralded the benefits of the new trade as exemplified by an expedition led by Stephen Cooper: "It is gratifying to learn that these enterprising adventurers have made a profitable trip. The party brings with it, in exchange for the merchandise it carried out, above 400 Jacks, Jennets, and mules, a quantity of beaver, and a considerable sum of specie [gold and silver coins]. The beaver, and the livestock will bear a profit by transportation to some of the older states, and the specie, in these troubled times, will serve to impart activity to the business of the county."[195] Coarse wool blankets and Spanish-style saddles were also imported into Missouri to some degree.

During the first ten years of the trade, one of the chief obstacles was interference from the Indians. The Santa Fe Trail crossed through the territory of the Osage, Kansa, Comanche, Kiowa, Pawnee, Arapahoe, Southern Cheyenne and Apache nations. As the number of caravans increased, so did the clashes between traders and Indians. Primarily, the warriors tried to steal or drive off the livestock, and occasionally traders and teamsters were killed. Reports such as this one in the June 17, 1823 issue of the *Missouri Intelligencer* were fairly typical: "We regret to have to state that the company whose departure *for* Santa Fe we mentioned about four weeks since, have sustained the loss of nearly all their horses. Some Osage Indians, conjectured to be about twenty, followed them eighty miles undiscovered, with a view, as appeared in the sequel, of committing outrage. On the morning of the first instant, at about dawn, while all the company were asleep except two, who, not apprehending danger, had retired from an advanced position to the campfires, they were alarmed by the discharge of guns, and the yells of the savages."[196]

By 1825, the Santa Fe commerce had become a major factor in the Missouri economy. However, newspapers like the *Missouri Intelligencer* printed articles decrying the "ruinous state" of the trade. It was simply a calculated bid to prevent outsiders from other states from cashing in on the trade. In January of 1825, Senator Thomas Hart Benton introduced a bill in Congress authorizing the President to appoint a commission to mark a road from Fort Osage to the boundary with Mexico on the Arkansas River. With the permission of Mexico, the road was to be marked on into Santa Fe. The commission was also to secure safe passage for the caravans from the various Indian nations along it.

President John Quincy Adams appointed Lt. Governor Benjamin Reeves, George Sibley and prominent fur trader Pierre Menard of Kaskaskia, Illinois, as commissioners. Menard declined and was replaced by Thomas Mather, also a Kaskaskia merchant. The Arrow Rock was the designated rendezvous for the expedition. "The commissioners (Col. Reeves and Mr. Sibley) left here (Franklin) on the 4th inst. Accompanied by their Secretary and Surveyor, immediately after our anniversary festival, and proceeded to Arrow Rock, the place of rendezvous. They would meet there the guard, (thirty men) chain carriers, waggons, &c."[197]

Sibley kept a journal of the trip and described some difficulty in crossing at the Arrow Rock ferry. "Tuesday 5th July — Left Franklin at 11 o'Clk. The day extremely warm. Col. Reeves & the Horsemen overtook us, and we all came up with the Waggons before they reached the ferry, & passed them. We crossed the Missouri at the Arrow Rock and went on to Reece's and halted. Nearly All the Horsemen got over the River this evening, but the wind was too violent to cross the Waggons, except two of them. It is 12 miles from Franklin to Reece's.

Wednesday 6th July — Tremendous Storm of Rain and Wind last Night. The Waggons all got safely over this morning, and now our Whole party is assembled ready to move on to the work assigned us. It consists of Col. Reeves & G. C. Sibley, Commissioners — Archibald Gamble, Secretary — J. C. Brown, Surveyor — Stephen Cooper, Supt of the Hands...."[198]

The commissioners met with the Osage leaders at Council Grove, Kansas, on the Neosho River on August 5 "...and there made a treaty with them for the passage of the road, and the unmolested use of the same to the citizens of the United States and the Republic of Mexico."[199] In return the Osage received an annuity of $800. A similar treaty was made with the Kansa. These treaties not only secured safe passage for the traders' caravans, they also took the remaining Osage and Kansa lands in Missouri and eastern Kansas and confined both nations to greatly reduced reservations. Much of their old territory was divided up and given to eastern Indian tribes being removed by the government.

For some unknown reason, the commission actually went to Taos instead of Santa Fe. They made markers along the way, but these succumbed to the weather or were destroyed by Indians. The surveys and maps were filed away in Washington, D.C. and were rarely used. Traders already knew the way, and caravans simply followed the ruts of previous ones. The work of the commission did bring national attention to the Santa Fe trade and efforts to extend the same types of protection to "inland commerce" as was given to "maritime commerce."[200] The Army Corps of Topographical Engineers found the commission maps useful in the 1840s and 1850s.

As the trade grew, the Arrow Rock ferry soon saw two-way traffic. Mexican merchants came to Missouri to trade. In 1826, the Franklin *Missouri Intelligencer* reported: "Six or seven new and substantial built waggons arrived in this place on Tuesday last, heavily laden with merchandise, on their way to New Mexico, owned … by Mr. Escudero, a native of that country … This may be considered as a new era in the commerce between Mexico and this country, and it is probable the example of Mr. E will be followed by others of his rich countrymen, who will bring hither large portions of their surplus wealth, for the same purpose…."[201] Trader Josiah Gregg reported that by 1843, fully half the merchants on the Santa Fe Trail were Mexican nationals.[202]

Oral tradition holds the Big Spring south of the Tavern was a watering stop for the early Santa Fe caravans. This may well be true as it was the first freshwater spring encountered after crossing the Missouri River. Some Santa Fe caravans outfitted in Boonville, and the road from Boonville to Arrow Rock passed directly by the spring. By the 1940s, the spring was frequently referred to as the "Santa Fe Spring" in tourism literature, although Big Spring has always remained its official designation. The spring is no longer in its natural state. To protect it from being trampled and muddied, the spring was fenced or enclosed multiple times beginning in the 19th century.

By 1831, Independence, a hundred miles farther upriver, had emerged as the main outfitting center for the Santa Fe trade. Franklin had largely been washed away by the shifting Missouri River, and Arrow Rock was still in its infancy. However, it is possible that some caravans outfitted here. Josiah Gregg wrote in 1844: "The town of Franklin on the Missouri River … seems truly to have been the cradle of our trade; and in conjunction with several neighboring towns, continued to furnish the greater number of these adventurous traders. Even subsequently to 1831, many wagons have been outfitted and started from this interior section."[203] Trading caravans have been documented as leaving Fayette and even Columbia as late as 1835. These would have crossed the river at or near Arrow Rock.

William B. Napton, Jr. makes Arrow Rock's connection to the Santa Fe trade clear:

> *... The relations between the people of old Franklin and Arrow Rock were very intimate, that is in their trade relations, it being only ten miles from the eastern terminus of the Santa Fe Trail....*[204] *A considerable number of citizens of this county [Saline] joined the caravans after they had crossed the river at Arrow Rock, to engage in the Santa Fe trade also, Colonel Marmaduke making at least four trips, finding the business quite profitable. Besides Marmaduke from this county, there was William and Darwin Sappington, and James W. Smith, son of General T. A. Smith. Their wagons for Santa Fe were loaded at old Jonesboro [now Napton], where the Sappingtons had a store for some years...This Santa Fe Trail, crossing the river at Arrow Rock, followed the old Osage trace across the county in a direct route to Grand Pass...*[205]

In 1824, Meredith Miles Marmaduke, an employee of Franklin merchant Augustus Storrs, accompanied the first large-scale caravan to use wheeled conveyances. The company consisted of "... seventy-eight men, who have twenty-three carriages, waggons and dearborns and on an estimate about two hundred horses."[206] Marmaduke kept a journal of the trip, the first to be made while traveling on the trail. Marmaduke was returning to Missouri and met George Sibley at Fort Osage on July 27, 1825: "This evening Col. Marmaduke arrived at my House with Mr. James Moore, direct from S[an]ta Fee. They came with a large Party, who bought a great number of Mules, Asses, &c. They were met by a Large Band of Osage Indians ... by whom they were robbed of about 120 head of Animals, & some other property...."[207]

After this trip Marmaduke moved to Arrow Rock Township. In 1827, he and his brother-in-law, Darwin Sappington, and Thomas McMahan formed a partnership "... to engage in the trade with Mexico."[208] Marmaduke suffered losses again in 1829 when Indians, probably Comanche, struck his caravan and made off with the entire herd. Senator Thomas Hart Benton wrote a letter to Marmaduke expressing his regrets. Incidents such as these caused traders to call for protection of the trade with military escorts. This loss and increased Mexican tariffs, along with a growing family, caused Marmaduke to quit the trade by 1830.

John Hardeman was a prominent agricultural experimenter who got involved in the Santa Fe trade and left his business affairs in the care of his son, John Locke. A slave named William was given the task of operating Fruitage Farm. Hardeman, Sr. had the financial backing of General Thomas Smith, and in May of 1828, ferried his wagons and merchandise across the Missouri below the Arrow Rock. Alphonso Wetmore was elected captain of the caravan and Hardeman second in command. In August, they reached Santa Fe and found trade to be "a bad prospect."[209] The market was glutted, and some of the party went farther down into Chihuahua and Sonora to sell their goods. John left the port of Matamoras for New Orleans on August 10, 1829. In New Orleans he contracted yellow fever where he soon died. Doctor Jonas Kerr fleeced his estate of $1,643.63 1/2 for treating the ailing Santa Fe trader.[210]

Philip W. Thompson was a prominent Arrow Rock merchant connected to the Santa Fe trade. "Mr. Thompson conducted personally some very large freight trains or outfits to Santa Fe and other points in the Southwest."[211] Mexican officials refused to accept Thompson's "Santa Fe papers" in 1837 and prohibited him from entering New Mexico. He petitioned Manuel Alvarez, the U.S. Consul in Mexico, "... to get Bicente Sancha and Gregorio Ortiz to certify them."[212] In 1847, the Arrow Rock Masonic Lodge No. 55 made the following resolution: "On motion resolves that as Bro. H. S. Mills is about to travel in foreign countries that this Lodge give him a certificate of membership, and that Bro. P. W. Thompson, now in Santa Fe, New Mexico be presented with a like certificate."[213]

Henry S. Mills, mentioned above, was another prominent Arrow Rock merchant and may have had some connection to the Santa Fe trade. New Mexico was still a "foreign country" at this time. Mills may have been making investments in Thompson's or another trader's ventures. Around 1845, Thompson became a business partner of Joseph Huston, who operated the tavern and a store in Arrow Rock.[214] It is unknown if Huston was involved in Thompson's Santa Fe trade business.

According to Thompson family tradition, an old trapper resided alone in a cabin on the estate, overlooking the river. Each spring when he returned from the West, Philip Thompson would first go out to the bluff to check on him. On one of his later trips, he went to the cabin and found a decomposing skeleton in the bed.

Around 1848, Thompson and his wife Brunette (Lawless) were divorced. Again, according to Thompson family tradition, he found his wife was pregnant when he returned from the West.[215] William B. Napton, Jr. simply wrote: "Soon after the close of the Mexican war Mrs. Thompson secured a divorce from her husband ..."[216] It is difficult to ascertain exactly what the circumstances were. Topics such as divorce and adultery were not openly discussed or recorded at this time. Huston, a widower since 1855, married Brunette Thompson in 1857.

Thompson continued to make annual trips to New Mexico and California up to 1861. That year, his caravan was supposed to have been "requisitioned" by State Guard troops under General Sterling Price.[217] Thompson's Greek-Revival style house, "Chestnut Hill," was built in 1844 on a 1,000-acre tract of land he purchased in 1826. The house is one mile west of Arrow Rock and remains in the possession of Thompson descendants. Traces of Santa Fe wagon ruts were visible near the house as late as the 1940s.

The Turleys were another Arrow Rock family with long-lasting ties to Santa Fe. In 1816, Samuel Turley brought his brothers and sisters from Kentucky, and they joined their brother, Stephen Turley, at the Jones-McMahan settlement south of Arrow Rock. Around 1819, Jesse B. Turley became involved in trade with the Osage Indians at "Three Forks," the junction of the Verdigris, Grand and Arkansas rivers in Oklahoma. Stephen was voted "commander of the guards" in a large wagon caravan that went to Santa Fe in 1827. In 1830, Simeon Turley moved to New Mexico and by 1831 had settled near Arroyo Hondo, 12 miles north of Taos.[218]

Simeon built a two-story mill and a distillery famous for producing liquor known as "Taos Lightning." He also had a prosperous ranch and gold mine and was soon the wealthiest man in New Mexico. He even applied for Mexican citizenship, though this seems to have never been approved. Jesse and Simeon formed a partnership, and nearly every year from 1834 on, Jesse and his son, Talton, would bring wagonloads of trade goods to Hondo Arroyo. Simeon then traded the merchandise from a store on his ranch. On April 18, 1843, Simeon sent a letter to Jesse in Arrow Rock informing him he was shipping him "200 buffalo robes and some beaver."[219] Simeon was described as an open-hearted, generous man and was well liked by visiting Americans, except for a Methodist preacher named

Joseph Williams, who said that he "...makes a great many drunkards."[220]

On January 19, 1847, Taos Indians and Mexicans rebelled against American rule of New Mexico, and Governor Charles Bent was killed. Simeon Turley believed he would be spared, but the mob headed for his ranch the following day and burned it. Turley got away, and a Mexican friend hid him eight miles from Arroyo Hondo. The following day, the man reported the hiding place to the mob, and Turley was killed. At the same time, Jesse Turley's wagon caravan was en route from Missouri and was attacked on the Arkansas River. Fifty-five oxen were driven off by Indians, allegedly Osage. Philip W. Thompson, Jesse Turley and Henry C. Miller, also of Arrow Rock, made a memorial to Congress asking for compensation for their losses. The memorial passed the Senate on March 24, 1852, and was sent to the House, but it never appears to have been voted on.[221] At the end of the Mexican War in 1848, Jesse settled Simeon's estate to provide support for Simeon's common-law wife, Maria Rosita Romero, and their seven children.

Jesse Turley then entered into partnership with Richens "Uncle Dick" Wooten, another famous trader. Wooten improved the trail over the Raton Pass in New Mexico and turned it into a toll road. In 1849, Stephen and Jesse were in a caravan leaving from Independence. While on the Cimarron River they learned of the gold strike in California. Stephen sold his outfit on the spot and headed for the gold fields. This apparently angered Jesse, who yelled, "All right, go to California and take that damn fiddle with you."[222] Stephen did well panning for gold and returned to Missouri in the fall of 1850. He set about building a fine brick house to replace his log cabin overlooking the Lamine River, but died soon thereafter. Jesse decided to permanently relocate to New Mexico in 1860. It was hinted he developed a relationship with the widow of Governor Charles Bent. He died at Mora Mora near Santa Fe in 1861.[223] Turley descendants remain in and around Arrow Rock today.

There were other Arrow Rock citizens with connections to "freighting on the plains." William B. Napton, Jr. himself accompanied a caravan down to Santa Fe in 1857, from a sense of adventure and for his health, rather than to make money. Billy Scott was an Arrow Rock old-timer known as "Uncle Billy." "During the war [Civil War], Uncle Billy had made a trip out to some fort on the plains, delivering supplies, for which he had a two horse wagon...."[224] Thomas Rainey reported in 1865, John

Leffler, "... old plainsman and freighter, with his three yoke of oxen carried freight along the Old Trail from Arrow Rock to Marshall, leaving upon it the last tracks of the old ox-wagon."[225]

By 1847, large freighting firms were contracted with by the government to supply the Army of the West. Firms such as the Aull Brothers in Lexington, Waldo and Hull in Independence and Waddell, Russell and Majors in Westport now dominated the trade. The day of the individual trader supplying two or three wagons from local merchants was rapidly coming to an end. It is clear many Boonslick citizens like Thompson and the Turleys continued to have ties with the trade long after this transition. However, wagon traffic on the trail that passed through Arrow Rock now represented a new wave of westward migration.

Francis Parkman noted this migration beginning early in 1846. During an eight-day steamboat trip from St. Louis to Independence, he wrote: "In five or six days we began to see signs of the great western movement that was then taking place. Parties of emigrants with their tents and wagons would be encamped on open spots near the bank, on their way to the common rendezvous at Independence."[226] This scene undoubtedly occurred in the great bend of the Missouri, where everyone was crossing the river. William B. Napton, Jr. also commented on this migration: "There was a great throng of emigrants through Saline County to California on the river road in 1849 and 1850. In the early spring of that year, the covered wagons of these emigrants were hardly ever out of sight at Arrow Rock."[227] Arrow Rock served as a rest stop and point of re-supply and wagon repair for many of those travelers.

Between 1822 and 1843, as much as $3,000,000 in profits resulted from the Santa Fe trade. As early as 1828, Governor John Miller said, "That trade is one of much importance to this state; the principal part of the silver coin in circulation, particularly in the western part of the State, is derived from that quarter...."[228] Of even longer term impact were the mules brought from New Mexico by Stephen Cooper and others beginning in 1823. These helped lay the foundation of Missouri's renowned mule industry. By the late 1880s, Missouri produced more than 34,000 mules a year that were widely used throughout the world into the early 20th century.

The Santa Fe trade was important in laying an economic foundation for Missouri. It had connections to the early fur trade in the Southwest and gave rise to the mule industry of Missouri. The direct role of Arrow Rock as a major outfitting center for the trade caravans remains undocumented. However, the involvement of citizens from Arrow Rock and vicinity in the Santa Fe trade is beyond question.

The Founding of Arrow Rock and Prominent Residents

"Whereas it is the opinion of many persons acquainted with the local situation of the Arrow Rock and the adjoining County around about that if a town be laid out at or in the Neighborhood of the said Arrow Rock that it would tend to the mutual advantage of the adjoining county by giving activity to trade, commerce and also to those who might be disposed to become residents of the same. To this end a meeting was held pursuant to publick notice, at the Arrow Rock ferry on the 23rd day of May [1829]." [229]

On the 10th of June 1829, Burton and Nancy Lawless deeded 25 acres, and John and Mary Bingham deeded 25 acres for the establishment of the town. Town commissioners Joseph Huston, Reverend Peyton Nowlin, Benjamin Huston, Rudolph Hawpe and Joseph Patterson received the deed of gift and employed Meredith Miles Marmaduke to survey and lay out the boundaries of the fifty-acre town site "immediately on the Missouri River and near to the Arrow Rock...." [230] Evidently taking a cue from the recent demise of Franklin, the commissioners wisely chose to locate their town on the bluff above the flood plain.

Marmaduke laid out the town in a conventional grid pattern reminiscent of Philadelphia, Pennsylvania. [231] Each block was laid out in 204-foot squares to contain exactly one acre. Main Street was the business street and ran east to west. High and Morgan streets paralleled it on the north, while Van Buren and Clay paralleled it on the south. The streets running north and south were numbered from First to Tenth, while the street closest to the Missouri River became, of course, Water Street. It is important to note some of the streets were never developed while others are now abandoned and reclaimed by the woodlands. The Public Square was located in the half block north of the Tavern, fronting High, Third and Fourth Streets.

On July 3, 1829, the following newspaper ad appeared in the Fayette

Missouri Intelligencer. By the choice of name for the new town, the commissioners evidently saw greatness ahead:

Town Of Philadelphia

THIS TOWN is situated in SALINE COUNTY, on the Missouri river, about twelve miles above Franklin, at a point known by the name of Arrow Rock. It is laid out on a high bluff, and commands a handsome view of the River, and has several excellent Springs adjoining. This point, as a place of business, possesses as great natural advantages as any other, having around it an extensive country of the best farming land in the State, with a good and rapidly increasing population of wealthy and enterprising citizens, which never fail of furnishing large quantities of surplus produce and articles for exportation, which forms a considerable part of our commerce. The main road from St. Louis to Liberty crosses at this point, and roads in every direction from this place will always be dry and good. Title undisputed, the land being purchased from the United States.

LOTS
Will be offered for sale on the premises to the highest bidder, on the 24th of July next. A credit of   months will be allowed to purchasers, by their giving bond with approved security. For the encouragement of those who wish to vest their funds in town property, the proceeds arising from the sale of lots are to be applied to the improvement of the Town.

        P. W. NOWLIN
        J. PATTERSON
        J. HUSTON
        R. HAWPE
        B. HUSTON
        Commissioners

    July 3, 1829   *49-3rv* [232]

On June 14, 1830, a special term of the Saline County Court received a petition "... presented for a road leading from Abram Smith's to Todd's landing at the big Arrow Rock and it is ordered by the court that the same be established on the most direct rout having regard to the ground through which the same shall pass."[233] On November 8, 1830, the court "... ordered that Elisha Ellis be appointed overseer of the road from Todd's landing at the Arrow Rock on the Missouri River to Philadelphia and thence to Abram Smith as laid out by the report of the commissioners and that William Becknell Esq. Designate the hands to work on said road."[234] This was the first civic improvement within the corporation.

Although the town was officially designated "Philadelphia," it periodically shows up in historical documents as "New Philadelphia." Apparently, this was a way outsiders tempered the presumption of greatness. This designation appeared April 14, 1833, in the journal of Maximilian, Prince of Wied, who also noted a problem with the name: "In a ravine before Arrow Rock Hill there is a new village which is called New Philadelphia though the inhabitants do not approve of this name."[235] Based on his description, it appears the earliest development of town was concentrated along the creek fed by the Big Spring, immediately south of town.

Since the locale had been known as "the Arrow Rock" for a century, it was hard to make the more pretentious name of Philadelphia stick. But even before the arrival of Maximilian, the General Assembly of Missouri took up the name issue on February 8, 1833:

> Be it enacted by the General Assembly of the State of Missouri [as follows]
> I.   The town heretofore called and known by the name of Philadelphia, in the county of Saline, on the Missouri river, shall hereafter be called Arrow Rock, and by that name shall be known and called in all the courts of this State. This act to take effect from and after its passage.[236]

Town growth was relatively slow at first, as many immigrants reaching Arrow Rock continued west toward the new towns of Independence and Liberty. Others continued settling in the Missouri River bottoms or along the Lamine and Blackwater rivers. An extensive number of people who became prominent in local, state and national affairs were associated with Arrow Rock Township. This prominence continued as the town grew. Following are some notable individuals from early in the town's history:

Dr. John Sappington (1776–1856) arrived in the area in 1819. He is credited with being the first physician in Saline County. He successfully mass-marketed quinine, treating thousands of people afflicted with malaria. Dr. Sappington was the patriarch of a family that had a profound influence in Missouri, Saline County and Arrow Rock politics. Two of his sons-in-law became governors, as did his grandson.

John Beauchamp Jones (1810 –1866) tended store in a log cabin from about 1834 to 1840. He wrote several popular books including *Wild Western Scenes* (1841) and *The Western Merchant* (1849) based on his experiences in Arrow Rock. Jones moved to Philadelphia, Pennsylvania, but, as a pro-slavery publisher, he began to fear for the safety of his family. At the beginning of the Civil War, he became a clerk in the Confederate Cabinet in Richmond, Virginia. He kept a diary of his activities in the cabinet, which has been reprinted several times.

John Locke Hardeman (1809–1858) was the son of John Hardeman, who developed the large experimental plantation "Fruitage Farm" across the river in Howard County. John Locke Hardeman moved to Saline County in 1830 and established a large farm west of Arrow Rock named "Lo Mismo." In 1854, he was elected state representative from Saline County. Hardeman was a bachelor, and after his death, his half-brother, Dr. Glen O. Hardeman, inherited the farm. "Lo Mismo" is currently undergoing restoration.

General Thomas A. Smith (1781–1844) was a career army officer and served during the War of 1812. Fort Smith, Arkansas, was named in his honor. When Smith retired from the army, he became the agent at the U.S. land office established in Franklin. In 1826, he established a large farm named "Experiment" several miles southwest of Arrow Rock. Like his friend, John Hardeman, Smith tried developing new crops and farming techniques. Smith frequently entertained a constant stream of relatives, political friends and even delegations of Indians traveling to St. Louis.

Nathaniel Beverley Tucker (1784– 1851) was a Virginian who immigrated to Missouri in 1815 and became a circuit judge. In 1830, he moved to Saline County and married Lucy Ann Smith, the daughter of General Thomas A. Smith. Tucker built a southern style plantation named "Ardmore" southwest of Arrow Rock (no longer standing). In 1833, he left Arrow Rock and served as Professor of Law at William and Mary College in Williamsburg, Virginia, until his death. He wrote several novels including *George Balcombe*, which was based on his view of Missouri plantation society. Tucker was a "Fire Eater," an early advocate of southern secession from the United States. In 1836, he wrote *The Partisan Leader,* a novel that eerily foretold a revolt by the southern states.

Dr. Charles Bradford (1817–1862) was born in New York City and educated at the University of Pennsylvania. In 1840, he moved to Arrow Rock and purchased a house from Samuel Miller at the corner of Main and Sixth Street. This house remains today and is an antique shop. Dr. Bradford married Lavinia M. Pearson, the granddaughter of Dr. Sappington, in 1841.

Dr. William Price (1812–1865) built a two-story brick house at the corner of Main and Seventh Street around 1840; it is still standing. Price married Mary Ellen Sappington, the youngest of Dr. John Sappington's nine children. He became a partner with his father-in-law.

Claiborne Fox Jackson (1806–1862) was Missouri's Civil War governor. Born in Kentucky, he moved to Franklin, Missouri, in 1825. By 1831, he owned a warehouse and store on the Arrow Rock riverfront. Jackson campaigned for Andrew Jackson's presidency and was rewarded by being appointed the first postmaster of Arrow Rock in September of 1832. Jackson expanded into banking and lived for a period of time at Fayette and was elected to the State Legislature. He returned to Arrow Rock in 1856 and was elected governor of Missouri in 1860.

Dr. George Penn (1800–1886) of Nelson County, Virginia, studied medicine at the University of Pennsylvania. In 1828, he purchased a farm near Jonesboro, and in 1832, formed a partnership with Dr. Sappington. He married Sarah Bella Chambers in 1831. She was the daughter of Colonel Benjamin Chambers, the first clerk of the Saline County Court. Penn launched a political career by successfully running for the State Legislature in 1834. He was elected a State Senator in 1838. Throughout the 1840s, he was involved in the Arrow Rock Academy and other civic projects in the town, where he had an office. In 1844, Penn was one of three commissioners who surveyed the Missouri-Arkansas boundary. From 1846 to 1847, he served in the Mexican War as a regimental surgeon in the Army of the West. Later, he was sub-Treasurer of the United States in St. Louis.[237]

Henry S. Mills arrived in Arrow Rock in 1837 and was a successful merchant and banker. For a number of years he served on the Town Board. He built a two and a half story house on Main Street in 1854, which is today a bed and breakfast establishment.

Anthony O'Sullivan (1808–1868) was an Irish emigrant who became a prominent resident of Arrow Rock from 1841 to 1851. He was initiated into the Arrow Rock Masonic Lodge and became the Grand Secretary of the Grand Lodge of Missouri from 1852 to 1866.

Meredith Miles Marmaduke (1791–1864) came to Missouri from Virginia in 1821. He was a son-in-law of Dr. Sappington. Besides his involvement in the Santa Fe trade, he surveyed the original town of Arrow Rock. In 1840, he was elected Lt. Governor of Missouri and assumed the governorship in 1844 upon the death of Governor Reynolds.

John Sappington Marmaduke (1833–1887) was the son of Meredith Marmaduke and the grandson of Dr. John Sappington. He was educated at West Point, became a Major General in the Confederate Army, and was elected governor of Missouri in 1884.

Dr. Matthew Walton Hall (1817–1894), a native of Kentucky, came to Arrow Rock from Salem, Illinois, in 1845. He was a long-term member of the Arrow Rock Board of Trustees, and was prominent in civic affairs and projects throughout Saline County. He was twice elected to the Missouri House of Representatives. His brick Arrow Rock home, built in 1846, remains as part of the Arrow Rock State Historic Site.

George Caleb Bingham (1811–1879), Missouri's most famous artist, was a resident of the Arrow Rock area from 1827. He painted portraits of many of the prominent citizens of Arrow Rock and the Boonslick Country. Even more important were his genre scenes, which depicted life on the Missouri River and the rough vitality of the new state of Missouri. Active in politics as well as art, Bingham had family ties in Arrow Rock long after his career took him to other cities and foreign countries. Bingham's Arrow Rock home is designated a National Historic Landmark and is part of the Arrow Rock State Historic Site.

The town commissioners were to continue managing the affairs of the new town "until the population should amount to twelve respectable householders, at which time it was required of the said householders to cause reasonable notice of a meeting of the citizens of said Town, for the purpose of electing Trustees and vesting in them the duties previously performed by said Commissioners."[238] Fourteen men voted in Arrow Rock's first town election held on August 1, 1840. Dr. William Price, William Roper and Jesse McMahan were elected the first Trustees of Arrow Rock. George Caleb Bingham and Burton Lawless served as election judges and certified the results.

The Board of Trustees got to work on August 26, organizing themselves and installing McMahan as president/treasurer, Dr. Price as secretary, and William Roper as superintendent of public works. They immediately set out to make improvements to the town: "It was ordered that a stone wall should be erected of sufficient length, breadth and height as would by filling the north side with dirt make main street a good pass way from Dr. Penn's office where the wall shall commence to near Mr. Houks shop where it shall terminate, and that the cost of said wall when finished be paid out of the Town fund."[239]

This stone wall runs along the south side of Main Street near the Academy Boarding House to the corner of First Street. Dr. Penn owned the lot where the boarding house sits. Mr. Houk was undoubtedly on the corner of First and Main. The Works Progress Administration (WPA) undertook extensive repairs of the Main Street wall about 1935. However, much of the original hand hewn stonework of 1840 is still visible, especially the bottom part of the wall.

The Board of Trustees also ordered an "appropriation be made for repairing the public well in such a manner as would be productive if practical of a sufficiency of water for all persons desiring to get water from said well."[240] This well was probably the one located behind the Main Street businesses on the Public Square. Burton Lawless had also granted free use of the Big Spring "in perpetuity" to the town. Many residences had their own individual wells and cisterns.

County Government and the Courthouse

In 1816, Howard County was formed to administer the vast western third of Missouri Territory, and Franklin was the county seat. As the land was filling quickly with settlers, new counties were formed out of Howard to facilitate and improve administration. In 1819, Cooper County was formed out of Howard and encompassed what is now Saline County. The Missouri Legislature created Saline County on November 25, 1820.[241] The Legislature ordered the first session of the county court to be held April 16, 1821, at the town of Jefferson, located in the "Big Bottoms" north of Arrow Rock. Needless to say, the session was held in a log cabin.[242] Missouri achieved statehood shortly thereafter, on August 10, 1821.

In January of 1822, the county court affixed the boundaries of three townships: Arrow Rock, Jefferson and Miami. Arrow Rock Township encompassed the entire southern half of the county.[243] At that time the southern boundary of the county extended to the Osage River. To police the growing population of slaves, in 1824 the county appointed John Hargrove, William Chick and Alexander Galbreath as "patrollers" of Arrow Rock Township.[244] This was the first of many such patrols enacted within the county to control slaves and minimize the chance for runaways.

The first circuit court was held February 5, 1821, in Jefferson though there was little business to transact. The first murder case occurred in August of 1822, when an old Frenchman named Jean Estelquay or John Starkey was murdered at the ford of Cow Creek a few miles north of Marshall. Starkey had been a veteran of the American Revolution and had traveled from Jack's Ferry (Lexington) to Boonville to collect his pension money. Another Frenchman, Andrew Turpin, apparently murdered and robbed him as he slept under a large elm tree, wrapped in a blanket. Turpin was apprehended and indicted in November. He was held in an outbuilding in Jefferson and feigned having frozen feet, whereupon he made his escape and fled to the western wilderness. On November 20, 1824, Judge David Todd held a trial though they had no prisoner. Sentence was pronounced, "...the said Andrew Turpin therefore shall be hung by the neck until he be dead."[245]

The site of the Cow Creek ford came to be regarded as haunted. Two years later, another Frenchman traveling through the area wrapped himself in a blanket and slept under the large elm tree. A horseman came along, and the prone object on the ground startled his horse. The man awoke, stood up, and began making inquiries of the rider in broken English and French. The terrified rider turned around and galloped away. Stopping at the first house he came to, he claimed he had seen the ghost of Starkey.[246]

In March of 1824, an important case developed when a slave named Jack sued William Chick, Sr. and William Chick, Jr., the "slave patroller," for assault and battery and false imprisonment.[247] Judge David Todd heard the case, and Abiel Leonard of Howard County provided legal counsel to Jack. Judge Todd warned the Chicks to permit Jack to "... have a reasonable liberty of attending his counsel and this court when occasion may require... and that he be not taken or removed out of the jurisdiction of this court."[248]

Before the case was tried, the Chicks gave Jack his freedom, and he in turn dropped the suit. Todd's handling of the case was contrary to what the U.S. Supreme Court did thirty-five years later in the infamous Dred Scott case. The court then made it clear a slave had no rights to sue for freedom. In contrast, Todd made it distinctly clear to the Chicks that although Jack was "a negro and held as a slave," he had "rights that they were bound to respect."[249] If the Chicks had not given Jack his freedom, it is possible this case from Arrow Rock Township would have developed national ramifications.

The circuit court issued the first emancipation of a slave in Saline County on December 15, 1827: "Know all men by these present, that I, Isham Reavis ... in consideration of the hitherto faithful servitude of my servant woman, Patience, about the age of 36 years, and for the further consideration of the sum of sixty dollars to me in hand paid, the receipt ... set free and at liberty the said negro woman Patience, and her young child, named Elizabeth Jane, about 18 months old, and also her future increase; and the said woman and child are hereby set free ...."[250]

The county seat was moved from Jefferson to Jonesboro (present-day Napton) in 1831. The Jefferson location was prone to flooding, and, in 1826, most of the inhabitants of the Big Bottoms fled because of spring floods. Many did not return. The location of the county seat was reflected in the density of the population at that time. Jonesboro was now considered the "capitol and metropolis" of Saline County. According to the 1881 History of Saline County "... it was a favorite outfitting depot and starting point for many traders, explorers and adventurers, who traveled to and from Santa Fe in early days."[251]

In January of 1833, the Missouri legislature created Pettis County, reducing Saline County to its current boundary.[252] Blackwater Township was also formed out of Arrow Rock Township. By 1839, the population was dispersing throughout the county, and the legislature authorized the removal of the county seat to the center of the county as near as practicable. Five commissioners selected the present site of Marshall, and on July 18, 1839, Circuit Judge William Scott approved their report. Judge Scott ordered an election to be held August 5th to select a temporary seat of government until the new seat was constructed. The votes were: Arrow Rock 217, Greenville 123 and Centre 67.

At the first session of the county court in August, the new permanent county seat was christened Marshall in honor of the late Chief Justice of the Supreme Court, John Marshall. The first term of the county court in Arrow Rock was November 11, 1839, and the circuit court met there the same month. Gilmore Hays and W. A. Wilson were the justices. William Scott was Circuit Judge, John Trigg, Circuit Clerk and David S. Wilson was the Sheriff. On November 12, 1839, the county court repealed the "Grocery and Dram Shop laws" and settled a suit between Alonzo Edwards and Thomas Davis. John Smith was sworn in as a Justice of the Peace.[253]

"These courts were held, and indeed almost all the other business of the county transacted in a double log building (to which was afterward added a frame), belonging to Benjamin Huston."[254] The small log building near the corner of Fourth and Main Street has traditionally been identified as the "Old Courthouse." The one story building may be one of the oldest structures in Arrow Rock. In January, 1840, Obediah Pearson purchased it from Jacob Coffman for $530.00.[255] Around this time, it probably received the wide weatherboarding and a Greek Revival style porch.

Clearly there are problems with the claim of its being the county courthouse. As far as can be ascertained, the building was never a double log building, although a frame addition survived until 1960. There is no record Benjamin Huston owned the property, and this author has been unable to trace the source of the oral tradition. Unfortunately, county records do not give the specific location of the court building in Arrow Rock. Barring the discovery of more conclusive evidence, it seems highly unlikely the "Old Courthouse" was indeed the Saline County courthouse. At best, it can only be presented as an early structure that has been furnished as a representation of how the county courthouse may have appeared.

The structure has also been widely claimed as the model for George Caleb Bingham's painting, *The County Election*, executed in 1851–1852. Again, the source of this tradition has not been found. Contrasting the courthouse in the original painting and the building in Arrow Rock reveals significant discrepancies in scale and architectural detail. Although people in the painting have been identified as Arrow Rock residents, the courthouse in the painting is likely a generic representation of Greek Revival structures common at this time period.

The Militia and Missouri's "Little Wars"
In 1792, Congress passed "An act more effectually to provide for the national defense by establishing a uniform militia throughout the United

States." This was the model for militia laws enacted in the state of Missouri. Every free, white male citizen between the ages of eighteen and forty-five was to be enrolled in the militia. Every citizen was to "...provide himself with a good musket or flintlock, a sufficient bayonet and belt... or with a good rifle, knapsack, shot pouch and powder horn, twenty balls suited to the bore of his rifle...."[256]

Congress and the general public were reluctant to maintain a large standing army. The feeling was strong enough for Missouri election laws to prohibit soldiers and sailors from voting in elections. However, in time of crisis, these same civilians often "decried the defenseless state they found themselves in."[257] The militia, "the citizen-soldier," appeared to meet the need for defense without the expense of maintaining a standing army. During the War of 1812, the militia, especially in the form of the "Rangers," formed the main defense of the Missouri frontier.

Company musters were held in every township at a convenient public place. General musters were usually held at the county seat. Jonesboro, southwest of Arrow Rock, was "the great mustering ground of the Saline County Militia, in which generals, colonels, majors, and captains became as plentiful as blackberries in their season."[258] The officers had to purchase their own uniforms. They were elected to the office, and it was customary to provide "refreshments" to the troops. The outcome of militia elections was often determined by the quality of the whisky served. Company musters undoubtedly took place at Arrow Rock. The general muster was probably held at Arrow Rock when it was the county seat in 1839 and 1840. Unfortunately, many of the state's early militia records have been lost.

Attendance at musters was required. Failure to do so without an adequate reason was supposed to result in a fine. For many it was cheaper to pay the fine than to leave their farms or businesses for military drill. "As not every man had a gun, numbers went through the manual of arms with sticks, cornstalks and other implements...indeed, general musters were only kept up...for a long time, on account of the 'fun' that always attended them...refreshment stands abounded; horse races were made and run; foot-races; wrestling matches... and many a fisticuff was fought on muster day. At all these things, and at the drilling and evolutions of the militiamen, the crowd stared and admired."[259]

An increasing number of "all volunteer" militia companies formalized the social aspects and camaraderie associated with militia musters. Soon the general musters came to be seen as troublesome, inconvenient and of no productive good. In 1847, the state legislature abolished the militia act. Following are some of Missouri's "little wars" in which men from Arrow Rock Township may have participated. These events present an idea of how the militia was employed. Some of these "wars" were comical farce while others had serious, bloody consequences.

Big Neck War — A band of Ioway Indians led by Great Walker (called Big Neck) was traveling to St. Louis to confer with William Clark in 1829. Settlers near Kirksville attacked them, and, in the ensuing fight, several Indians and whites were killed. The state militia was assembled in Fayette and marched north, spending several unfruitful weeks scouring the countryside. Great Walker eventually surrendered to authorities and was placed on trial for murder. A jury ruled the Ioways had acted in self-defense and absolved Great Walker of any crime. For the rest of his life Great Walker wore black paint on his face to mourn his family and friends killed in the fight.

Black Hawk War — In June of 1832, about 1,000 Sauk and Fox Indians clashed with settlers in northwest Illinois. They had returned to their old village and found it occupied by white settlers. Rumors soon circulated that Black Hawk, the Sauk leader, was building a coalition of Indian tribes as Tecumseh had done 23 years earlier. Panic consumed the frontier and various states activated their militias. Osage hunting parties still entered western Missouri, and the Kickapoo tribe had a large reservation in the southwestern part of the state. Rumors flew that these tribes were going to join Black Hawk and attack the Boonslick settlements. The Saline County militia prepared to repel the supposed invasion of hordes of Indians.

General Stephen Trigg was ordered to take the militia and scout to the west and southwest of Saline County. "Each man was to provide his own horse, arms, accouterments, and rations"[260] as required by the law. A company of forty rangers was raised in Saline County, a number of them from the neighborhood of Arrow Rock. Henry Becknell was chosen captain.[261] Jacob Nave (Neff) was 1st Lieutenant, Ben E. Cooper, 2nd Lieutenant, and William Wolfskill, Ephraim McClaine, Henry Nave (Neff), William Pruntin and Ephraim Prigmore served in the ranks.[262]

Trigg's command started out in mid-August ascending the Lamine and Blackwater rivers. They traveled south past Knob Noster and reached the Osage River where they made camp and were resupplied. Several bands of Kickapoo were encountered, and it was alleged "...they were well armed, and bore other indication of being on the war path. These were turned back without a fight, and made to understand that it would not be healthy for them if caught out on the same business again. The camps of the Osages were visited, and the occupants found to be to their own legitimate business, and entirely friendly."[263] The Saline County Company returned to Jonesboro after being in the field 21 days and was disbanded.

For all the fear the Black Hawk affair generated, no fighting materialized in Missouri. Perhaps the most memorable part of the local campaign was the personality of the commanders. General Trigg was described as "a mighty pert man, and a good judge of Indians." Captain Becknell, also a Ranger in the War of 1812, was remembered as being "not of a religious turn of mind at all...Many a settler remembers how volubly and with what wonderful force and power he could swear."[264]

Heatherly War — A gang of bandits led by the Heatherly family terrorized settlers along the Grand River in 1836. They stole some horses from some Ioway Indians who gave chase. Fearing that one of their men would talk and bring federal retribution, the gang murdered him. To cover the murder, they spread the alarm and claimed the Ioway had killed him. Militia units were sent to the region but could find no sign of Indians. When the truth was learned, the gang was arrested and tried for murder.

Osage War — The remnant of Osage land in Missouri was taken by the Treaty of 1825. However, small parties of Osage continued to hunt bears in Missouri because they were more plentiful here. In the spring of 1837, one hunting party was accused of killing settlers' hogs, even though the Osage detested hogs and would not touch their meat. Rumors of an "Indian invasion" followed. Governor Lilburn Boggs ordered the militia to evict all Indians from the state, including "mixed-bloods." Even the Indian mission schools were ordered closed. Federal soldiers protected Harmony Mission when state militia tried to close it. This was the only time shots were almost fired in the so-called war.

Second Seminole War — Many of the Seminoles of Florida resisted deportation to the Indian Territory in 1837. The federal government requested volunteers to subdue them. Colonel Richard Gentry of Columbia raised a company of volunteers from the Boonslick Country. Allegedly, he boasted the Missourians would teach Florida how to handle their "Indian problem." Several Osage and Delaware Indians served as scouts for the militia. The Battle of Lake Okeechobee on Christmas day in 1837 resulted in 138 casualties among the soldiers, many of them Missourians. Colonel Gentry was killed, but reportedly, none of the Saline County volunteers were injured or killed. Unscathed, the Seminoles melted into the Everglades, where they continued to resist the military for nearly 20 more years. Their descendants still remain in Florida.

Mormon War — In 1832, Joseph Smith led several hundred Mormons to Jackson County, Missouri. After a series of bloody clashes with the locals, the Mormons fled north and established communities in Caldwell, Daviess and Carroll counties. Far West in Caldwell County became the seat of Mormon government. In the summer of 1838, the Mormons purchased land at DeWitt, across the river from Saline County. The river landing there was regarded as a convenient point to land supplies and immigrants bound for the Far West. A public meeting was held at Carrollton, and it was decided to remove the Mormons from the county. When a "committee" approached Mormon leader, George Hinkle, he reportedly "drew his sword and defiantly flourishing it, threatened the extermination of all those who should attempt to disturb the peace of himself and the saints."[265]

Violence broke out between Mormons and anti-Mormons throughout the state. Governor Boggs ordered the extermination of all Mormons in the state. Captain William Durrett of Arrow Rock led the militia company from Saline County. Carrollton anti-Mormons, led by Dr. Austin, marched on Dewitt, threatening to kill every Mormon who remained in town after October 1. Twenty-five mounted "rangers" from Saline County under Captain William Wolfskill scouted east of DeWitt and turned back small groups of Mormons trying to reach the town. On October 4, the anti-Mormons launched their attack using a piece of artillery but found the Mormons had fortified the town.

A "peace commission" met with Hinkle and the Mormons on October 6, and they agreed to leave. Hinkle allegedly said he "could easily have cleaned out Austin and his crowd, had it not been for the 'damned bear hunters' from the other side of the river," a reference to the Saline County men.[266] More than likely, this was a Saline "ranger" bragging for the county history rather than a comment by Hinkle. At the close of the DeWitt affair, the Saline County men went home though anti-Mormon hostilities intensified elsewhere in the state.

Honey War — In 1839, Missouri and the Iowa Territory disputed a nine-mile wide strip along the boundary line. Governor Boggs ordered the enforcement of Missouri laws and tax collection in the strip. Iowa governor Robert Lucas issued a proclamation countermanding Boggs' order. A Missourian cut down three "bee trees" for honey and was fined $1.50 by an Iowa court. A Missouri sheriff then attempted to collect taxes in the strip and was arrested by Iowa officials. In late November, both the Missouri and Iowa militias were called out to confront each other. While the men froze in deep snow, cooler heads decided Congress or the Supreme Court should determine the boundary. A haunch of venison labeled "Governor Boggs of Missouri" and another "Governor Lucas of Iowa" were riddled with bullets and solemnly interred before the militias marched home derisively wearing their coats wrong side out as a badge of their service.

Mexican War — The United States went to war with Mexico in 1846 over a dispute involving the border of Texas. Boonslick men flocked to volunteer for the expedition to take New Mexico. They believed if Mexico won the war, the lucrative Santa Fe trade could end. Victory meant commercial domination and homesteading opportunities in a million square miles of the American Southwest.

The First Regiment Missouri Mounted Volunteers under Col. Alexander Doniphan was made up of 850 volunteers from the Boonslick Country. Dr. George Penn of Arrow Rock was appointed the regimental surgeon. Company D was composed of 82 men from Saline County, several from Arrow Rock. The Missourians captured Santa Fe without firing a shot. They pressed on 300 miles to capture Chihuahua. At the Battle of Sacramento they overwhelmed an entrenched army three times their size. They joined up with forces under General Zachary Taylor, "Old Rough and Ready," in Saltillo.

However, the war fervor did not last long as a June 1, 1847, letter from Arrow Rock reveals:

> *We had quite a patriotic day in our town on the 27th. There was a call on the county for volunteers. But they met with but little success they did not get even as many as one volunteer. It was quite different to what it was last year when it was who should and who should (not) volunteer. It will be sometime yet before this war will be brought to a close. I am fearful the worst is to*

*come it is really heart rending just for one to think how many
lives have been lost which could so easily been avoided. I suppose
old rough and ready will be all the go for president with you
next year.*[267]

Susan Shelby Magoffin, the wife of a Santa Fe trader, gave an unflat-
tering report of the Missourians in 1847:

*I saw [Chihuahua]...filled with Missouri volunteers who though
good to fight are not careful at all how much they soil the property
of a friend much less an enemy. The good citizens... had never
dreamed...that their loved homes would be turned into quarters
for common soldiers... the fine trees of their beautiful alamador
[public walk] barked and forever spoiled, and a hundred other
deprivations....*[268]

On June 5, 1847, the Missourians left Mexico and headed towards New
Orleans. By July 4th, the Saline volunteers had all arrived home. "On the
last named day [July 4] the returned volunteers were given a grand recep-
tion by the people of the county...A procession was formed...It was
regularly marshaled and marched, with music and banners...forming
quite an imposing pageant. A magnificent barbecue dinner was served."[269]
Patriotic speeches and toasts were made and "In the evening there was
a grand ball in a large hemp warehouse at the foot of Main street, Miami,
which was largely attended ... by the best people of the county."[270]

The Missouri River: Artery of Commerce

"The economic and social progress of a people depends to a large
extent upon the existence of facilities for the transportation of goods and
the communication of ideas."[271] This statement was true of Arrow Rock and
the Boonslick Country as a whole. The Missouri River was the region's
vital artery of transportation and communication.

The Franklin *Missouri Intelligencer* observed in its December 11, 1821
edition: "Missouri ...has outdone all her competitors — the produce of
her soil is now on its way to the great emporium of western trade, borne
on the bosom of great rivers that have their origin in her own country, and
in strong boats, the workmanship of her own hands. During the last
week, the people of St. Louis witnessed the no less uncommon than gratifying sight of several flat-bottomed boats, laden with produce from the

country high up on the Missouri, descending the Mississippi, destined for New Orleans. These boats compose the van of a much greater number, that are on their way down, from the Boonslick settlements."[272] To a lesser extent, dugout canoes and keelboats were important conveyances of river commerce as well.

It was the steamboat, however, which would exponentially increase the prosperity of the Boonslick Country. The Franklin *Missouri Intelligencer* made the following announcement and correctly predicted its impact in its May 28, 1819 edition:

> *With no ordinary sensations of pride and pleasure, we announce the arrival, this morning, at this place, of the elegant STEAM BOAT INDEPENDENCE, Captain NELSON, in several sailing days (but thirteen from her time of departure) from St. Louis, with passengers, and a cargo of flour, whisky, sugar, iron castings &c being the first Steam Boat that ever attempted ascending the Missouri. She was joyfully met by the inhabitants of Franklin, and saluted by the firing of cannon, which was returned by the Independence . . . boats may ascend the turbulent waters of the Missouri to bring to this part of the country the articles requisite to its supply and return laden with the various products of this fertile region. At no distant period may we see the industrious cultivator making his way as high as the Yellow Stone, and offering to the enterprising merchant and trader a surplus worthy of the fertile banks of the Missouri, yielding wealth to industry and enterprise.*[273]

A little over two weeks later, the steamboat *Western Engineer* passed through the area. It was part of the Yellowstone Expedition under Major Stephen Long. The boat was known as "Long's Dragon" because the bowsprit was in the shape of a serpent. The smokestack was vented to the head so smoke belched through the mouth and nostrils. The display was intended to awe the Indians as the boat churned its way upriver. The Saline County history of 1881 gave an account of its passing: "Some Indians who were at the Arrow Rock when the boat passed that point, gazed upon the seeming monster with astonishment. A band of them followed it from Arrow Rock to the Miami bottom, expecting it to 'give out' they said, pretty soon, for it was so short of breath, and panted so!"[274] This story is probably apocryphal as the Long expedition did not note the presence of any Indians until they reached present-day Nebraska.

In the next decade, only about 15 steamboats went up the Missouri River. By 1831, there were five fast, light "packets" operating on the Missouri River. These were: *Car of Commerce*, the *Chieftain*, the *Globe*, the *Liberty* and the *Missouri*.[275] They delivered goods and produce in a fraction of the time and cost of those hauled by keelboats and flatboats. By 1849, fifty-eight steamboats were operating on the river. Within a decade, that number more than doubled.

The 1850s and 1860s were the golden age of the steamboat, and river commerce was at its apex. By this time, the boats were often conveying Oregon and California bound passengers to departure points at Independence or St. Joseph. These steamboats could carry 300 to 400 passengers and up to 700 tons of freight. A boat might cost $50,000 to $75,000 to build, but this could be made back in one good season.[276]

While the Missouri River was the water highway of the American West, it was a dangerous, noisy highway. "Often I heard the bank [of the Missouri] undermined by the current, cave in amid the loud noise resembling the report of the cannon fired at some distance. At night this noise, together with the roar of the river and its whirlpools and the creaking and grinding of drifting trees, caused a horrendous uproar," wrote one traveler.[277] The dangers of river navigation experienced by Lewis and Clark had not lessened in the steamboat era. The boat pilot had to have a sharp eye to avoid having the bottom of the craft ripped open by submerged logs or running aground on hidden sandbars. The cost of freight usually had 10% added for insurance against boat wrecks.

Almost three hundred steamboats wrecked on the Missouri River between 1819 and 1918. One hundred of these sank between 1830 and 1860 alone.[278] Loss of life was usually minimal, as passengers could often swim or simply wade ashore. Wrecks typically occurred in shallow, not deep water. Regardless, the sinking of a riverboat was a devastating economic loss and a traumatic experience, perhaps similar to the loss of an airliner today. But the river was not the only source of peril for steamboats. The boat itself was very dangerous because of the high-pressure steam boilers that sometimes blew up.

The explosion of the steamboat *Sultana* is classified as one of the worst maritime disasters in United States history and demonstrates the dangerous nature of the boats. Although this tragedy occurred on the Mississippi River, its impact was felt in Arrow Rock. Ida Brown Gambrell was the youngest of 12 children of Judge Bernis Brown, one of the early settlers of Arrow Rock. Ida was educated at McPherson Female College in Lexington, Missouri, and at Joshua L. Tracey's Adelphi College in Boonville. She returned to Arrow Rock and on July 26, 1855, married W. J. Gambrell. He was involved in the shipping business, and they moved to Kansas City. In 1863, they relocated to St. Louis where he purchased an interest in the *Sultana*. After Union forces captured Vicksburg, Mississippi, the boat began making profitable runs between St. Louis and New Orleans. On April 27, 1865, at Vicksburg, the *Sultana* took on about 2,000 Union soldiers who had just been freed from prisoner of war camps. A few miles above Memphis, Tennessee, the boilers exploded, and over 1,500 persons perished; blown to bits or scalded to death. Many bodies, including that of Mr. Gambrell, were never found. Mrs. Gambrell returned to the family farm at Arrow Rock where she lived the remainder of her life.[279]

Most boats simply fell prey to the snags that filled the river. On May 6, 1820, the side-wheeler *Missouri Packet* struck a snag at Hardeman's Island near the mouth of the Lamine River. This was probably the fifth steamboat to ascend the Missouri, and the first to sink in the river. The Howard and Cooper County history of 1883 reprinted a "letter" that said $250,000 in specie was aboard the boat and could not be salvaged. The "letter" contained discrepancies, and it is difficult to believe this amount of gold coin was being shipped into the wilderness. Even the payroll for the 60 plus soldiers at Fort Atkinson would fall below this amount. The Army paid in scrip, which could be spent with the fort's sutler, not specie. However, numerous attempts were made to locate and salvage the boat, the most recent being in 1987. "Unfortunately, the boat was seriously damaged in the futile search for lost treasure."[280]

The stretch of river near the mouth of the Lamine was known as "Slaughterhouse Bend," and at least five boats went down there. In 1826, the *George Washington* sank at Hardeman's Island, near where the *Missouri Packet* went down. Other boats that sank in this bend were the *Radnor* (1846), the *Sacramento* (1849), the *T. L. Crawford* (1857) and the *John Golong* (1862).[281] Most of these boats fell prey to snags. The first boat to sink near Arrow Rock itself was the *John Aull* in 1845. The *New Sam Gaty*, an impressive side-wheeler of 367 tons, was built at Louisville, Kentucky, in 1860. On June 28, 1868, it was heading down river and ran against the bank opposite Arrow Rock, striking a projecting log. The resulting hole in the starboard side began filling with water, and the boat listed to such an extent the boilers fell down, setting fire to the steamer and completely destroying it. Loss was reported at $17,000.[282]

Damage was not always limited to the boat itself. In August of 1864, sparks from the stacks of the steamboat *Isabella* set fire to the riverfront at Arrow Rock, destroying four warehouses.[283] This was an economic blow the merchants of Arrow Rock could ill afford, as the Civil War had already seriously crippled the economy. The safety record of the boats does not appear to have improved with the passage of time. A small sternwheeler steamer, the *Plow Boy No. 2*, was destroyed by fire at Arrow Rock in 1877. The *Tom Rodgers*, a large sternwheeler, was destroyed by fire while lying up for the night at Arrow Rock in 1887. Its loss was reported at $15,000.[284]

River navigation was usually closed from November until March, owing to ice floes and the river freezing over. The ice was often thick enough to support teams and sleighs but crossing could be a risky venture. The Arrow Rock *Enterprise* reported in 1892: "...the hack and mules running between this place [Miami] and Miami Station...had broken through the ice and were in the Missouri River...when nearing the Carroll [County] shore, the ice gave away dropping the mules and hack to the bottom of the river. Fortunately, the water at that point was only two or three feet deep and everything was soon extracted without damage."[285] During freezes, mules were outfitted with cleat shoes to prevent their slipping on the ice. They would pull a special plow designed for cutting river ice into blocks. These were packed in sawdust at the icehouse located somewhere down the hill from the end of Main Street. Thus, throughout the latter half of the 19th century, ice was available in the summer months.

The opening of spring navigation on the river was a much-anticipated event as the Arrow Rock correspondent for the Marshall *Weekly Democrat* reported on March 4, 1858: "Our town at present presents a rather gloomy appearance; nothing new stirring. Several of our merchants have left for the East and St. Louis; others will leave in a few days. Next week things will look up, our merchants will be receiving their spring stock of goods, and the people may expect goods at very low figures, as many of the merchants are going to sell for cash ...The ice is still running, but in a few days we may expect steamboats."[286]

The appearance of the first steamboats transformed the town.

> *With the opening of navigation business has been resumed on an*
> *extensive scale, and drays, carts and wagons are constantly*
> *traversing the streets between the steamboat landing and the*
> *business portion of the town, carrying hemp and other products*
> *of the farm for shipment, and returning with lumber groceries, or*
> *other goods for the country, or to be stored in the extensive ware-*
> *houses "up town." The town presents a business aspect at this*
> *time that would do credit to some of far greater pretensions as*
> *"commercial centers," "shipping points" and "business places"*
> *than Arrow Rock.*[287]

Newspaper ads by merchants advertised a variety of goods and luxuries.
Some were formerly expensive and difficult to obtain, but now readily
available owing to steamboat traffic:

> *Fresh Arrival — Sugar and Coffee*
> *Just received by the Steamer Ogden,*
> *A lot of superior N[ew].O[rleans]. Sugar, at 12 1/2 c per lb.*
> *A few bags of prime Rio Coffee.*
> *HUSTON & THOMPSON.*[288]

> *Stein & Block, Arrow Rock have just received their spring and*
> *summer stock of goods, and desire to let the people know that they*
> *are prepared to give better bargains than any other establishment*
> *of the kind. They buy their goods in New York, which, they say,*
> *enables them to sell cheaper and better goods than their rivals.*[289]

The river landing, of course, was a focal point of the Arrow Rock
Board of Trustee's business. It was the economic heart of the town. "Be it
ordained that the sum of three hundred Dollars be and is hereby appropriated towards building a wharf at the steamboat landing of the Town of
Arrow Rock," October 18, 1849.[290] Such ordinances and committees deal-
ing with access to the river and the construction and repair of the wharf
are a recurring item of Town Board meetings, demonstrating the importance of the river to the growth and prosperity of Arrow Rock.

"It was resolved that the ordinance of October last, appointing Henry
S. Mills and W. W. McJilton commissioners for building a wharf at the

Steam Boat Landing be and is hereby rescinded ... Resolved that H.
S. Wilhelm and M. W. Hall be appointed a committee to wait on H. S.
Mills and ascertain what he will sell as a right of way thru his Lot to the
River." February 14, 1850.[291]

The right of way to the river was an important issue for the town.
Within a few months, the right of way is dealt with again. "On motion be
it resolved that the Secretary be and is hereby authorized to contract with
Mr. Mills for a public right of way from the bridge across his lots to the
landing on the river and to procure from him a good and sufficient deed
for the same — June 6, 1850."[292] Yet, for the next several years, Mills sometimes grants the right of way, and sometimes he doesn't.

There were an extensive number of warehouses at the wharf from the
1830s up to the turn of the century. Claiborne Fox Jackson, Dr. W. L.
Boyer, the Sappington brothers, Jesse McMahan and others had warehouses at various times. On January 1, 1859, Joseph Huston, Jr. and Will
H. Wood sold their respective businesses and formed a partnership as
forwarding and commission merchants. For the next ten years, half of the
grain, livestock and hemp shipped from Saline County and a substantial
share of Cooper and Pettis counties came through their warehouse at
Arrow Rock. They also received and handled merchandise shipped in to the
same territory. "John Huston and Nelse Robertson, 'John and Nelse,' colored, were the faithful warehouse keepers."[293] In 1869 Joseph Huston, Jr.
and Will Wood closed out their commission business in Arrow Rock. In
1874 they opened the Wood & Huston Bank in Marshall.[294]

The Arrow Rock landing briefly saw service as a boat-building yard. In
1867, German immigrant Louis Moehle established a sawmill and boat
yard on the Lamine River in Cooper County. His son, Gustav, eventually moved to Arrow Rock. Between 1890 and 1909, Gustav and his sons
built boats on the river landing. These included the *Guy Hunter*, the
Minna, the *Nadine*, the *Laura* and the gasoline-powered *Roy L.*[295] The
Moehle family also operated a flour mill on the west side of town.

As Arrow Rock's prosperity declined, the riverfront was gradually abandoned. By the turn of the century, the warehouses were gone, and property
titles became murky. The bend in the river steadily moved away from the
old landing, leaving it to be reclaimed by nature. Although the traces of the
road to the ferry landing remain, timber, marshland and beaver ponds
are now found on the site of the once thriving and bustling riverfront.

Living Off the Land: Agriculture, Minerals, Manufacturing and Slavery

While the Missouri River was the artery of Arrow Rock, the area's agriculture, and to a lesser degree, mineral wealth was its lifeblood. Farmers in the Boonslick found adequate rainfall and rich soil. The periodic floods of the Missouri River made the bottomlands some of the richest soil in the nation. "I am in a promised land where you have no need to work for the land is so rich you may plant a crowbar at night and it will sprout ten penny nails by morning," wrote Robinson Garrett Smith to relatives in Kentucky.[296] By 1821, the Boonslick Country was fast becoming the major agricultural center of the state.

The early settlers to the Boonslick were simply concerned with putting food on the table. Hogs and corn were the primary foods of sustenance. Corn was ground into meal or soaked in lye and made into hominy. Smoking and salting were done to cure hog meat. A limited amount of vegetables such as potatoes were grown. Flax and even cotton were grown in small quantities to provide fiber for clothing. As the region became more developed, there was a shift in agricultural production. Many farms continued to produce livestock and began growing wheat in addition to corn. But many others began cultivating hemp and tobacco and developing into plantations.

"Hemp grows luxuriantly all through this country, the prairies appear beautiful when clothed with hemp eight feet high, and the great number of [hemp] breaks a going preparing the hemp for market at this season of the year," James Tate wrote in April of 1849.[297] Will H. Wood reported that in 1858, Arrow Rock shipped 7,135 bales of hemp, equaling 1,427 tons, for a total value of $128,120.[298] The Marshall *Weekly Democrat* of Feb. 14, 1859, carried a report from apocryphal correspondent "Podajcah Peasly" that underscored the importance of hemp in the Arrow Rock economy: "The streets of our town present quite a business; the hemp comes rolling in as it has done for the last few weeks; and from the excellent arrangement of Wood & Huston they can bale it as fast as it arrives … their entire business … is receiving, baling storing, and shipping hemp."[299]

First, the stalks of hemp were allowed to rot in the field so the fibers could be broken down. Water rotted hemp was considered superior, but more costly to produce. The rotted hemp was pressed into bales for shipping. These bales were sent to "rope walks" where the fibers were spun into rope. Most of it was shipped to the Deep South where it was used as cordage for tying cotton bales. A smaller amount of the hemp rope was used for the mast rigging of sailing ships. Thus, the Missouri hemp industry was inextricably linked to the cotton culture of the Deep South.

The cultivation and processing of hemp and tobacco was tedious, backbreaking labor. Since land was relatively abundant, most people in the Boonslick owned their own farms, which meant there was a shortage of labor for the growing number of hemp and tobacco plantations. The first settlers in the Boonslick had brought slaves with them, and, by the 1830s, the demand for laborers sharply increased. By 1849, there was one slave to every two white persons in Saline and Howard counties. Needless to say, the majority of slaves were located in the countryside.

Slaves were expensive to own and maintain. One of the earliest notices about purchasing slaves in the neighborhood of Arrow Rock appeared in the Franklin *Missouri Intelligencer* newspaper:

> *Wanted to Purchase*
> *A NEGRO GIRL*
> *Between 12 and 20 years of age, for which cash will be given.*
> *Should there be any children, they will also be purchased. The*
> *subscriber has about eighty head of cattle, which, together with*
> *some cash, he will barter for young Negro property.*
> *William Ish,*
> *Saline County, hand of Bearer*
> *Fish Creek, Oct. 2, 1824.*[300]

An early bill of sale for a slave in Arrow Rock dates to 1831. "I Joseph Huston of Saline County Missouri in consideration of the sum of four hundred dollars to me in hand paid & acknowledged to have been received have & by these presents do bargon sell & convey to Benjamin Huston a negro man named Armstrong aged thirty two to his heirs and assigns forever warranting and defending the right of title of said man, and that he is healthy and sound witness my hand and bill this second day of May 1831."[301]

Slave auctions occurred throughout the region, but no records have been found pertaining to Arrow Rock. There was no known "auction house" in Arrow Rock such as existed in large cities like St. Louis, Memphis and New Orleans. Slaves were probably traded and sold locally, as the Huston invoice demonstrates. It is possible itinerant slave traders would bring shipments of slaves upriver on the steamboats. Oral tradition states the front step of the Huston Tavern was used as an auction block for slaves. The earliest photographs of the Tavern do not show the same step as is there now. It appears a large stone block at the edge of Main Street was moved to the door of the Tavern in the 1920s.

Nearby Boone County provides an idea of what the slave market was like in 1835: "Negroes are selling astonishingly high — common negro men are in demand at $800 — women and boys from 10 to 12 years old at $500 ... they will be real scarce in this neighborhood this Fall."[302] Closer to Arrow Rock, John Locke Hardeman was managing "Ardmore," the plantation of Nathaniel Beverley Tucker and wrote to him in 1845, "... I have bought two negroes ... a man and girl of 14 years at $500 and $350 which I expect to realize out of my hemp (profits) etc. in April and May."[303]

After crops had been harvested and shipped to market, it was a common practice for owners to "rent out" their slaves to perform other jobs. Besides being laborers, some of the men were skilled tradesmen such as carpenters, masons, blacksmiths, coopers and wagon wrights. This is evident in Arrow Rock as African American craftsmen undoubtedly labored on many of Arrow Rock's structures. The women, besides doing fieldwork, performed domestic chores such as cooking, sewing and washing. Often, they were instrumental in raising the children of their masters.

In this respect, the life of slaves in central Missouri was not quite as monotonous as it was for the field hands of the Deep South. In fact, the threat of being "sold south" was a tactic used by many owners to keep their slaves obedient. Enslaved persons were considered property and could be sold away from their family and loved ones at any time. The most compassionate of slave owners were ultimately forced to make choices based on economic reasons, not the needs of the slaves. Thus, even in the very best of circumstances, life for Missouri slaves was still uncertain and highly restrictive.

It is clear slavery fueled the economic wealth of Arrow Rock and created much of the leisure time enjoyed by upper class whites. Records tend to deal with bare economic statistics, and little was recorded about the lives of enslaved peoples themselves. Many history books have not dealt with the subject, and primary documentation is rare. Consequently, archaeology becomes a key method for investigating the past.

During the summer of 2003, the University of Missouri–St. Louis conducted a three-week archaeological field school at "Oak Grove" plantation about 8 miles southwest of Arrow Rock. George A. Murrell started "Oak Grove" in 1852. He married Sophia T. McMahan in 1859 and built for her a Greek-Revival style house. In many respects, Murrell's plantation could be considered as typical of plantations/large farms in Saline County.[304]

Murrell owned 640 acres, and the 1860 census reveals livestock included 17 horses and mules, seven milk cows, five oxen, 12 other cattle and 100 swine. Cultivated crops included 200 bushels of wheat, 3000 bushels of corn, 600 bushels of oats, six bushels of peas/beans and 40 bushels of potatoes.

Other products included 350 pounds of butter, 10 tons of hay and 10 bushels of grass seeds and 350 tons of hemp. For labor on his farm, Murrell had 13 African American slaves, who occupied three separate quarters.[305]

An interesting item recovered from the excavation site was a cache of freshwater mussel shells. These were probably eaten then deposited by the doorway, but they may also have a spiritual connotation. Shell caches have been found in Chesapeake Bay African American sites and at Ulysses S. Grant National Historic Site in St. Louis. Mussel shells were interpreted as a charm to protect the house from evil spirits. In West African culture, shells have connections to the afterlife. This and future excavations will help piece together the neglected story of African Americans in the Arrow Rock area.[306]

The profitability of agriculture impacted the economy beyond the plantation owners. J. A. J. Aderton operated a large mercantile and commodities business in Arrow Rock. In 1847, he purchased 9,000 bushels of wheat at 50 cents per bushel and sold it in St. Louis for 95 cents to $1.20 per bushel. His employee, W. A. Beeding, wrote to his cousin Norman Lackland in St. Charles: "There is money to be made in this upper country speculating…We have everything that is needed or a man can wish for as a little exertion is all that is needed for a man to get along… Saline County consists of a great deal of wealth it is mostly all well improved and thickly settled by intelligent and respectable people."[307]

The late 1840s to the mid-1850s was a time when many local industries converted to steam technology. For instance, Henry Bingham and Joseph Huston had both opened steam-powered sawmills in Arrow Rock around that time. Lumber of consistent dimensions could be produced quickly and easily. This probably led to a housing boom, as frame houses were cheaper to build than brick and allowed more flexibility in design than brick or log structures. Elisha Ancell made a business of home building in the 1850s and 60s. He would build houses, live in them two or three years, then move on and build another. Several of his houses survive in town.[308] Lumberyards, such as the one operated by the Ancell brothers, even began importing sawn lumber such as yellow pine and sawn shingles.

By 1855, the town of Arrow Rock had purchased a hay scales. Operation was rented out to the highest bidder, and all hay, hemp or coal bought or delivered in Arrow Rock was to be weighed. Saline County had rich deposits of cannel coal, a hot burning bituminous, and mining became a fairly profitable activity. Most of this mining was done relatively close to the surface as opposed to deep shaft mining. Coal was burned in blacksmith forges and heated some buildings as well. A small amount of coal will burn longer and provide greater heat than a larger amount of wood. Judging from their small size, some of the fireplaces in the Tavern and Academy Boarding House evidently burned coal. In the late 1850s, Claiborne Fox Jackson contracted with a St. Louis mining company to extract ten thousand tons of coal per year from his farm. His annual yield from the mineral was $7,500.00.[309] Vincent Marmaduke agreed to pay the Town Board of Arrow Rock $6.00 per month for use of the town wharf to ship his coal downriver in June of 1862.[310]

Gold fever struck Arrow Rock in 1858. This time, the field of opportunity was not in distant Colorado or California. It was right in Arrow Rock's backyard! The Marshall *Weekly Democrat* printed a letter from an Arrow Rock correspondent in its October 1, issue:

> *"Arrow Rock, Sept. 28, 1858 Friend Democrat: Drop your pen and scissors, buy a sifter and milk strainer and hasten to the new Eldorado! Gold has been discovered within four miles of our little town, and the excitement is immense. The town is nearly deserted — men, women and children have left for the gold diggings, intent upon making their fortunes. On last Saturday a gentleman (whose name we are not allowed to use) brought into town specimens of black sand and quartz, in which pieces of gold were discovered. Mr. Davis our jeweler, tested them in several different ways, and pronounced it the pure stuff. We should never have given credence to the story, but we saw the gold with our own respective eyes, and*

*handled it with our individual fingers, as also the said sand and
quartz, and we are fully convinced that it was gold.*

*In connection with this startling discovery, staring us in the
face, we have several Indian legends proving that there are gold
deposits in Slough Creek. The citizens of Howard (County) having
heard the report are rushing to the diggings. The ferry-boat is laid
up, as the captain and all hands have emigrated to the gold region,
and many of the Howard gold seekers are crossing the river on a
log, while others are swimming over. Several steamboats which
have landed here have been infected, and officers crews and passengers have deserted them and repaired to the gold regions. Gold!
Gold! Gold! Is all the cry and we feel that the rest of the citizens in
the county should derive some benefit from the discovery.*

*Citizens of Saline, arise! And protect your interests! Drive
these outsiders off, and if they must dig gold, let them find it in
their own counties.*

*We suggest every man come to the mines armed to the teeth, to
drive off the intruders. Already the "Rangers, Company J" have
answered the call, and are on the ground to meet any emergency.
Rally around their standard, and we will show these foreigners
that we can protect our rights. Yours, truly, VERACITY.*[311]

A subsequent issue of the *Weekly Democrat* quickly deflated all hopes of
striking it rich. The true origin of the gold was discovered:

LATER FROM THE MINES

*A stranger, representing himself to be a pedlar, has made oath
before a justice that the gold dollar found in Slough Creek, is his
individual property, and that it was lost from his pocket while
crossing Slough Creek during one of his late pereginations. Our
Howard friends are making back tracks, and the "Rangers" have
evacuated their camp. The excitement is somewhat allayed, and
peace and quiet reign triumphant.*[312]

There was no explanation of how the gold ended up being mixed with
black sand and quartz. Perhaps that was a figment of overzealous report-
ing. The site of the supposed "gold mine" was on a farm owned by Mary
Ellen Price, wife of Dr. William Price and daughter of Dr. John Sappington. It was marked on a branch of Slough Creek in the 1896 Saline County

plat book, and the owner in the patrons' directory was listed as S. B. Spates. In a satirical acknowledgment of the 1858 incident, Mr. Spates called his property "Goldville Farm."[313]

The true "gold" of Arrow Rock's economy was the rich agricultural production of the surrounding farms and plantations. An itemized list published in the Marshall *Weekly Democrat* in 1860 demonstrated the over-arching importance of regional agriculture to the prosperity of Arrow Rock:

> *Shipments from Arrow Rock 1859*
> *We are indebted to Mr. Will H. Wood, commission merchant for the following statement of the shipments made from Arrow Rock for the year 1859:*
>
> *Hams* *1,117*
> *Wheat, sacks* *3,319*
> *Bacon, cks.* *20*
> *Lard, bbls.* *64*
> *Hides* *1,213*
> *Peltries, pkgs.* *25*
> *Wool, bales* *75*
> *Tobacco, hhds* *19*
> *Barley and rye* *648*
> *Corn.* *249*
> *Green apples, bbls* *275*
> *Dried fruit, sacks* *475*
> *Hogs.* *500*
> *Beans, sacks* *30*
> *Hemp seed, sacks* *40*
> *25,000 gall[ons] stone ware* [314]

The stoneware came from the Arrow Rock pottery works owned by Newton G. Caldwell. Vital for storing food, stoneware was the "Tupperware" of its day. Caldwell's works may have been the third largest pottery works in the state at this time. Charles McGuffin and his wife, Amanda, daughter of Joseph Huston, Sr., owned Block 30 on the north side of Morgan Street. McGuffin died in 1854; his loan was defaulted and picked up at auction by Caldwell in 1855. The 1860 industrial census for Saline County shows Caldwell had invested $4,000, had 200 cords of wood worth $500, and had five employees and one slave. In addition, the factory was "horse powered." Thirty-five thousand gallons of stoneware were valued at $2,800 that year.[315]

In 1863, the pottery works was sold to Dr. William Price as Caldwell moved to Callaway County to assist in operating his father's pottery factory. When Price died in 1865, the property passed on to his heirs, then to his brother-in-law, William B. Sappington. The pottery works went out of business around 1870. After the Civil War, stoneware declined in use with the invention of the Mason jar and metal containers.[316] Extensive archaeological investigation of the site was conducted from 1996 to 2001, revealing a beehive kiln, the remains of several work structures, and thousands of pottery shards and fragments.

Arrow Rock was still shipping substantial amounts of agricultural commodities as late as 1869. The *Saline County Progress* reported on August 3rd of that year: "Wood & Huston have shipped from this place, over 16,000 bushels of wheat and more is continually coming night and day…The oat crop which is a very heavy one, has just commenced coming to market. The peach crop is very light — apples very plenty. The *St. Luke* still noted for her prompt arrivals is our favorite packet."[317]

Lead mining, which had been carried on in the area intermittently since the 1820s, saw a resurgence. The same edition of the *Saline County Progress* carried a report from an Arrow Rock correspondent: "Mr. Dills, 4 miles south of here is succeeding with his new lead mines beyond all expectations. His cash price for the 40 acres already developed is $1,000 per acre. You are respectfully invited down to examine for yourself and get a 'chunk' for seeing is believing."[318] Despite this glowing, perhaps exaggerated report, lead mining did not develop into a lasting economic boon for the area.

Town Growth and Development

On December 10, 1847, the Saline County Court ordered the Town of Arrow Rock to be incorporated. The Court appointed Joseph Huston, Sr., Dr. Matthew W. Hall, P. W. Edwards, Dr. William Price and J. A. J. Aderton as Trustees to the board. Joseph Huston was elected as chairman. The board met again on December 13, and their first resolution was to appoint John S. Jones the Town Constable and Assessor.

Dr. Hall and Dr. Price were appointed to draw up a set of "laws" and submit them to the board on or about December 23, 1847. Most of the board's "laws" are rather mundane and establish how the board is to conduct its business. A few are rather interesting and perhaps even amusing by today's standards:

> *Article 6th*
> *Any member having a motion to make, a resolution or ordinance to introduce shall rise from his seat, read the same, address the chairman in an orderly and respectful manner, and no member shall be allowed to speak more than twice nor longer than thirty minutes upon the same subject.*
>
> *Article 7th*
> *It shall be the duty of all members of said Board of Trustees to be present at every meeting, and for failing so to do, shall forfeit and pay the sum of fifty cents, unless excused from said fine, upon a reasonable cause given for said absentee absence.*
>
> *Article 8th*
> *For disorderly conduct or a violation of the foregoing bylaws a majority of the Trustees may require such penalty as they may think coequal with the offense, and this shall apply to strangers as well as Trustees.*[319]

A grim side of human nature was revealed at this first meeting of the incorporated board. The gentlemen on the board were of Southern extraction and owned slaves. Because of the growing abolition movement in the North and the slave rebellion of Nat Turner in Virginia in 1831, slave insurrection was on their minds. They wanted to be certain the African American population stayed under control: "Be it ordained &c that John Thornton be appointed Captain of the Patrol and that he be empowered to select two other persons to act with him, and it shall be the duty of said Patrol to guard the Town and prevent unlawful meeting of Negroes, and see that no Negro is out from home after 10 o'clock at night without a pass, and if so found shall receive a whipping not exceeding ten lashes."[320] There are no records of the town ever imposing this penalty, but the board continued to periodically reauthorize the slave patrols.

A transcript of the minutes of the Town Board exists from August, 1840, through January 19, 1875. Jean Tyree Hamilton borrowed the original records from Mrs. Watson Diggs and her sister, Mrs. Mary Davis, for transcription in 1960. Their grandfather, Henry S. Wilhelm, had served for nineteen years on the Town Board, twelve of them as Chairman, and had preserved this set of books. Some pages were missing. A copy of Mrs. Hamilton's transcript is in the library of the Arrow Rock State Historic Site. References to minutes from later years are sometimes found piecemeal in various archives.

An examination of the Records of the Town of Arrow Rock provides a snapshot of the activities occurring as well as the character of the town. Arrow Rock was decidedly a rough and tumble western frontier town. Multitudes of people from different states and social and ethnic backgrounds continually streamed through Arrow Rock by boat or on the overland trails. Despite this mixing, clear social distinctions existed based on factors such as race, creed, education, gender and class. Southern values and attitudes held preeminence.

As in all growing communities, the Town Board needed and wanted revenue. On January 20, 1848, the property tax for improved or bare land in town was raised to a whopping (for the time) 2 1/2%. At the same time, owners of wagons that did hauling for the public were required to pay a tax of $1.50 for an ox-pulled wagon and 75 cents for a two-horse wagon. A July 25, 1857 ordinance directed "all flatboats landing at the wharf loaded with lumber or wood shall pay the town $1.00 per landing and any articles remaining on the wharf for 48 hours or more shall be charged $1.00 per day." The following year, steamboats had to pay "$2.00 for docking at the Arrow Rock Wharf on the trip up river and none to dock on the trip down river."[321] Failure to pay was to result in a $100 fine, to be collected by the constable who also doubled as the collector.

Duke Paul of Wuerttemberg on his third and final trip to the United States again passed through Arrow Rock on December 7, 1851. He reported the growth of the town as outpacing its neighbors: "... At daybreak we reached Marshall, a small place which is just now being built, crossed the small Saline Creek over a good bridge, and detoured over a retched road to Arrow Rock. I have long been acquainted with its landing place due to my earlier journey. It is a flourishing little town and like the majority of places on the west bank is growing more rapidly than those on the northeastern bank."[322]

By 1851, Arrow Rock's communication with the outside world was no longer limited to steamboat, stagecoach and the U.S. Postal Service. On

February 7 of that year, a telegraph line ran from Boonville to Arrow Rock and then on to Marshall. By the end of March, the line reached all the way to Lexington, Missouri.[323] News from across the state and nation could now be received and sent in a matter of minutes or hours, instead of days or weeks. For the time, it was a quantum leap in technology.

Continued growth led to the Town Board exploring new ways to increase town revenues. In 1858, a $1.00 poll was charged to all white men residing in Arrow Rock over the age of 21. The Trustees also approved a new liquor license and tax of $75.00, valid for one year. Failure to obtain the license was to result in a fine of $100.00. Even recreation was eventually subjected to taxes. On March 10, 1868, the Town Board taxed all billiard tables at $10.00 per year, to be paid in advance. The board even felt their authority extended beyond the corporation limits. Billiard tables within one half mile of town, if any, were to be taxed as well. Most of the funds collected went into the improvement and maintenance of the streets and the river wharf and paying for the town constable and collector.

The Town Board minutes clearly hint at Arrow Rock's rowdy nature. River boatmen, wagon teamsters, wharf and warehouse laborers undoubtedly sought diversions from the monotony of their daily tasks. The consumption of alcoholic beverages was perhaps more widespread and accepted than even today. Gambling, such as betting on horses, was another passion. Drinking and gambling and the resulting "ruckuses" evidently occurred with enough frequency to cause the board to pass the following ordinance in January of 1849: "Be it ordained &c that any one guilty of fighting, or loud and boisterous quarrelling, or engaging in any mob, or making unusual noises, furious or violent riding within the corporation, upon conviction before a magistrate shall be fined in any sum not less than two dollars and fifty cents and not more than twenty dollars."[324]

Fighting and rowdiness evidently continued to be a problem. On February 4, 1856, the Town Board passed an ordinance increasing the penalty for fighting and rowdy behavior. This meeting of the board was held at Dr. Matthew Hall's office, but apparently it was to no avail. The following year, Dr. Hall sold his home and property to Fountain Durrett for $2,000 and relocated to a farm near Marshall. According to Hall family tradition, he sought to remove his children from "the evil influence of a river town."[325]

Other illicit activities may have been occurring which induced Dr. Hall to leave. The minutes of the Town Board on August 12th, 1867, reveal this problem: "On complaint of Mrs. Tipping, Mr. & Mrs. Luther & several other persons and from evidence sufficient, we the Board of Trustees declare the house adjoining the corporation of Arrow Rock & owned by Mr. R. Butler a Bawdy House and kept by two black women known as Mary Butler and Sarah Reeves, and that A. Coiner, Town Constable shall be ordered to close the house & turn the occupants out."[326] A "bawdy house" was a house of prostitution. Although there are no records, it is possible this activity occurred sporadically in Arrow Rock long before the breaking up of this particular operation. Prostitution occurred in larger river towns, although it was not openly discussed in 19th century society.

Starting in the 1850s, Arrow Rock churches attempted to curb liquor consumption and its attendant social problems. An Arrow Rock "correspondent" to the Marshall *Weekly Democrat* mocked the temperance movement in March of 1858: "The temperance cause has made considerable change in affairs here. The traffic has been abandoned, and all hands are duly sober, and some rather dry. Our town may truly be called a temperance town; not a drop of the critter for sale. But the opening of the navigation and appearance of steamboats may change the appearance of things. The Rev. Wm. Wheaton delivers an address on temperance tonight, a very good time to make a haul."[327]

Noise was a problem, and undoubtedly much of this was fueled by liquor consumption. In September of 1858, the Town Board received several complaints "relating to letting off firearms in the streets to this corporation, frightening horses, etc." The board passed a new ordinance "that any person guilty of firing or setting off fire works, fire crackers or throwing turpentine and gass balls ... shall on conviction be fined not less than one or more than five dollars for each offence ...."[328] "Throwing turpentine" involved lighting it before tossing it in the air. "Gass balls" may have referred to filling a container with carbide gas, then causing it to explode. Such merriment was especially popular around the holidays. Christmas was an especially favorite time to discharge guns and fireworks. This type of merriment was still a problem in December of 1868, for the Board of Trustees "Ordered that the Chairman procure such assistance for the Town Constable during holidays as may be deemed necessary by him."[329]

Ever fearful of slave revolt, the Trustees of Arrow Rock continued to focus on enslaved African Americans. On January 6, 1849, they reauthorized the slave patrols: "Be it ordained &c that there shall be appointed three persons to act as patrols for the Town whose duty it shall be to patrol the town and any negro found out from home after 10 o clock at night without a pass shall receive a whipping not exceeding 10 lashes."[330] This was merely a continuation of an ordinance passed in 1847.

The Town Board passed a littering and loitering ordinance on April 16, 1859, stating "any person or persons placing any obstruction or depositing any kind of dirt, ashes or other things In Main Street or unnecessarily obstructing the sidewalks shall on conviction for any such offense, pay a fine of not less than five nor more than fifty dollars… any person who shall remain in this corporation without visible means of support and annoying the peace and quiet of the citizens on conviction shall be termed a vagrant and fined not less than two nor more than fifty dollars and failing to pay the same be compelled to work out the amount at fifty cents per day for the benefit of the Town of Arrow Rock…."[331]

Dogs have always had a special place in the history of Arrow Rock. They have periodically been and continue to be a subject of Town Board meetings. This intriguing reference to dogs was in the minutes of August 1, 1853: "Resolved that the ordinance in regard to killing dogs passed the last meeting be rescinded." Unfortunately, no explanation is given for the rescision and minutes of that previous meeting are missing. The dog problem surfaced again in 1855. On May 14, the board declared all out war: "All dogs or sluts running at large in the streets or alleys of said Town during the said 60 days shall be killed by the constable of the Town and cause the same to be removed outside the town limits for which he shall receive 50 cents per head…."[332]

The board again tried their hand at dog control on March 3, 1856: "All dogs must be confined. Constable shall have the right to kill all dogs running loose."[333] One correspondent reported to the Marshall *Weekly Democrat* in May of 1859: "As further evidence of the vigilance of our 'Board,' Main Street is now obstructed by the heaps of inoffensive curs, who have fallen victims to their displeasure, under the dog-law, and our friend Jerry is now busily engaged in the war of extermination."[334] After a couple of decades without a mention, the board minutes of August 3, 1892, simply report, "Dog law needs enforcing."[335] Before being too critical of past board actions as cruel, it must be considered that nearly everyone in town owned horses and often kept a cow, hog or chickens on his lot.

Packs of free-roaming dogs could be a real menace to livestock. They carried the threat of rabies, which was then untreatable.

Town improvements continued at an accelerated pace in the 1850s. In 1853, plank sidewalks were constructed on the north side of Main Street from First to Sixth Street. Stepping-stones were set across the streets to connect the walks. Over the next two decades, the Town Board expanded the system of plank walks where brick sidewalks did not already exist. On January 16, 1855, the Town Board meeting was held at Dr. Hall's office, and a new ordinance was passed to prohibit the burning of coal bits within the town limits. Evidently structure fires had been a problem, although no specific records of property loss from fires have been found. A committee was formed to study the construction of chimneys for forges "in order to render them most secure against Fire to themselves and other fixtures about them...."[336]

Typically, the streets of Missouri towns were dirt. After a rain, they turned into mud deeply rutted by wagon wheels. Arrow Rock was progressing over neighboring towns in this area as well. Increasingly, traffic in town was regulated to collect revenue and fund street improvements:

> *Be it ordained that from and after the First day of May 1850, no carriage, cart, wagon, dray, or other vehicle be allowed to carry loading, or passengers, or a passenger, for hire within the limits of the town of Arrow Rock, without being licensed for six to twelve months for that purpose by the Secretary of the Board of Trustees.*
>
> *Be it ordained that the following rates be and are hereby established for granting licenses. For every cart for 6 months 50 cents for 12, $1. For every ox wagon for 6 months, 75 cents, & for 12 months, One dollar & 50 cents. For every 2 horse wagon for 6 months, 75 cents, & for 12 months, one dollar and fifty cents. For any other four wheeled vehicle, for six months, One dollar, & for 12 months two dollars — April 11, 1850.*[337]

On September 7, 1857, the Town Board purchased two yoke of oxen, two ox carts and one plow for the "grading and paving of the street."[338] James Huston was employed to "oversee the work and hands and teams & working utensils, also to hire suitable hands for work...."[339] He was allowed one dollar for his services. Paving consisted of "macadam," or crushed gravel, laid down on Main Street. Macadam did not eliminate mud, but it provided a firmer surface and reduced the rutting caused by wagon wheels.

Public works projects can cause emotions to run high, and it was no different in 19th century Arrow Rock. On October 12, 1857, the Board of Trustees resolved "that James Huston shall proceed to take sufficient dirt or earth from Main Street on the present grade to fill up the hollow at the Rock Wall on grade with said wall."[340] This action caused Jesse McMahan, President of the Board, to protest the proposed work. Failing to halt the action, McMahan "tendered his resignation as trustee of the Town of Arrow Rock, whereupon the same was accepted."[341] James A. Boyer was immediately elected President of the Board.

In August of 1858, the Town Board entertained bids to construct stone gutters along Main Street. This would further improve the surface of Main Street by rapidly draining runoff from rain. The board awarded the contract to James and William Kelly, who were paid the rate of $1.50 for each of 22 feet of gutter laid.[342] The Arrow Rock Masonic Lodge has a daguerreotype of a man named William Lamb, a Scottish emigrant. Early handwriting on the back of the picture credits Lamb with building the gutters.[343]

According to oral tradition, slaves did much of the actual labor of cutting and laying the stones that are set 18 to 24 inches deep. It would not have been unusual for the Kellys to rent slaves from their masters to perform the actual labor while they "supervised." Perhaps Lamb was supervising stone cutting at the quarry, since he was a Mason.

The stone gutters run on both sides of Main Street from First to Seventh. They at once impart a 19th century ambiance to the town while striking terror into the heart of the present-day motorist trying to cross them. For horses and high-wheeled wagons, they were not a problem. They are not a problem for an automobile that crosses them slowly at a 45-degree angle. The gutters remain as a testimony to the skill of African American laborers at the pinnacle of Arrow Rock's prosperity.

The Marshall *Weekly Democrat* reported, "In the spring of 1858, Arrow Rock had the air of a boom town, with a group of warehouses on the levee, and Main Street lined with stores. Drays, carts, and wagons are constantly traversing the streets between the steamboat landing and the business portion of the town, carrying hemp and other products of the farm for shipment, and returning with lumber, groceries and other products for the country, or to be stored in the up town warehouses."[344]

Like all prospering and influential communities, Arrow Rock had its own newspaper, several times. None of the papers lasted very long, but even more unfortunate, no complete editions from the earliest papers survive. Newspaper reports about Arrow Rock generally come from the surviving papers of neighboring towns. If more papers were to turn up, undoubtedly many questions about persons and events in Arrow Rock's past would be answered.

Saline County Herald, 1859–1861. This was a weekly paper, which had moved to Arrow Rock from Marshall. James Allen was the publisher. The only part of this paper to be discovered was an article addressing Union Army Captain Nathaniel Lyon's capture of Camp Jackson at the beginning of the Civil War.

Democratic Cable, 1871–1872. A weekly paper, which had moved from Miami. A man named Reynolds published it.

Arrow Rock *Enterprise*, June 1877–1881. A weekly paper started and published by Scott Mills.

Arrow Rock *Times*, 1881–1891. A weekly paper started and published by N. H. Rugg.

Arrow Rock *Enterprise*, July, 1891–October, 1893. A weekly paper published by R. S. Sandige. A complete run of this paper survives.

Arrow Rock *Statesman*, November 1893–1919. A weekly published by R. S. Sandige. This was taken over by the Diggs brothers in 1897 and operated by Bascom Diggs after 1898. Charles G. Patterson published the paper its final year of existence.

Arrow Rock *Times*, 1920–1921. Although it was the most recent paper to be published, little is known about it.[345]

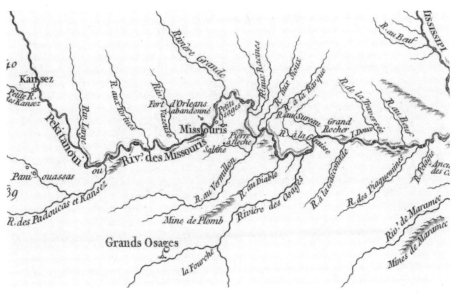

Excerpt from "Carte de la Lousiane" drawn in 1732 by French cartographer d'Anville, published in 1752. This map contains the earliest known reference to the name Arrow Rock, "Pierre à fleche." *David Rumsey Map Collection*

"Passing Franklin and Arrow Rock on the Missouri." This pencil sketch by Karl Bodmer on April 15, 1833, is the earliest known picture of the Arrow Rock bluff. *Joslyn Art Museum*

Portion of the Arrow Rock bluff today as seen from the Big Muddy National Fish &
Wildlife Refuge's Lewis & Clark hiking trail to the Missouri River. *Missouri
Department of Natural Resources*

Mahinkacha, "Maker of Knives," painted
by Karl Bodmer in 1834. One of only two
illustrations of a Missouri Indian known to
exist. *University of Missouri Press*

Aketa tonkah, "Big Soldier," Second Chief of
the Little Osage. "Big Soldier" was born at the
village upriver from Arrow Rock. He was a key
negotiator with George Sibley at Arrow Rock
in 1813. *University of Missouri Press*

George Champlin Sibley, U.S. factor at Fort Osage and Arrow Rock, Santa Fe Trail commissioner and founder of Lindenwood University in St. Charles, Missouri. *Lindenwood University*

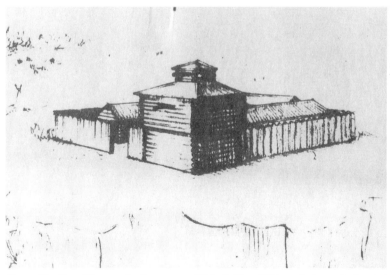

The Osage Trading House, also known as Sibley's Fort. This artist's rendering is based on Sibley's written description of the installation. It is also representational of the small civilian forts and blockhouses which dotted the area during the War of 1812. *MDNR*

Judge Frederick Hyatt and his wife. Hyatt lived in the Jones-McMahan settlement south of Arrow Rock. He traveled to Kentucky in 1813 to obtain his bride. *Friends of Arrow Rock, Inc.*

Saline County Seal, c. 1832. The only known illustration of an early salt works. *MDNR*

A scene on the Missouri River, 1872. This etching shows a variety of craft used for navigating the "Big Muddy." *MDNR*

A ferryboat on the Missouri River, c. 1900. The earlier versions of the Arrow Rock ferry were probably similar to this. *MDNR*

The ferryboat *Hope* at the Arrow Rock crossing, c. 1900. *FAR*

Arrow Rock river landing and warehouses, c. 1868. *Mark Gardner Collection*

The Arrow Rock landing, c. 1910. By this time, trees were reclaiming the once-bustling waterfront. *FAR*

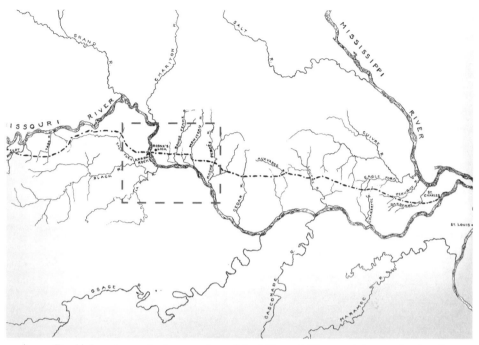

Arrow Rock's location at the intersection of the Missouri River and the overland trail system made it a prime site for a town. The boxed area represents the core area of the Boonslick country. *State Historical Society of Missouri*

General Smith's home at "Experiment" farm, near Jonesboro (Napton). One cabin of this "dogtrot" house is still standing (2004), making it the oldest building in Saline County (1826). *FAR*

General Thomas A. Smith, veteran of the War of 1812, agent at the U.S. land office in Franklin, Missouri, and owner of "Experiment" farm. *FAR*

Henry and Amanda Nave (Neff), considered the first truly "permanent" white settlers in Saline County. *FAR*

Eleanor F. Chapman

The Neff Tavern as it appeared based on the description of Jesse Bingham Neff. *FAR*

Meredith Miles Marmaduke, veteran of the War of 1812, Governor of Missouri, Santa Fe trader, Saline County judge and surveyor. *MDNR*

Portrait of Governor Claiborne Fox Jackson, being viewed by two members of the Daughters of the American Revolution in the Arrow Rock Tavern, 1961. *MDNR*

Dr. John Sappington (1776–1856), daguerreotype taken in the late 1840s to c. 1850.
Mrs. Jane Breathitt Sappington (1783–1852), daguerreotype taken c. 1850.
These two photographic images were a 2003 gift to the Friends of Arrow Rock from
Eleanor Price Ledogar, great-great-granddaughter of Dr. and Mrs. Sappington. *FAR*

Dr. John Sappington, by George Caleb Bingham, 1834.
Jane Breathitt Sappington, by George Caleb Bingham, 1834.
These are the earliest extant paintings by Bingham, who would later become known as
"The Missouri Artist." They are on display at the Arrow Rock State Historic Site Visitor
Center. *MDNR*

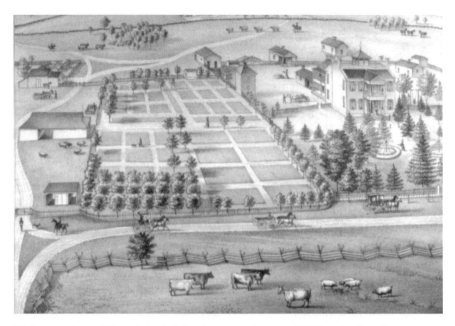

Bird's-eye view of "Prairie Park," the plantation home of William B. Sappington, from the 1876 *Illustrated Atlas Map of Saline County, MO.*

The Marmaduke brothers, c. 1868. John S. is seated in the center, and Vincent is seated to the right. *FAR*

John Sappington Marmaduke, c. 1880, Confederate general and one of three Missouri governors from Arrow Rock. *FAR*

Burton Lawless, one of the two founders of the town of Arrow Rock. *FAR*

John Percy Huston, Jr. viewing the portrait of his great-grandfather, Joseph Huston, in the Tavern, c. 1960. Joseph Huston was one of the founding town commissioners. *FAR*

D and Martha Lawless. The Lawless farmhouse at the edge of Arrow Rock has been restored by the Friends of Arrow Rock, Inc. *FAR*

Nathaniel Beverley Tucker, owner of "Ardmore" plantation and Professor of Law at the College of William and Mary, Williamsburg, Virginia. *FAR*

Dr. George Penn, from a "carte de visite" c. 1859. Dr. Penn was a partner of Dr. Sappington, active in Arrow Rock's civic and political affairs and a regimental surgeon during the Mexican War. *MDNR*

Henry S. Wilhelm, member of the Arrow Rock Board of Trustees and president of the Arrow Rock school board. He was responsible for preserving many of the town's early records. *FAR*

Dr. Matthew Walton Hall, physician active in civil and political affairs in Arrow Rock and Saline County. Born in Washington County, Kentucky in 1817, he came to Arrow Rock with his family in 1845. *FAR*

Dr. Matthew Hall House. This Greek revival style house was built in 1846. *MDNR*

George Caleb Bingham, the "Missouri Artist" from a daguerreotype, c. 1858. *State Historical Society of Missouri*

George Caleb Bingham house, c. 1920s. *MDNR*

George Caleb Bingham house after Works Progress Administration (WPA) restoration in the 1930s removed the second story and ell. *MDNR*

Daguerreotype of Mattie and Sallie Cobb, c. 1859. Thirteen-year-old Mattie died in the Tavern where her parents were the managers. *MDNR*

Remains of a hemp press near Malta Bend, c. 1955. This device pressed the hemp into bales for shipment. *FAR*

"Park Place," home of the Kuhn family, c. 1890. Located on the east end of Main Street, it was typical of small, middle-class homes common in Arrow Rock in the 19th century. No longer standing. *MDNR*

A tintype taken in Arrow Rock. This unknown man is probably a Union sympathizer. He is dressed in attire typical of the late 1850s through the mid 1860s. The revolver and the hand resting on the book on a Corinthian column may be meant to evoke an image of defending the law or the Constitution. *MDNR*

A tintype taken in Arrow Rock. This unknown man is probably a bushwhacker. He is wearing what appears to be a Confederate uniform jacket and has long hair typical of Missouri guerillas during the Civil War. *MDNR*

Societal Development

Religion and Churches

The first ministers in Saline County were Reverend Thomas Kinney in 1816 and Reverend Peyton Nowlin, who arrived a short time later. Both were Old Baptists, popularly known as "Ironsides" or "Hard-shells." They traveled a circuit to preach, as there were no established congregations during the early period of settlement. Reverend Nowlin became one of the town commissioners of Arrow Rock. Methodists were the next Christian denomination to come into the area, followed by the Presbyterians.

Few of the early pioneers made any pretensions to being particularly religious. Rev. Nowlin would hold meetings in forests, homes, barns or anywhere "two or three gathered together."[346] When one of the preachers arrived in a neighborhood, residents would gather to hear the Gospel preached. Guns would be stacked in the corner of a cabin, and at the conclusion of the sermon, a jug of whisky might be passed around. Even the preachers were known to indulge. It was considered common courtesy to accept a drink, if offered, and imbibing was not necessarily viewed as sinful conduct. Afterwards, the men would go hunting or hold a shooting match.[347] Sunday services also gave the women and children an opportunity to socialize with neighbors they seldom saw.

Camp meetings were common as the area became more settled. Once a camp meeting was called, members of all denominations participated. Favored places for early camp meetings were at the farm of Rudolph Hawpe just south of Arrow Rock, on Cow Creek, and on the Blackwater River.[348] People would sometimes travel twenty or thirty miles to attend the meetings that might last several days or more. Frequently, a large brush arbor was erected for holding the meeting, and the participants camped in tents nearby. At some of these meetings, a phenomenon known as the "jerks" sometimes manifested itself. Members of the congregation

"...would jerk violently from side to side and backward to forward, sometimes shouting 'Glory to God.'"[349] In other cases, people would faint. Generally, the ministers and most of the people attributed these to manifestations of the Spirit of God. Besides meeting spiritual needs, the camp meetings provided an opportunity for social interaction among neighbors.

A notable preacher in the area around 1831 was Jacob Montgomery, a slave owned by James Montgomery. Jacob was a powerful preacher, and he ministered to both black and white audiences. A group of youths went to a meeting to "hear Nigger Jake" preach and have some fun by scoffing at him. However, three of the party made an open profession of faith in Christ. One of the youths declared, "...there must be a God and religion a reality" else how could a "...poor illiterate black man... preach with the force and effect which he did."[350]

On the night of November 12 and 13, 1833, there occurred a meteor shower that provoked an emotional, if not religious, response from many who saw it. Visible throughout the United States, "meteors fell as thick and fast as snow-flakes in a heavy snow storm."[351] The luminous trails remained visible for minutes at a time and a few of the larger ones for up to a half hour. Many did not understand what was happening and concluded the "Day of Judgment" had arrived. One terrified local woman awoke her husband exclaiming, "Get up old man, quick! The day of judgment has come!" Grumbling and turning over in bed, her husband replied, "O, lie down and go to sleep you old fool, do you suppose the judgment *day* is going to come in the *night?*"[352]

A dance attended exclusively by the slaves of the neighborhood was in progress on a farm near Arrow Rock. When the shower began, one person ran into the cabin and announced, "The Lord is coming with fire and glory." When the dancers ran out, they fell to their knees in prayer at the sight of the "sudden and awful supernatural visitation." Elsewhere, James Reavis and another party had been engaged in a lawsuit over possession of a black man named Ben. Under advice of his lawyer, Reavis kept Ben under guard. When the star shower began, the fearful guard fell on his knees to pray, but Ben "...got up and lit out for his friends on the other side of the case, making good his escape."[353]

The establishment of regular congregations and meeting places signaled a significant transition in frontier society. People were becoming more settled, looking for permanence and stability in their lives, as well as moral guidance. Churches helped provide a stable social order and fellowship with kindred spirits. The first church organized in Arrow Rock Township was Zoar Baptist formed in 1825 by Reverend Peyton Nowlin. There were nine members of this Baptist congregation located north of present-day Napton.

The Arrow Rock Methodist Episcopal Church was formed in 1831 and met in a log cabin. One of the early ministers was Reverend Jesse Green, who was also a cabinetmaker. George Caleb Bingham was an apprentice in Rev. Green's shop for a period of time. In 1843, a white frame building was built on the corner of Sixth and High Streets for $2,200.00. Although remodeled extensively through the years, the structure remains in use today as the Arrow Rock Federated Church.[354] United States Senator Thomas Hart Benton reportedly attended a service at this church. "Old Bullion," as he was known, was so politically powerful that ministers were intimidated to preach. One unnamed old minister rose and said, "Brethren we ought to be ashamed. Tom Benton is a greater man than any of us, but God Almighty is greater than Tom Benton ... From what I learn, Tom Benton needs preaching about as bad as anyone on this ground and who knows but the sermon today may save his soul."[355] The preaching proceeded, and Benton is said to have listened with approval.

In 1835, the Methodist Episcopal conference for the western district was held at Arrow Rock. Over one hundred preachers were in attendance, some from as far away as the Arkansas border. Average daily attendance of the sessions numbered about 1,000 people, five times the number of people then living in Arrow Rock. Among those in attendance were Christianized Indians from the Indian Territory (Kansas), primarily Delaware, Wyandotte, Shawnee and Kickapoo. Clad in their curious mix of native and white clothing, they were reported as "...paying close attention to the services and deporting themselves in every particular as devout Christians ... who saw God in the clouds and heard Him in the wind."[356] They were objects of much attention and curiosity during the ten-day conference.

The churches often sought to counter some of the more coarse or rowdy aspects of frontier society. For example, the Methodist Church became the focal point of efforts to curb liquor consumption in Arrow Rock. The Reverend Dr. Prottsman organized a series of temperance lectures in the late 1850s. The Temperance Society was formed in Arrow Rock, and they held a huge barbecue, which nearly 600 people attended. In April of 1861, the Sons of Temperance held their semi-annual conference at the Arrow Rock Methodist Church.[357]

Churches were established throughout the surrounding countryside as well, but many of these no longer exist. A few had close associations with names well known in Arrow Rock. The Concord (Christian) Church was erected in the countryside northwest of Arrow Rock in 1845. Reverend Thomas Allen dedicated it, and some of its members included Daniel Thornton, Santa Fe trader Philip W. Thompson, William Roper, the town saddle maker, and Charles Wood, the father of Arrow Rock merchant and civic leader Will H. Wood.

The Arrow Rock Presbyterian Church was organized on April 3, 1840. Reverend Gary Hickman was pastor of this congregation from 1842–1852. Apparently, the congregation did not have a building and met in other locations. Rev. Hickman also helped operate the Arrow Rock Female Academy during this period. The Cumberland Presbyterian Church was organized December 12, 1853. In 1857, they erected a frame building on the northwest corner of Seventh and Main Streets. In 1900, the building was sold to the Zion Evangelical and Reformed Church, who continue to hold services there.[358]

The Baptists were one of the first Christian congregations in Arrow Rock, owing to the presence of Reverend Nowlin. Ironically, they had no building but met in the open for years, probably using brush arbors. On December 1, 1853, they purchased a lot on the corner of Second and High Streets from Meredith and Lavinia Marmaduke and built a church there. This building burned in 1872, but a new structure was soon built in the Gothic style. During church services in the new building, African American residents occupied the balcony.

Thomas Rainey told the story of the conversion of John Bobbitt: "Owing to his hard swearing he had remained out of the fold of his favorite church, the Hard-Shell Baptists … But during their annual 'association' meeting he became deeply convicted of his sinful life and offered himself for membership, to the great joy of the faithful…."[359] It was the practice of the Baptists before admitting a member to require that he relate his "experience" to the assembled church. Bobbitt was unused to speaking before company, but when called upon, stood near the pulpit to relate his experience.

In an almost inaudible tone he began: "I dreamed a dream, I dreamed I was sitting out in my orchard under the shade of an apple tree, and I heard a voice from heaven saying, 'John Bobbitt, your prayers have been answered, and your soul is saved.'" An older man sitting three seats back cupped his hand to his ear and said, "Will the brother speak a little louder; I failed to hear him distinctly." Embarrassed, Bobbitt repeated the story, a little louder, but another man further back cupped his hand to his ear and said, "I would be glad if the brother would speak a little louder. I did not hear more than half of what he said." Still embarrassed and now irritated, Bobbitt repeated the story word for word very loudly. Finally, a man on the back row that Bobbitt did not like very well, stood up and said, "If the brother will speak so we can all hear, we will be glad." Thoroughly enraged, Bobbitt shouted, "I dreamed a dream! I dreamed I was sitting out in my orchard under the shade of a tree! And I heard a voice from Heaven saying, 'John Bobbitt! Your prayers have been answered and your soul is saved!' Now I reckon you hear that damn you!" Rainey assured his readers that Bobbitt's relapse was only temporary.[360]

Following the Civil War, the Disciples of Christ sought a location for a church building. The town's gunsmith, John P. Sites, and his wife Nancy, donated the ground on which this building now stands. The first entry to the church record book is April 10, 1876: "We the undersigned do mutually agree…to unite in forming a congregation of the Church of Christ at Arrow Rock, Saline County, Missouri."[361] Brother C. Q. Shouse was ordained an elder, and John Sites and Asa Ulmstattd were appointed deacons. Rev. Shouse preached at the rate of $12.50 per month. Services continued until 1949. In 1962, the Arrow Rock Craft Club began the restoration of the church building under a five-year lease agreement with the Christian Church of Mid-America, Inc. The Friends of Arrow Rock secured a 99-year lease in 1982 and completed additional work then. The Christian Church is furnished and interpreted as a church of the 1870s. It is still used for special services, weddings and receptions.[362]

Until the 1940s, the Arrow Rock churches were strong enough to maintain their own congregations. After 1945, the Baptist, Methodist and Christian churches took turns holding services for all three congregations. In 1948, the congregations were unable to care for their buildings, and it was decided the three churches should federate. Albert Hogge was appointed chairman and Dorothy Kruger clerk to execute this transition, which was completed by October, 1950. The Arrow Rock Federated Church continues to meet in the original Methodist Church building.[363] The Baptist Church was sold to the Lyceum Theater in 1960.[364] It is now the front lobby and concession stand of the Arrow Rock Lyceum Theater. However, the original structure retains much of its architectural lines.

"Religion played a major role in Arrow Rock's African American community as a center of spiritual and social activities."[365] Both facets helped blacks maintain a sense of dignity in a society in which segregation was the order of the day. In the case of the white Baptist Church, blacks were permitted to sit in the balcony for worship services. It is possible other churches allowed African Americans to attend services under restricted conditions, although documentation has not been found.

Much information about church life in the black community comes from oral histories of lifelong African American residents, Ruth and Dennis Banks. Mary Burge, a member of the Friends of Arrow Rock, began recording their stories in the 1970s. In addition to relating the church histories, the Banks enjoyed reminiscing about some of the humorous events that occurred in relation to the congregations.

The first African American church built in Arrow Rock was the Arrow Rock Free Will Baptist Church. Construction started in 1869 on property north of the city limits of Arrow Rock, adjacent to Blocks 30 and 39. "White and colored men worked to build it, and white and colored women cooked enormous meals to feed the workers."[366] William B. and Mary Sappington deeded the site to the "Ruling Deacons in the Colored Baptist Church of Arrow Rock" in 1871 for one dollar. According to oral tradition, the first minister was Reverend John Brown and the church was probably named "Brown's Chapel" after him. Brown was twenty-five when he began preaching at the church in 1870. William Carry, also a Baptist minister, appeared in the 1870 census and may have preached some at the church.

The church is now located on Block 12, Lot 30 on High Street. John Brown and Zack Bush, acting as Trustees of Brown's Chapel, purchased this lot from Dr. William Price in 1882. Oral tradition says Zack Bush moved the church building to the site with a team of mules. The Trustees, Zack Bush, John Brown and Robert Brooks deeded the former site of the church to Rev. John Brown. Brown's Chapel served as the first schoolhouse for Arrow Rock's African American community from 1869 to 1892.

"At one time there was an enrollment of 192 in Sunday School. Until the 1900s there was no piano in the church but fiddles and jaw harps were used before this."[367]

Reverend Harrison Green owned a home in Arrow Rock and also served as Bishop of the black Baptist churches in Saline County. Records indicate he was performing marriages in Saline County as early as 1868. All the black churches wanted him to preach, and he was getting weary. Consequently, a church law was passed in Arrow Rock stating a minister could serve no more than two churches at a time. Reverend Green was highly influential in the Arrow Rock community. In addition to being a minister, he was Worshipful Master of the Masonic Lodge Number 22 A.F. & A.M. He also taught school at the Brown's Chapel from 1874 to 1890.

Brown's Chapel was very active in county, state and national conferences. "There have been as many representatives from Arrow Rock Brown's Chapel church at national conferences as much from any church in Saline County."[368] Bishop Emeritus M. H. Williams recalled some of these Association meetings held in Arrow Rock during the 1920s. The meetings would begin on the first Sunday in August and run for an entire week. There were as many as 300 people attending these meetings.

Church membership began declining in the 1930s, but this was true of most institutions in Arrow Rock, white and black. An active congregation remained at Brown's Chapel until 1988, and Reverend Raymond Todd was the last pastor. Trustees Erma Huston, Thelma Conway and Pearl Adams sold the church and lot to Ted and Virginia Fisher of Arrow Rock. In 1996, the Fishers donated the church to the Friends of Arrow Rock on condition it be restored and used to interpret Arrow Rock's African American history. The restoration was completed in May of 1998, through fundraising events and tax credited donations through the Neighborhood Assistance program of the Missouri Department of Economic Development. The restored parsonage remains next door, but it is a private residence. A "Homecoming Celebration" is now held every other year at the chapel for the descendants of Arrow Rock's African American community.[369]

The second black church constructed was the African Methodist Episcopal (A.M.E.). This church was built of logs on Second Street, north of the city limits but burned sometime during the 1870s. Dennis Banks said after the Methodist church and parsonage burned, the congregation held meetings in brush arbors for several years. "The minister would ride or walk in on Saturday and spend the night with a member. One of the early ministers of this black church was Rev. Dennis Peyton Banks, whose name was derived from Reverend Peyton Nowlin and the Banks family."[370]

The A.M.E. church was rebuilt in 1877, further north on Second Street but still outside the corporate limits. It was a white frame building built with the help of donations from the community. Ruth Banks told of a revival meeting held there in the 1890s:

> *Revivals were frequently held and greatly enjoyed. This was a time for feasts, singing, visiting and much fainting. Jake and Esau Banks were twins and very lively young boys, always in mischief. At this one revival Dennis Banks and Phoebe Adams were to go early and open up. Lanterns and candles were used, and they were to light them. They were also to lead the devotional and prayers. They had written their prayers on paper and were hurrying through the dark. Unknown to them, Jake and Esau had slipped on ahead, and with sheets covering them were waiting in front of the church. When Dennis and Phoebe lit the candles there were two ghosts. The papers were dropped and they ran out yelling, "Ghosts!" That ended the revival for the night.*[371]

Tragedy struck the A.M.E. church. The Arrow Rock *Statesman* reported on November 30, 1917: "On Sunday morning the colored Methodist church and parsonage burned down. The fire started in the parsonage at about 7:30 and is supposed to have caught from a defective flue. The church and parsonage were located close together and in a few minutes both buildings were a mass of flames. There was no insurance on the buildings and nothing was saved except the seats in the church."[372] According to Dennis Banks, "Reverend Payne was the minister. He said as he was leaving for another town — 'Well, Payne is leaving, but your misery stays here.' And he was right, as the congregation was never strong enough to rebuild. The members met in homes for a few years, and then joined the Baptist Church, which was still strong."[373] There are no readily visible remains of the A.M.E. church or parsonage.

The Banks noted there was a bit of a rivalry between the Baptist and Methodist churches. The Baptists never felt the Methodists were saved. They wondered, "How could a drip of water on the head save a black sinner?" The two churches were within earshot of each other. One time the Methodist group was singing, "*Will There Be any Stars in My Crown?*" As soon as they finished, the Baptists began singing "No, Not One." The Methodists thought it was planned, although it was a coincidence. The next Sunday, a Baptist meeting was to be held, and some members went over to borrow some benches. The Methodists refused, saying they didn't lend to people who made fun of them.[374]

Dennis Banks recalled, "The Baptists always baptized by immersion and used several places. The slough in the (river) bottom was a favorite place."[375] Other popular places for baptisms were "the old sinkhole," and ponds on the Edwin Barger and the Henry Hogge farm. The sinkhole is possibly the one located in the picnic area of Arrow Rock State Historic Site. The Barger pond is now Big Soldier Lake in the state historic site. The Hogge pond was about 1/2 mile north of town. Dennis described the baptism of resident Richard Mury. "It was a bitter December day and ice had to be cut before he could be immersed. When Dick come up he was most froze, and he yelled …There was much yelling, and crying and fainting at these baptisms. These baptisms were great occasions and many came, by horseback, buggy, and on foot. There was much singing, and the favorite songs were *Standing in Need of Prayer*, *Shall We Gather at the River?* and *Oh, Them Golden Slippers*. Weather made no difference — summer or winter, when someone got 'the feeling' there was a baptism."[376]

The churches held dinners or picnics known as "Rally Basket Dinner" or "Homecoming Basket Dinners." Hundreds of people would turn out for one of these events. According to Pearl Adams and Hortense Nichols, everyone brought "a washtub of food."[377] Another favorite event was Gospel Choir Day each spring. Choirs of all ages would sing from 8:00 a.m. to midnight. Arrow Rock's black congregations were very dynamic in expressing their faith.

Recreation and Entertainment

The isolation, monotony, hard physical labor and long hours of work in the early 19th century left little time for recreational pursuits. Raising crops, caring for livestock and securing fuel for heating and cooking was a dawn to dusk job. All family members, including children, were involved. Food preservation, preparation of meals and producing fiber for clothing were often all day tasks for women and their daughters.

Sometimes community endeavors became a cause for recreation. Neighboring women might periodically gather to make yarn, linen or sew quilts. But this social activity ultimately had a very practical side to it: providing warmth and clothing. For young girls, such gatherings were a learning session of a needed survival skill. Likewise, men and boys engaged in hunting and fishing, but these activities also sought to supplement the food larder. Still, the people occasionally ceased their labors for a chance to socialize and engage in recreation for enjoyment's sake.

One of George Caleb Bingham's famous genre paintings is *Shooting for the Beef*, painted in 1850. This is based on a scene he undoubtedly witnessed many times while living in the vicinity of Franklin and Arrow Rock. Edmund Flagg described this popular pastime for men in 1838:

> *As I rode along through the country I was somewhat surprised at meeting people from various quarters, who seemed to be gathering to some rendezvous, all armed with rifles, and with paraphernalia of hunting suspended from their shoulders. At length, near noon, I passed a log cabin, around which were assembled about a hundred men: and, upon inquiry, I learned that they had come together for the purpose of "shooting a beeve" [or beef], as the marksmen have it. The regulations I found to be chiefly these: A bull's-eye, with a center nail, stands at a distance variously of from forty to seventy yards; and those five who, at the close of the contest, have most frequently driven the nail, are entitled to a fat ox divided into five portions. Many of the marksmen in the vicinity, I was informed, could drive the nail twice out of every three trials.*[378]

Bingham also depicts forms of recreation that were popular. Card playing is depicted in *Raftsmen Playing Cards*. Popular games of the time included whist and euchre. Even Indians had learned to play cards from the whites as evidenced by the packs of playing cards listed in George Sibley's trade records at Arrow Rock. Gambling of some form was often attendant with card games. Bingham showed two "common" men in a tavern playing checkers in *Checker Players*. Chess was also played, although it was probably a game of the more sophisticated merchants and planters.

In his painting *The County Election*, Bingham shows even politics had a social aspect to it. The election gathering clearly shows an almost carnival-like atmosphere as men drink and socialize even while engaging in the important process of electing government officials. In the foreground of the picture, two small boys are playing a game of mumble peg. In mumble peg a wooden peg was driven into the ground with about two inches protruding above the surface. A jackknife is thrown to the ground in a variety of techniques. If the blade sticks in the ground, the player advances to the next throw. The loser was required to pull the peg from the ground with his teeth.

Other popular games for children included jacks and marbles, hopscotch and Americans and English, similar to tug of war. In the first half of the 19th century, toys were extremely rare for children, and nearly all were homemade. For a child to own a "store-bought" toy in the latter half of the century was a special treat. In the collection of Arrow Rock State Historic Site there are a variety of toys dating from the 1830s through the 1880s. These include porcelain-head dolls, a knife with a wooden blade and corncob handle, and a "Dancing Sam" toy. This item manufactured in 1863 represents the transition to "store-bought" toys. A stereotypical depiction of a black man jumps and dances when a paddle is pushed. A cast iron lamb pull toy manufactured in 1881 represents an era when mass manufactured toys became more commonplace. Regardless of their degree of sophistication, nearly all these 19th century toys required the exercise of a great deal of imagination.

Horseracing was also a popular communal activity. Races might be an impromptu event that occurred in a street or a farm field, usually accompanied by wagering. There was also organized horseracing in the area. This notice appeared in *The Western Emigrant* newspaper, published in Boonville in 1839:

NEW FRANKLIN & BOONVILLE RACES
Will commence on the 9th day of October next and continue four days.
First day, 2 year old colts & filleys, purse of $50
entrance money $10 and a silver Tumbler to the winner worth $10
Second day, two mile heats, a purse of $150
Third day, three mile heats, a purse of $250
Fourth day, three best in five, one mile heats, proprietors purse $100, and the entrance money....[379]

As technology improved and the settled areas developed, opportunities for leisure time increased. Slowly but surely, recreation became more sophisticated, compared to what it had been in pioneer times. Wealthier merchants and planters, of course, had more leisure time than the common laborer or yeoman farmer. Still, much of the recreation remained community oriented. Even a political rally became a cause for social interaction and relaxation as reported in the Marshall *Weekly Democrat* September 10, 1858:

> *The Arrow Rock Barbecue*
> *MR. EDITOR: I fear that I have hardly complied with my promise of giving you an account of the Arrow Rock barbecue in time for your present week's issue…But the barbecue. The day was a glorious one; the rain of the evening previous had cooled down the atmosphere…*
>
> *About 8 o'clock the guests began to arrive, and before eleven every road, avenue and path leading to town was crowded with persons from every portion of the county and counties adjoining, and before twelve the town was literally full. The old, the young and the middle aged were all there. Men, women and children — Democrats, Americans and Whigs…*
>
> *About one o'clock the dinner was announced; and such a dinner it was too, as the good people of Arrow Rock know how to get up. The long table literally groaned under its load of good things served up in the best style. The meats were, we believe, the best prepared we have ever noticed on an occasion of the kind…*
>
> *After the dinner had been fully and fairly discussed, and every body seemed well satisfied at the result a stand was prepared and speeches appropriate to the occasion were made by Col. C. F. Jackson, V. Marmaduke, R. C. Harrison, J. W. Bryant, Wm. Davis and Col. Robert Snell…*
>
> *When the day had cleared and night had drawn her sable curtain over the face of nature, the young people assembled at the old brick seminary, and to the strains of music sweet, "tripped the light fantastic toe" till dewey morn.*
>
> *Thus I have given you a synopsis of the beginning, continuation and end of the Arrow Rock barbecue….*[380]

Starting in 1838, circuses and menageries began touring Missouri on a regular basis. "Whether traveling in wagons or on boats, the circuses exhibited almost entirely in the populated river counties."[381] As they followed the Missouri River, they would perform in the communities on one side of the river during their westward trek and then the other side on their return trip. Most of these circuses were small organizations that gradually became more elaborate with animal acts, parades and bandwagons.[382]

Typical prices for a tent show in this period were fifty cents for adults and half price for children and servants. In 1845, the Great Philadelphia Zoological Garden toured the river towns of central Missouri, and Arrow Rock was on their itinerary. Advertising for the Philadelphia Menagerie stated, as they approached Boonville, the elephant would be pulling its band car followed by horses and 21 wagons. As a special treat the animal trainer would harness and drive a large Nubian lion.[383] Although an advertisement for the Arrow Rock performance does not survive, it is likely the same procession entered town.

Evidently traveling shows came frequently enough for the incorporated town board to take action to regulate them on December 23, 1847: "Be it ordained &c that any Agent or Proprietor of a Company wishing to exhibit any Theatrical slight of hand or other small amusements shall first pay into the Town treasurer the sum of two dollars and get a permit from the secretary, and the Agent proprietor or company of any Circus, Menagerie &c shall first pay into the treasurer three dollars and get a permit from the secretary to make such exhibition." [384]

In July of 1858, the Levi J. North Circus featured an ear-splitting calliope described as a "mammoth chariot of music … sweet and harmonious as that of a church organ and to be heard ten miles off." In view of the power of the instrument, the management promised the performance would be "chaste."[385] The *Weekly Democrat* in Marshall carried the following ad on August 7, 1868:

> *THE GREAT ORIENTAL CIRCUS & EGYPTIAN*
> *CARAVAN Circus with 12 Arabian Camels! And Bedouin*
> *Arabs among its attractions will perform at Arrow Rock on*
> *Saturday, August 15, 1868.*[386]

During the 1850s, the young gentlemen of the town organized a literary and debating society called "The Philomatheans."[387] In March of 1858, they put on a humorous play called *The Toodles*. "The large hall over the store of Messrs. Will H. Wood & Co. was converted into a temporary theatre with an elevated stage, drop curtain and proscenium." [388] The play was such a hit the Philomatheans considered organizing a regular Thespian society. It is not known if they followed through with their plans.

Even shopping for needed supplies had a certain recreational quality to it. Thomas Rainey recalled farmers came to town "on horseback or in a two horse wagon. Often when he lived quite a distance away, he would bring his whole family, with a great basket of fried chicken, broiled ham, pickles, cakes, pies and all sorts of good things to eat, and make a holiday of it. The merchant would be invited to join their picnic and all would have a good time of it." [389]

Rainey recalled: "…the desire for amusement and a social life found an outlet frequently in small neighborhood parties, and now and then larger assemblages at the old brick Tavern in Arrow Rock…These parties would include a due proportion of elderly people who met in the parlors, while the younger set would 'on with the dance' in the large hall, also used as a dining room…the music was inspiring and dancing elegant — a source of pleasure even to those not engaged in it; and it also served as a training school for the younger people in developing sprightly, graceful carriage, and composure in the presence of company." [390]

Cultural and recreational pursuits such as cotillions held in the Tavern and the presentations of the Philomatheans demonstrate a growing sophistication and increase of leisure time. However, a certain degree of Arrow Rock's coarse frontier quality still seemed to linger. At the Town Board Meeting of June 2, 1871, the Trustees considered a problem relating to recreational pursuits: "Complaint having been made by Mr. L. D. Lindsay that the players of the game of Croquet frequently indulge in profane and obscene language near his premises. Ordained that the Constable be instructed to suppress the game of Croquet near Mr. Lindsay's house." [391]

In reminiscing about the social life of Arrow Rock, Rainey also revealed clues as to why so little of women's role in area history was recorded. "I hesitate to enroll the names of the ladies I remember (at the dances) because such as are living may not enjoy seeing their names in print. Nearly all of them were of pioneer families, modest, dignified and bewitching dancers. Many of them never attended higher school than the vicinity afforded, but they had mothers at home, who sent them into society with such manners and training as would place them at ease…A great deal has been written complimentary of the distinguished men who once belonged to the Arrow Rock community and deservedly: but not enough has been said in praise of the pioneer mothers. They were not only remarkable housekeepers, but they were highly intelligent and refined ladies, contributing their full share to the high tone and gentle manners prevailing. They were modest homebodies and their influence yet survives in their descendants."[392]

Social Organizations

"Grass-roots institutions such as mutual benefit associations, fraternal organizations, and religious groups not only helped families with basic survival needs, but created and sustained bonds of fellowship … Fraternal and mutual benefit societies, in particular, provided funds and other resources to members in need and to the poor generally…."[393] Fraternal organizations were a significant part of Arrow Rock's social life.

The oldest and largest fraternal organization was the Masonic Lodge. A petition was submitted to the Grand Lodge of Missouri on November 2, 1841, seeking a charter for Arrow Rock. Arrow Rock Lodge No. 55 was established October 4, 1842. Freemasonry may be described as a secret society because its meetings are closed to the uninitiated. While membership was open to all men of good character, the Masons traditionally drew most of their members from the more intellectual and influential in the community.

This tradition was reflected in Lodge 55's early membership rosters which included: Rudolph Hawpe, Benjamin Huston, William Roper, Joseph Huston, Sr., Thomas McMahan, Henry Nave, Jr., Judge Bernis Brown, Bird Lawless, John Piper, Dr. William Price, Dr. Charles Bradford, Philip W. Thompson, Wyatt Bingham, Henry S. Wilhelm, Dr. Matthew W. Hall, Dr. Oscar Potter, Anthony O'Sullivan and Henry S. Mills.[394] Governor Meredith M. Marmaduke, although a member of another lodge, was a periodic visitor to the Arrow Rock Lodge meetings.

On May 12, 1851, Anthony O'Sullivan offered a resolution that, "… the Charter, Jewels, etc., of Marshall Lodge No. 65, to be delivered to this Grand Lodge, the members having removed, they ceased to work."[395] In effect, the lodge was defunct. Apparently, the officers and many members of the Marshall Lodge had gone to California for the Gold Rush. O'Sullivan moved to St. Louis thereafter, where he attained the prominent office of Grand Secretary of the Grand Lodge of Missouri.

The location of the first lodge room is unknown, although they explored the possibility of renting an upper room of the Academy, then under construction. They met at an unknown location until August of 1842, when they appropriated $105 to build a lodge room over William Roper's saddle shop. Roper's shop was a frame building directly across the street from the Tavern.[396] This apparently remained the meeting location until the Civil War. In August of 1866, a committee was appointed to investigate construction of a lodge building. On February 8, 1868: "The building committee reported through their chairman, Bro. H. S. Mills, a plan or draft for a new two-story building of brick 24 x 50, the upper story to be used exclusively for the A.F. & A.M. lodge, the lower floor to be rented for benefit of said lodge. Estimated cost of the building not to exceed $3,000."[397] The building was constructed on the corner of Fifth and Main Street, and the building continues to function as planned. Arrow Rock Lodge No. 55 A.F.& A.M. meets upstairs, and the Arrow Rock Craft Club has its shop downstairs.

Friends Lodge No. 40 of the Independent Order of Odd Fellows (I.O.O.F.) was organized in Arrow Rock on August 23, 1849. The Odd Fellows organization was started in England by working-class men for social activities, to provide members assistance in finding work, and to provide economic aid to a member's family in time of illness or death. The motto of the Lodge was "Friendship, Love and Truth," symbolized by three links of a chain. The lodge in Arrow Rock became well known for its winter oyster supper and summer fish fry.

New members were voted on by casting marbles. A white marble was cast in favor of admission; a black marble was cast against it. Thus, if a person were "black-balled," he was kept out the Lodge. Collars were worn denoting the office held in the organization. The auxiliary organization for women was called the Rebekah Lodge. A large number of Arrow Rock merchants and middle-class citizens belonged to Lodge 40. Some of the notable members included: J. A. J. Aderton, Henry V. Bingham, Benjamin Hawpe, James Ancell and George Caleb Bingham.

The Odd Fellows probably met in various members' homes or places of business. In May of 1868, a two-story brick building was constructed for $3,000 by the firm of Ancell & Fitzgerald. The Odd Fellows met in the upstairs portion from 1868 until 1927. The downstairs was rented out to various business interests, including a newspaper. J. C. B. Ish had a wholesale and retail drug and pharmacy business in 1870. Due to the declining population and subsequent decline in membership, the Arrow Rock Lodge merged with the Marshall Lodge in the 1930s. The Friends of Arrow Rock, Inc. now owns and maintains the building. The Grand Lodge of the Missouri I.O.O.F. furnished the upper floor as a museum. The lower floor is set up as a press museum and is supported by the Missouri Press Association.

The Grange is the nation's oldest national agricultural organization. Formed after the Civil War, their goal was to improve the economic and social position of the nation's farm population. The Grange had an adversarial relationship with the railroads at first, because the railroads speculated and manipulated grain prices to the detriment of farmers. The Grange became known for its work in opposing these railroad policies. The Grange is also a fraternal order, the Order of Patrons of Husbandry. It evolved to include rural non-farm families and communities. Worthy Grange No. 99 was formed in Arrow Rock on March 26, 1873, the first in Saline County. They built a building in 1876 at a cost of $1,000. The location is unknown.[398]

The Grange was one of the first organizations to formally admit women as equals. They also served as officers in the organization. This may have occurred because many women had to run the farms during the Civil War while their male relatives were in military service. Charter members of Worthy Grange No. 99 of Arrow Rock included: James West, the town's liveryman, J. R. Dickson, John Neff, W. H. Huston, James Thornton, W. S. Jackson, Nick Huston, R. T. Huston, John Bingham, Mrs. T. W. Russell, Mrs. W. S. Jackson, Miss Kate Dickson, Mrs. A. E. Price, Mrs. Mary Price, Mrs. M. Edwards, Mrs. Louis Neff and Miss Delia McMahan.[399] It is not known when the Grange closed in Arrow Rock.

Arrow Rock Lodge No. 489 of the International Order of Good Templars was organized January 21, 1881. Not to be confused with the Masonic Knights Templar, the Good Templars were a temperance group. Their goal was to promote worldwide prohibition of liquor and individual abstinence. The lodge met in a brick hall, possibly by renting from one of the other fraternal organizations. There were thirty-eight members when the lodge organized. Some of them included: C. M. Sutherlin, a prominent merchant,

Miss Ida Bradford, J. M. Green, Miss Nena McMahan and Frank West.[400]

Arrow Rock blacks could not participate in any of the town's organizations or social events unless they were working there as a servant or cook. Therefore, in the late 19th century, there was a trend towards the development of fraternal organizations in the African American community. These organizations, along with churches, provided for social and ritual activities. Perhaps more importantly, the members had a place to govern themselves, free of white control. Arrow Rock had four African American lodges that included Grand United Order of Odd Fellows of America Lodge No. 3201; C. R. Smith Lodge No. 170 of the United Brothers of Friendship; Sherman Lodge No. 17 of Lincoln Sons and Daughters of Freedom, No. 60, and Brown Lodge No. 22 of Ancient Free and Accepted Masons.[401]

The Odd Fellows lodge was formed in 1890. Originally, they met in a house but then moved to a new building on the corner of Main and Third streets in 1899. The women's auxiliary was known as the Household of Ruth. There was also a children's corps that included both boys and girls.[402] The Lincoln Lodge was formed in 1896 at the northern end of Sixth Street on the northwest corner of Block 29. Dennis Banks was a long-time secretary for the Lodge and kept a ledger dating back to 1906. The United Brothers of Friendship were established in 1911 and rented the Lincoln Lodge for their meeting hall. Dennis Banks served as secretary of this Lodge in 1920. The women's auxiliary group was called Edwards Lodge No. 17 of the Sisters of the Mysterious Ten. Members included Mrs. Minnie Parker as Worthy Princess and Mrs. Eva Taylor as Worthy Secretary. A juvenile corps known as the "Pride of Arrow Rock No. 75" had 28 children divided equally between boys and girls.

The earliest of the black lodges was the Masonic Lodge No. 22 of A.F. & A.M., established in 1877. Known as the Brown Lodge, it seemed to be the most prestigious. Thelma Conway, a former resident, remembered them as the "big shots" of the fraternities.[403] This lodge can trace its roots to Prince Hall, an 18th century free African American. After serving in the American Revolution, Hall established the first all-black Masonic lodge in Boston, Massachusetts. However, the white lodge in Boston refused to grant him a charter, so he obtained it from the Grand Lodge in England.[404]

The Masonic lodge hall was built in 1881 on the corner of Morgan and Sixth streets on Block 30. William B. Sappington had divided the block and sold a portion of Lot 106 to the trustees of the Brown Lodge for $30.00. Brown Lodge enrollment at this time was 27 members. In 1890, the "Worshipful Master" or leader of the lodge was Harrison Green, one of the first black teachers in Arrow Rock and later a minister. In 1890, the Masons formed a women's organization called the Mt. Herman chapter of the Heroines of Jericho.[405]

The first floor of the Brown Lodge may have been used as a restaurant or store. After the 1920s, documentation clearly indicates it served this purpose. The site was also the location of the annual "Emancipation Day Picnic" held on August 4th. Blacks from all parts of Saline County gathered at the lodge hall for a goat roast. Fielding Draffen recalled, "It was considered a day you kind of reflected on what your ancestors came through and you just kind of enjoyed the day."[406] Very likely other community events occurred at the Brown Lodge. Membership began to decline in the 1920s, and the lodge was disbanded in 1931. The Emancipation Day Picnic seems to have faded by the beginning of World War II.[407]

The Brown Lodge is the only structure still standing on Block 30. This site was also the location of an Arrow Rock pottery works and has been the focal point of a major archaeological study conducted from 1996 through 2002. The excavations served a dual purpose: to discover how the pre-Civil War pottery works functioned and to gather information about African American life in Arrow Rock. The lodge building was vacated in the 1950s. Even by then, it had severely deteriorated and by 1998 was barely standing. Ted and Virginia Fisher gave the Friends of Arrow Rock, Inc., the lodge building. In 2001, the Friends undertook a complete restoration of the structure. The building is used as a museum of Arrow Rock's African American history.

The Huston Tavern and Other Hotels

In 1914, Thomas Rainey wrote, "I first saw Arrow Rock in the fall of 1865 ... My first night was spent in the old brick tavern, then as now, the most notable building in the town...."[408] Indeed, of all the buildings in the community, the Tavern is the one that signifies "Arrow Rock" to most people. It is the structure around which the historic preservation of the town grew. It was also one of the first acquisitions in what is now the Missouri state park system. A few visitors will wrinkle their noses at the Tavern, believing it to be a bar. However, in 19th century terminology, a

Tavern was not merely a "dram shop,"[409] it was also a hotel and restaurant and community center.

Joseph Huston of Virginia, who settled in Arrow Rock in 1819, built the structure. Huston was a civic leader in the community and one of the original town commissioners. He also served at various times as an election judge, Justice of the Peace and Saline County Court Judge. "Tall and spare of build, he was a friendly and popular man."[410] On November 23, 1833, he purchased all four lots of Block 17 for $89. The low price suggests the property was unimproved.

Huston was a carpenter by training, and in 1834, he began construction of a two-story, four-room brick structure in the Federal style of architecture on the northeast corner of the block. Family tradition states Joseph's brother Benjamin, brother-in-law Andrew Brownlee, and future son-in-law William McJilton, all helped build the structure. Tradition also states family slaves sawed lumber harvested from nearby forests and made and fired the bricks on the construction site. For them to do preparation and rough carpentry work while their masters did the finish and detail work would be fairly typical.[411]

The structure's original design suggests it was meant as a family residence, and perhaps it evolved into use as a tavern. As already noted, thousands of people were passing through Arrow Rock each year on their way west. Huston's home, on the corner of Main Street and Third Street, which connected to the Boonville Road, would have been an attractive location for weary travelers to stop and ask for accommodations. Charles van Ravenswaay of the Missouri Historical Society had been involved with the Tavern's restoration in the 1950s. Based on remaining features he saw, he believed the original brick structure might have had one or more frame or log additions. There also may have been a second-story porch across the south side of the brick building. This author has seen and photographed evidence during restoration work that suggests a porch. Huston may have started out by charging travelers a nominal fee to stay in one of these additions.

The first clearly documented instance of the structure serving as a hotel comes from Dr. Glen O. Hardeman. Hardeman recalled his first visit to Saline County in 1840: "I took lodging only at the hotel kept by that well-known and popular citizen, Joseph Huston Sr.... I was charged the sum of 12 1/2 cents or, I should say a 'bit.' On my return ... I dined at the same hotel and was charged another 'bit' for an excellent dinner. The currency of that day was exclusively of Mexican or Spanish coin."[412] A "bit" was obtained by cutting a dollar into eighths. The Mexican currency demonstrates the impact that the Santa Fe trade still had on Missouri's economy.

Accommodations were Spartan in 19th century frontier hotels, and the Tavern was probably no exception. One steamboat traveler complained in his diary when the boat stopped for the night, "Wednesday, February 11th 1857 — Reached Arrow Rock & stopped for the night in a miserable establishment called a Hotel."[413] Rooms were often shared with complete strangers. If no beds were available, one could get a pallet on the floor or possibly even in the attic for a reduced price. However uncomfortable that may sound, it was better than sleeping outside in the rain or in a cold wind.

There was a detached or summer kitchen along with the original brick structure. This arrangement was common among southern households to keep the heat and cooking odors out of the house in the summer time. It also kept a majority of the flies away from the house. In 1964, the kitchen underwent restoration, and the remains of a stairwell to an attic were found and reconstructed. This indicates that a household slave or "domestic" lived in the loft, a common occurrence among southern households. In the restoration, an open-hearth fireplace used for cooking was discovered behind a false wall. Wood cooking stoves were expensive and fairly rare on the Missouri frontier until the 1840s. The kitchen is now restored to appear as it may have looked in 1834. The Daughters of the American Revolution have loaned a variety of artifacts from this early period to furnish the kitchen.

Booker Rucker, an employee of the State Park Board, analyzed paint samples in the kitchen during the 1964 restoration. It was determined the woodwork was originally painted a "teal blue." In 1988, this author took samples and conducted a basic analysis in several other rooms. Teal blue appears to have been the original color of woodwork in the front lobby and doorframes in the Huston Store. Other areas were inconclusive, having been stripped clean or the trim completely replaced at an earlier date.

Sometime between 1837 and 1840, Huston constructed a brick addition on the west side of the original brick structure. The first floor housed his "grocery," or mercantile store. No ledger of the store survives, but it would have sold everything from foodstuffs to clothing to hardware, truly, the "Wal-Mart" of its day. Around 1845, Huston entered into partnership with Philip Thompson. Joseph Huston, Jr. became active in his father's mercantile business until 1850, when he left for the gold fields of California. He returned the following year, and he and John C. Thompson entered the mercantile business as "Huston and Thompson."[414]

The second floor of the addition served as a ballroom and meeting hall. Originally a stairwell connected the second floor to the street, but this was removed around 1920. During restoration work in 1955, Mary Lou Pearson, the D.A.R. hostess of the Tavern, discovered the remains of stenciling on the ballroom walls. Stenciling is very rare in Missouri, and it probably demonstrates Huston's affinity for Virginia culture. The remnants of the original stenciling have been preserved, and the pattern has been reproduced in the room.

Thomas Rainey recalled the dances held "in the large hall, also used as a dining room" in the 1860s. Several invitations to social events survive. The earliest is a hand written invitation to a New Year's Eve Ball:

> *The pleasure of your company is solicited at J. Huston's on Friday the 31st instant at 5 o'clock P.M. Managers H. C. Miller, J. M. McMahan, W. W. Finley, J. L. McCutcheon, A. C. Maupin, L. Chambers, T. L. Sites, W. Landis, J. S. Long, Arrow Rock Dec. 13th 1841.*[415]

Later invitations were fancier, in that they were printed:

> *Grand Ball of the Season*
> *To be given at the Arrow Rock Hotel on Tuesday evening, Dec. 27, 1870, at which your company is respectfully submitted, A first class string band will be in attendance and every effort to make the occasion one of pleasure.*[416]

Sometime after 1850, and possibly as late as 1880, yet a third addition was made to the Tavern. This was a frame addition that incorporated the detached kitchen into the building. The area between the kitchen and the store was converted into a dining hall. Three bedrooms were located on the second floor. Another large frame dining hall and kitchen extended to the south of the building.[417] A dining porch replaced this addition in 1923, and that porch was replaced with a new dining hall and kitchen in 1955. These and other changes made by other owners have obscured details of the building's original construction.

A cupola on the roof contains the Tavern bell surmounted by a weathervane in the shape of a fish. The original fish is in the Arrow Rock State Historic Site's museum collection, but it appears to date from the early period of the Tavern's existence. A rope runs from the bell through the roof and into the lobby. There are several stories as to the purpose behind the bell. One popular story is the bell was rung to remind people to take their quinine pills to combat the shaking ague. However, there is no documentation from that period to authenticate this assertion. It is likely the bell announced mealtime to patrons who were conducting business elsewhere in town. There is evidence from Charles van Ravenswaay the bell was used to rally townsfolk for emergencies. "Years ago a traveler arrived at the Tavern one dark night and finding no one around, rang the bell. Very soon, to his astonishment, the whole town began crowding in to learn what calamity had occurred."[418]

In 1853, Joseph Neill took over management of the hotel portion of the building, which then became known as the "Neill House."[419] The minutes of the Town Board on March 6, 1854, revealed an election for five trustees of the corporation was to be held the following month at "Joseph Neal's Tavern."[420] Huston apparently continued to operate the store portion of the building. It is possible that his son, Joseph, Jr., became involved in the store about this time. On April 17, 1858, Huston sold the hotel portion to John W. Levy for $2,500, a hefty sum for the time.

Even before the sale was final, Thomas H. and Anna E. Cobb purchased an interest in what was now known as the "Arrow Rock Hotel." On April 7, 1858, Cobb moved in as the new manager, a position he held until early in 1861. The only surviving 19th century ledger from the Tavern is from the Cobb administration.[421] On February 25, 1858, the *Weekly Democrat* reported: "The Arrow Rock Hotel will 'be born again' soon. The present incumbent sells all the inside running gear of it 4th April next, and friend Cobb is hunting up new feathers, and bed quilts to reclothe it."[422] Tragedy struck the Cobb family during their tenure. Within an eleven-month period, four of their children died at the Tavern: 13-year-old Mattie died May 12, 1859, seven-year-old William died August 26, 1859, 16-year-old James died January 15, 1860, and ten-year-old Thomas died April 9, 1860.[423] Only daughter Sallie escaped the childhood plagues that claimed the lives of her siblings.

Mrs. Vanice managed the Tavern after the Cobbs' departure in 1861. Mrs. E. P. Scripture assumed management by 1865, the same year Federal authorities sought her son as a guerrilla. After a hunting competition between Arrow Rock and Marshall in 1868, Jay M. Potter auctioned the game at the "Scripture House" followed by "one of the best oyster suppers ever given in Arrow Rock, and gotten up as only our generous landlady, Mrs. Scripture, can get them up."[424]

ARROW ROCK HOTEL
E.P. Scripture, Proprietor.
Arrow Rock, MO
The Table will always be furnished with the best the
market affords, and every comfort and convenience
possible extended to guests.
[Jan 3, 1868] [425]

The Tavern passed through new owners and managers in fairly rapid succession, and these changes are not well documented. Perhaps this was a reflection on the town's gradual but steady decline. The August 27, 1869 edition of the *Saline County Progress* advertised yet another proprietor for the building:

CITY HOTEL
R. HORN, Proprietor.
Arrow Rock, — MO.
This house has been fitted up and refurnished, and is
now prepared to entertain customers in the best style.
Tables supplied with the best the market affords.
Good stable in connection with the House.
Thankful to the public for their liberal patronage
heretofore, we solicit a continuance of the same. [426]

Joseph Huston's daughter, Rachel (Huston) McJilton, became the proprietor of the hotel from 1876 to around 1881. After her tenure, ownership and management of the building becomes even sketchier. Arrow Rock's decline had accelerated, and the old building no longer enjoyed the preeminence it once had. Along with the change of owners, there seemed to be a change of names.

The earliest reference to the building's name found is the invitation to the New Year's Eve dance held at "J. Huston's" in 1841. The Saline County Masonic Lodge records also identify the building. "August 5, 1842. The Committee...to contract...carpenter work of the lodge room over Bro.

Roper's shop...sum of $105. [Roper's Saddle & Harness shop was in the first story of a two-story frame building across the street from the Tavern.]"⁴²⁷ The Arrow Rock Lodge held its semi-annual meeting on June 24, 1843, after which "...the lodge repaired to Brother Huston's Tavern, where after partaking of a social hour and dinner, the following officers were publicly installed...."⁴²⁸ It seems clear the building was originally named either "Huston's Tavern" or "J. Huston's Tavern." By 1923, the Daughters of the American Revolution were calling the building the "Old Tavern." In more recent years, it has also been called the "Arrow Rock Tavern," or the "Historic Arrow Rock Tavern."

Because Joseph Huston was a town founder, important civic leader and the builder of a structure that is now recognized as a focal point of Arrow Rock and Missouri history, it is worthwhile to examine a chronology of his life.⁴²⁹ It also provides a window on the types of lives led by upper class southern citizens who were not planters, but who dominated the town's development:

- 1784 Born in Philadelphia, Pennsylvania.
- 1789? His father died, and his mother moved the family to Augusta County, Virginia.
- 1805 Joseph married Sarah Brownlee, March 21. Five children born to this marriage: William, Susan, Amanda, Rachel and James.
- 1819 Moved his family to Missouri and settled near the Arrow Rock bluff.
- 1825? Wife Sarah died.
- 1826 Married widow Elizabeth (Humphreys) Lawless. Four children born to this marriage: Joseph, Jr., Samuel Humphreys, Erasmus Darwin and John Jackson.
- 1826–1834 Served as Justice of the Peace and Saline County Court Judge.
- 1831 Elected Presiding Judge of the Saline County Court.
- 1833 Purchased the following lots in Arrow Rock:
  Block 10 – Lot 19   Block 17 – Lot 59, 60, 63, 64
  Block 16 – Lot 16   Block 20 – Lot 69, 85, 86
- 1834 Constructed a four-room brick structure on Block 17, designed as a moderate house of the period rather than as a hotel.

- 1837 Applied to the County Court for a license to operate a grocery store in Arrow Rock. He may have then started construction of the two-story brick addition, which houses the store and ballroom.
- 1840 First documented reference as a hotelkeeper.
- 1840–1850s Owned and operated a steam-powered saw mill.
- 1843 Served as trustee of the Arrow Rock Female Academy.
- 1845? Entered into partnership with Santa Fe trader Philip W. Thompson. The mercantile business, known as "Huston & Thompson" was in the brick addition and possibly supplied some goods for the Santa Fe trade.
- 1845 – 1848 Joseph appointed postmaster of Arrow Rock. The store undoubtedly doubled as the post office, a common practice of the time.
- 1855 Wife Elizabeth died.
- 1857 Married Brunette (Lawless) Thompson, ex-wife of P. W. Thompson.
- 1858 Sold the "*tavern or residence*" portion of his building to John W. Levy. Mercantile store remained separate and continued operation as "Huston & Thompson." Possibly the store was being operated by the sons of the two men at this time.
- 1865 April 10 – 15? Huston died and was buried in the Arrow Rock cemetery.

The main competition for the Tavern came from the Union Hotel, at Main and Sixth streets. This is where the Downover Bed & Breakfast is now located. N. B. Noble & Co. advertised the establishment for auction on July 2, 1858:

PUBLIC SALE
IN ARROW ROCK
MONDAY, AUGUST 2, 1858

Will be sold to the highest bidder on Monday, August 2nd (Election Day) the property known as the UNION HOTEL, in Arrow Rock, together with the ground attached, which is known as being parts of lots No. 111, 112, 115 and 116, all in block No. 33.
    The house is a two-story frame, consisting of seven large rooms

*and a good cellar, also a large, convenient kitchen, consisting of
four rooms. There is also a huge cistern on the premises… house is
situated on Main Street, in the most pleasant part of town.*

*Household and Kitchen Furniture,
Consisting in part of the following articles: Dining Tables, all
kinds of Table Ware, Bedsteads and Bedding, Carpets, Chairs,
Small Tables, Wash Stands, Stoves, Looking Glasses, Wash Bowls
and Pitchers, and a great many other articles too numerous to
mention…*

> *This is a rare opportunity for any person who wishes to go
> into hotel or boarding business. We have from fifteen to twenty-
> five regular boarders all the time, and a liberal share of the
> transient custom. We have been doing a very good business,
> and our only reason for selling is that we intend going to
> California….*[430]

Little else is known about the Union Hotel. Evidently the original structure was gone by 1900, about the time the current house on the lot was
built. Another important tavern was about six miles west of Arrow Rock.
Isaac Neff (Nave), who had settled in Cox's Bottom in 1820, moved to
that area in 1836. By 1837, he built a two-story log and frame structure
alongside the Santa Fe Trail to accommodate passing travelers. The Neff
Tavern became a stage station and up until the Civil War was a post office
called Bryan. Jesse Bingham Neff, the grandson of Isaac, "remembered
sleeping there under a buffalo robe with the dry snow blowing in beneath
the clapboard shingles."[431] This tavern was standing until 1890, when it was
torn down. A smokehouse built of limestone still remains and is now
listed on the National Register of Historic Places.

Over the years, claims have been made for many famous people staying
at the Arrow Rock Tavern such as frontiersmen Kit Carson and Daniel
Boone, author Washington Irving, and even presidential candidate
Abraham Lincoln. There are no records to substantiate these claims.
Furthermore, Boone died in 1820, and Irving passed through Arrow Rock
in 1832, both long before Huston even purchased the lots. Noted historian Charles van Ravenswaay challenged these assertions as early as 1938.
He wrote the Tavern Board of Managers: "During the past number of
years I have watched with growing concern the development of various

'legends' regarding its [Tavern] history... Surely few buildings in Missouri can, with more honesty, claim a richer history than the Tavern. Sometimes called a 'textbook of Missouri history' it needs only a sympathetic hand to make true this not-at-present realized claim."[432] In more recent decades, the focus has turned back to the building's real history.

Education and the Academy

Education in Missouri was a haphazard affair in the first half of the 19th century. There were no standards or state provisions for education. If a settlement wanted a school, it had to establish its own. In the earliest schools, a minister might be a teacher. The Bible was sometimes used as a textbook, not only for its value as moral instruction, but because textbooks were exceedingly rare. Frontier people did not always see schooling as necessary or valuable. Even as late as 1870, nearly half of Missouri's population was functionally illiterate.

As an area became more settled, public, or "common schools," were often formed in a centralized cabin or house. Teachers were usually men, but gradually more women were hired as instructors for a meager wage. Instruction was usually limited to the basics of reading, writing and arithmetic. Readers and primers from eastern states found their way into these schools more frequently. As communities progressed and wealth increased, some formed "subscription schools." Parents would pay to send their children to these schools where they could receive extra instruction in the arts and humanities.

Arrow Rock had both common and subscription schools. According to deed records, Arrow Rock's first public school was constructed prior to 1846 on Lot 96 of Block 25, near the corner of Sixth and Van Buren streets. Archaeological excavations in 1977 and 1980 determined that two buildings were superimposed on the site. The first was a saddlebag log building with a limestone foundation. After 1865, this building was replaced with a brick building. Artifacts recovered included inkbottles, metal desk frames, pen nibs, slate fragments, graphite pencils, toys and personal objects. Archaeologists found the amount of domestic materials recovered from the site was higher than to be expected for a schoolhouse. This suggests the building may also have been used as a residence or for other community functions.[433]

This school remained in use until 1892, when it was replaced by a new brick building located on Main Street. The school building burned in 1910. It was insured for $10,000, and a new brick building was built for that amount on the Main Street location. The school building burned again in 1923 and again was rebuilt on the same spot. By 1954, Missouri's rural population had declined to the point that many rural districts were consolidated. The Arrow Rock school district became part of the Hardeman R-10 district. The 1923 brick school building survives today and functions as the Stolberg-Jackson Community Center with the lunchroom serving as a cafe.

At a meeting held at an unspecified time in 1842, the Town Commissioners took steps to establish a subscription school in Arrow Rock. They appropriated four hundred dollars "for the building of a Seminary of learning in said Town."[434] On February 24, 1843, the Missouri legislature passed an act incorporating the Trustees of the Arrow Rock Academy. Some of the provisions of the act were as follows:

> *1. That an academy be and the same hereby established, in the town of Arrow-Rock, In the county of Saline; to be called the Arrow Rock academy,*
>
> *2. That Charles W. Wood, E. C. M'Carty, Daniel Thornton, Joseph Huston, Geo. Penn, O. B. Pearson, Wm. Price, Charles M. Bradford, Wm. Roper, Henry C. Miller, M. M. Marmaduke, Thomas H. Harvey, Jesse B. Turley, Bird Lawless, Burton Lawless, Randolph Haupe [Rudolph Hawpe], De Witt McNutt, Robert Isaacs and John Lewis, be and are hereby appointed and constituted a body politic And corporate, by the name and style of trustees of the Arrow-Rock academy, and by that name, shall have a perpetual succession and a common seal, and may contract and be contracted with (and) may sue and be sued in any court of law or equity....*
>
> *4. The said trustees, or their successors, shall have power to meet at any time and place, in the town of Arrow-Rock, a majority of whom shall have power to appoint a president, librarian, treasurer and such other officers as may be necessary. The aforesaid trustees and their successors or a majority of them, shall also have power, from time to time to make such by laws, rules and regulations for the government of said academy, as they may deem necessary, not contrary to the constitution or laws of the United State, or of the State of Missouri.[435]*

This Arrow Rock Academy, no longer standing, was a large two-story brick structure on Third Street, directly east of the Tavern. In addition to having classrooms, the building was also used for social gatherings and meeting space. On October 1, 1843, the Town Board appropriated money to plaster the "town room" of the Arrow Rock Academy and "for such work as might be necessary to make the room comfortable."[436] Apparently, this is where the Board of Trustees held their meetings. In 1844, the board appropriated funds to purchase a new stove for the Academy and $25 for the purpose of making three writing desks for the institution. There were high hopes for this institution and its ambitious program, but it succumbed to debt within three years.

In 1848, the buildings were taken over by the Lebanon Female Academy under the direction of Rev. Gary Hickman. Hickman was also the pastor of the Arrow Rock Presbyterian Church. The August 26, 1848 edition of the Jefferson Inquirer advertised the Academy as being located in "large and commodious buildings" and having a yard and garden "beautifully ornamented, affording a delightful retreat during the warm weather."[437] The Lebanon Academy was short lived as well. On January 2, 1851, the board called for relinquishment of the Academy.

Professor Joshua L. Tracy launched the Arrow Rock Female Seminary in 1856. Tracy was well known for his work at Adelphia College in Boonville. A Mrs. Vanice was in charge of boarding pupils. A handbill published between 1857 and 1859 noted, "a limited number of pupils will be received into the family of the Principal." Oral tradition holds the adjacent two-story log and weather boarded house served as the boarding house. There are indications the house was part of the Academy grounds at this time. Dr. George Penn and then Reverend Hickman owned the house.

On February 1, 1859, it was announced, "that Mr. Tracy has resigned the presidency of the Arrow Rock Female College."[438] He left on good terms and went on to St. Louis where he assumed other roles influential in developing state education. Miss Helen Belknap, the former head of the English and Music departments, succeeded Professor Tracy as president of the Academy until the outbreak of the Civil War in 1861, when it closed for good.

The brick academy is mentioned in accounts as late as 1860. After that, its fate remains unknown. The building itself was probably gone before the turn of the century. The log house, now known as the Academy

Boarding House, sits on the intersection of lot lines in the middle of Block 14. This may mean it was built before the town was surveyed and platted in 1829. An attempt at dating the age from the tree rings in the logs was inconclusive but pointed towards a date early in the 1830s. The original structure was a single story, double pen cabin with an open breezeway in the center. The second floor was probably added within a few years. Some of the logs showed evidence of being recycled from other structures. The structure is restored as it may have appeared circa 1843 and is now part of Arrow Rock State Historic Site.

The Marshall *Weekly Democrat* gave a glowing report of the state of Arrow Rock's education in March of 1858: "Among other advantages, Arrow Rock enjoys the benefits of good schools. In the hub-bub and turmoil of business they have not forgotten to provide for the generation to come after them. Saturday being a holiday, we did not enjoy the privilege of visiting the different seminaries of learning, but we are told that their schools are not only well attended, but indicate an advancement gratifying to the friends of education."[439] On January 26, 1861, the Missouri legislature voted to extend the limits of the Arrow Rock school district, believing the growth and prosperity of the community would continue.

African American residents were disenfranchised from the education process. Laws in the antebellum period made it illegal for black people to learn to read or write. Education was the first steppingstone for black independence, and African American schools were created soon after the Civil War. James Milton Turner was a St. Louis slave who had been secretly educated during his youth. Turner was appointed by the Missouri Secretary of Education and the Freedmen's Bureau to establish African American schools in the state. He is credited with starting 39 schools in the state, including Lincoln University.

Like their white counterparts, early black schools were connected with churches. The first black school in Arrow Rock was founded in 1869. James Milton Turner came to town on November 9th of that year because the Arrow Rock school board had failed to build a school for black children. Henry S. Wilhelm, the board supervisor, explained that the school district had not received funds to build a school building. Wilhelm offered district funds to operate the school in Brown's Chapel, then under construction.[440]

Turner requested that the State Superintendent send a twenty-day notice that the school had to be in operation, or the board would be in violation of the law. He then called a meeting of the black community and made them promise to complete the church building in fifteen days. Turner traveled to Marshall to look for the money that had not been delivered to Arrow Rock. He told the Superintendent he expected the school to open in 25 or 30 days. There were 65 African American children and a few adults enrolled when the school opened.[441]

In 1890, the Arrow Rock School District purchased 1/2 acre for a black school north of Block 17. The first school building for blacks was not constructed until 1892. The Arrow Rock *Enterprise* reported on August 5 of that year: "The old school house has been torn down and brick and lumber conveyed to the lot in the northern part of town where the work of erecting a Negro school is progressing rapidly."[442] The *Enterprise* reported the "colored school" opened on October 14 of that year. Most likely, it was a frame building with a brick foundation.

The first teacher for this school was John Thomas Trigg. He was the first African American teacher in Arrow Rock who was born a free man. His name appeared in a teachers' "Register" in 1889, when he was 20 years old. For the next 20 years, he is the only African American teacher registered in Arrow Rock. Trigg continued teaching into the late 1920s and was remembered by his former students as a "competent, demanding teacher and a strict disciplinarian."[443]

Records are extremely sketchy regarding the "African Public School,"[444] but indications are it burned down twice. In 1939, a brick building was constructed for the school when it burned. This school caught fire again on December 26, 1948. Apparently enough of the foundation and walls remained for the building to be reconstructed the following year. The Supreme Court ruling *Brown vs. Board of Education* ended school segregation after 1954, and full integration occurred by 1956. The African public school then became a private residence, and it remains so today.

Public education in Missouri began progressing more rapidly after the Civil War. In addition to its public schools, Arrow Rock continued to host a private school. The McMahan Institute opened in 1865 or 1866. In 1891, the Arrow Rock *Enterprise* carried this ad:

McMAHAN INSTITUTE
Arrow Rock, Mo.
THE TWENTY-SIXTH ANNUAL

TERM WILL BEGIN
MONDAY SEPTEMBER 14, 1891
A FEW BOARDERS WILL BE RECEIVED
Boarding with Rooms, Fuel, Lights, etc., for term of six months
.... $120
Tuition in English Branches for term................ 30
Music and use of instruments....................... 40
Pupils can be entered at any time during the year.
A. M. R. McMAHAN
J. E. KIBLER
M. M. TURLEY[445]

Anna (Reid) McMahan was the eldest daughter of Jesse and Margaret Reid. The Reid family had been original settlers in the Jones' settlement south of Arrow Rock. Anna had attended a school taught by George Fenwick in her neighborhood, but she was largely self-taught. By 1858, she was teaching at a small school in her neighborhood. After her first year of teaching in Arrow Rock, half the pupils of Arrow Rock were enrolled with "Miss Anna." Within a few years, pupils were sent to her from throughout the countryside, until she no longer had room to accommodate them.

"What she knew she seemed to know more clearly than the average teacher, and she possessed the gift of imparting it in that impressive and original manner which enlisted the interest and attention of her scholars. She not only watched over the progress of her pupils in their lessons, but exacted of them good behavior in and out of the school room."[446] Anna educated her four younger sisters, and some of them became her assistants. Jessie Kibler was her sister, and it is possible, "M. M. Turley" was also her sister.

Anna's husband, Templeton C. McMahan, died in 1890. After that, she retired from teaching. She was remembered not only as a "successful teacher, but her influence was always devoted to the social, moral and intellectual advancement of the community in which she was born and spent the greater part of her life."[447] At present, the location of the McMahan Institute is not known. Possibly, it was continued in the brick academy building adjacent to the Tavern. If so, it is possible that the dismantling of the brick building coincided with the closure of the McMahan Institute.

Accidents, Death, Disease and Medicine

While in some respects 19th century life appeals to 21st century Americans as a "kinder and gentler time," a serious examination of medical and cemetery records alone would quickly dispel that notion. The losses suffered by the Cobb family while managing the Tavern were not unique. Childhood diseases such as scarlet and rheumatic fever were the dread of every parent. Mortality rates for infants were high, as they were for women giving birth. Therefore, it is not unusual to find men who married two or more women in their lifetime, due to deaths rather than divorce.

Nineteenth century life was rough by modern standards, and accidents were fairly common. Beyond one's own common sense, there was no such thing as safety precautions for everyday life. Nearly everyone depended on horses or mules for transportation. A bystander could be kicked or trampled or a rider thrown, especially if the animal were "spooked." Accidents involving wagons and horses were not unlike automobile accidents of today. Following are several examples demonstrating the dangers from the common mode of transportation for the day:

"We regret to learn that Maj. C. F. Jackson, of our county, Bank Commissioner of Missouri, met with quite a serious accident in St. Louis, on Friday afternoon last. He was thrown out of a buggy... and so severely injured ... that he was almost entirely unable to move without assistance. The horse he was driving, though usually a gentle one, became restive and frightened at some object, started to run and capsized the buggy...." Marshall *Weekly Democrat*, September 30, 1859.[448]

"Accident — Last Sunday evening as Mr. John P. Sites of this place [Arrow Rock], in company with his wife and a little girl, daughter of Mr. J. J. Webb, of Brownsville, was riding in a buggy, a short distance from town, the horse became frightened at some hogs on the side of the road, and ran away, upsetting the buggy, fracturing the collar bone and otherwise injuring the little girl. Mr. and Mrs. Sites fortunately escaped without serious injury. A complete wreck was made of the buggy." Marshall *Weekly Democrat*, October 10, 1860.[449]

"RUNAWAY — On last Wednesday morning, as a team belonging to Mr. Crockett the livery stable keeper in Arrow Rock, was going down the steep grade of Main street in that place, the wagon bed slid forward, causing the horses to take fright and run. In the pell-mell down the street one of the horses fell, and the wagon passed over him, and broke his back bone, Mr. Crockett seeing from the nature of the injury the utter helpless condition of the horse ended his misery by shooting him in the head." *Saline County Progress*, July 29, 1870.[450] This accident may have actually occurred on First Street, a steep grade connecting Main Street to the river landing.

At least two freak accidents occurred in Arrow Rock because of lightning. The minutes of the Town Board record on May 10, 1872: "It being represented to the Board of Trustees that Moses Lapsley having been struck by lightning and instantly killed the family is left in destitute circumstances. The Board appropriated Twenty-Five dollars to their relief." The Arrow Rock *Enterprise* reported, "Mr. Town Scott had a fine mare killed by a stroke of lightning during the storm on Wednesday. Mr. Scott was driving along the Marshall road about three and half miles west of town...The stroke instantly killed one of the horses and seriously injured the other."[451]

There were accidents that resulted from careless human hands. One particularly tragic accident, that shook the Arrow Rock community and all of Saline County, occurred on May 15, 1860:

> *MOST DISTRESSING ACCIDENT*
> *It is with feelings of deepest sorrow that we attempt to record the most heart-rending accident that has ever occurred in our county. A number of gentlemen had convened at the post-office in this place, about six o'clock yesterday evening. One of them had purchased one of Sharp's patent pocket pistols, which was in the hands of Mr. Vincent Marmaduke, who was examining it, when the trigger was sprung, and the load in one of the barrels was discharged. The ball entered the forehead of Mr. Henry Gaines... Brains and some pieces of bone exuded from the wound...*
> *A deep gloom pervades our village. The sensitive feelings of Mr. Marmaduke can be better imagined than described, in having accidentally shot one of his most intimate friends, and one of our most highly esteemed citizens... Mrs. Gaines has, for several days past, been confined to a bed of sickness, and we fear this sad calamity will go hard with her.*[452]

Henry Gaines was comatose until his death on May 20th. He had been a merchant in Arrow Rock, and just prior to his death, was the superintendent of the Marshall school. Despite extensive coverage of the death in later editions, there was no further mention of his wife, daughter, and parents or of Vincent Marmaduke. Because two prominent and popular families were involved, it is likely coverage was muted, out of respect. Apparently, no charges or civil suits were ever filed against Marmaduke. Possibly, the Marmaduke family made economic restitution to Gaines' survivors.

Most of the early graves of Arrow Rock were in small family plots, too numerous to mention. Many have been lost to the ravages of time and nature as the families have moved on. One such family plot to the south of the Academy is that of Jacob and Mary Shroyer. They were early settlers of Arrow Rock, and little else is known about them. Mary died in 1842 and Jacob in 1844. In 1935, the WPA built an elaborate mausoleum over their gravesites, not so much to commemorate them, but to provide work for the unemployed during the Great Depression.

As an established community with a growing population, Arrow Rock needed a common cemetery. Also, there were periodic deaths among the thousands of westward immigrants passing through. In May of 1849, the Town Board voted "to pay George Fall Twenty dollars for one acre of ground purchased from him for a Burial Ground."[453] A plank fence and two gates were added in the fall of that year. The fence and gate were necessary to keep out livestock, especially hogs that could root up the graves. In September of 1856, additional acreage was purchased for the cemetery and plotted out for graves. In 1892, Mr. Ed Gilpin was contracted to build a "substantial fence" around the cemetery. A group of local ladies formed the Arrow Rock Cemetery Association in 1911 to manage the grounds. Located one mile west of town on Route TT, the Arrow Rock Cemetery remains open to interments.

One of the most unusual graves in the area is that of William Henry Ashley in Cooper County, about five miles south of Arrow Rock. Ashley was Missouri's first Lieutenant Governor, serving from 1820 until 1824. To finance his political aspirations, Ashley engaged in the Rocky Mountain fur trade beginning in 1822. He retired from the fur trade a wealthy man in 1826. Although he failed in a bid for governor in 1836, from 1831 to 1837 he was a Missouri U.S. Representative. He purchased an interest in Pierre Chouteau's Spanish land grant along the Lamine River. As a U.S. Representative, he helped Chouteau secure Congressional confirmation of the 1799 land grant. However, Ashley had no time to enjoy the property or profit from it. He died March 26, 1838, and was buried atop one of the large

Indian mounds on the tract overlooking the Missouri River.[454]

Segregation of the races was a fact of life and in death as well. African Americans were buried in cemeteries of their own. Like many of the white cemeteries, these were small, and many have been lost altogether. However, a major black cemetery survives five and a half miles southwest of Arrow Rock. Oral tradition says that prior to 1856, Dr. John Sappington gave approximately two acres to Emanuel Banks, a highly regarded servant, to be used as a cemetery. It was identified as the "Sappington Negro Cemetery."[455]

Since the mid-nineteenth century, over 350 Arrow Rock citizens of African American descent have been interred in the cemetery. Among them are members of the Banks, Brown, Bush, Harvey, Parker, Switzler and Williams families; names that date back to the early period of Arrow Rock's history. Initially slaves, then free men and women, the descendants of these and other Arrow Rock black families continue to use the cemetery, which is now under private care.[456]

Medical knowledge and patient care were extremely minimal compared to today. For example, dentistry was in its infancy in the 19th century. The first dentist of record was Dr. J. E. Keith, who became a resident of Saline County in 1859. He made a circuit, traveling between Miami, Marshall and Arrow Rock.[457] Information regarding Dr. Keith's practice has not been located. However, an ad for "J. Dow, Surgeon Dentist" in *The Western Emigrant* newspaper may provide some idea of what Dr. Keith's practice was like:

> *"INCORRUPTIBLE TEETH*
> *Inserted in the best manner — teeth filled with gold and war-*
> *ranted — teeth and fangs of the most difficult kind extracted in*
> *a new way, with a lateral motion, probably with more ease and*
> *safety than has ever been discovered before. Scurvy and all sorts*
> *of scrofulous diseases cured. Young persons should have their teeth*
> *often examined and attended to before it is too late to save them.*
> *No charge will be made for examining teeth and giving advice.*
> *— Ladies will be waited on at their residence if desired. The*
> *most choice medicine and dentifrices kept on hand, and for sale*
> *at his shop on Morgan street, Boonville, Mo.*
> *July 11, 1839*[458]

"Missouri did not enjoy the reputation of being a healthful place in which to live."[459] Illness is a frequent topic of discussion in letters to family "back east." A letter sent from Arrow Rock on June 1, 1847, is all too typical: "I have been very sick since I last wrote to you but have now nearly recovered. I have had the ague and fever now for nearly eight months and it appears almost impossible for me to be rid of them. If it were not for the unhealthyness of the state I would be much better pleased with it."[460]

Hygiene was poorly understood, and the existence of bacteria and germs was unknown. People not only suffered maladies and injuries such as broken bones and colds, they suffered plagues of highly communicable diseases. Since most of the state's population was concentrated along the river systems, it was easy for epidemics of smallpox, measles, cholera, scarlet fever and dysentery to spread from community to community along a river. Arrow Rock was no exception. "Consumption" was a disease in which people appeared to gradually waste away. Usually, it was tuberculosis or a cancer.

A disease widespread in early America was Asiatic cholera. It is an infectious disease caused by bacteria and is prevalent in areas where public sanitation is poor. It affects the intestines causing diarrhea and severe fluid loss. If untreated, it can result in death. In the last stages, patients actually turn blue because of asphyxiation. In 1844, Dr. John Sappington wrote, "This disease has carried terror and desolation wherever it has gone, perhaps more than any other disease."[461] Outbreaks of the disease often caused people to flee, "panic-struck, as if an all-devouring demon had visited them."[462]

Successful treatment of cholera consists of re-hydrating the body, and treating with intravenous antibiotics. Of course, treatment in the 19th century was considerably different. Dr. Hardin M. Weatherford of Louisville, Kentucky, published *A Treatise on Cholera* in 1833, which was widely followed in the western states. He recommended "alkalies taken into the stomach … soda and tartaric acids … a grain of opium."[463] If the disease worsened, Port wine and more opium could follow the "soda and effervescing draught."[464] Finally, a patient whose condition continued to worsen was to be given cayenne pepper and French brandy. Hot mustard plasters, ground mustard rolled into a flour paste, were placed on the pit of the stomach. If all else failed, more opium could be given generously.

Cholera was highly contagious, and death could follow within a few hours of infection. Several waves of cholera swept through Arrow Rock and the Boonslick Country. The first wave broke out among soldiers and militiamen returning home from the Black Hawk War of 1832. After ravaging St. Louis, the disease followed the Missouri River. That year, six died from the disease in the neighborhood of Arrow Rock. Dr. Sappington and Dr. Penn successfully treated 35 cases in Arrow Rock in 1833. They "used large and repeated doses of laudanum [opium]; large and repeated draughts of strong, hot toddy; essence of pepper-mint; camphor, and red-pepper tea."[465] In 1835, Dr. William B. Price, Dr. Sappington's son-in-law, successfully treated 16 or 18 cholera victims in Arrow Rock, using Dr. Sappington's methods.[466] Indians on the Great Plains fared much worse when the disease reached them. Some tribes experienced the loss of nearly half their population within the space of weeks.

Cholera reappeared in the spring and summer of 1849. The new epidemic was so virulent that between 4,000 and 6,000 people died in St. Louis alone, including Dr. Penn's son, Lawson Penn.[467] "Arrow Rock, Saline City, Cambridge, Miami and Marshall were all visited by the dreadful scourge and there were many cases in the country. There was the greatest alarm throughout the county. Farmers...feared to visit the towns, even to procure family supplies or medical attendance. When they came in, they would ride up to the front of a store, call for what they wanted, receive it, and without dismounting, gallop hastily away."[468]

In June of 1849, the Town Board of Arrow Rock exhorted citizens to keep premises clean, "especially during the prevalence of cholera among us."[469] At least 50 people died in Saline County. Among them was Dr. Burrell Thompson, son of Philip W. Thompson. Dr. Thompson graduated from the St. Louis Medical College in 1848.[470] He contracted the disease while treating cholera victims housed in the Tavern and died in the space of about six hours.[471] According to the Glasgow *Weekly Times*, other physicians in Arrow Rock "had advised the inhabitants to abandon the place."[472]

Although the cause of cholera was not understood, it was known it usually appeared first in passengers disembarking from steamboats. On July 12, 1850, the Arrow Rock Board of Trustees passed the following resolution to deal with the reoccurring epidemics:

> *"Be it resolved that _____ be and is hereby appointed health officer of Arrow Rock, whose duty it shall be to board all Boats coming to the Landing and cause all persons sick with contagious*

*disease who may be placed ashore at this point to be immediately
taken to a place herein after specified and placed under the care
of the person who may be employed as nurse to attend the sick.*

*Be it resolved that _____ be and are hereby appointed com-
missioners to select a site on the north side of the town of Arrow
Rock upon which they shall cause to be erected, sufficiently
removed from all families, a house 16 x 20 feet made by planting posts & planking upright the same with 2 doors & 2
windows, plank floor & board roof & that they report to the
trustees as soon as convenient or necessary.*

*Be it resolved that Mr. William Chase be and is hereby
appointed public nurse to attend the sick who shall have power
to employ a suitable person as assistant and that he be allowed
2 dollars per day for his services while engaged as nurse.*[473]

On July 15, 1850, the Town Board approved payment to William Martin of $3.00 for hauling off sick persons. Presumably, these were cholera victims taken to the sick house. The last cholera outbreak in Arrow Rock occurred in 1866, killing 30 within the space of a month. After that time, increasing medical knowledge and understanding of hygiene reduced the frequency and severity of epidemics.

Next to cholera, smallpox was perhaps the second deadliest scourge. Those not killed were often left with terrible scarring from the pox marks. Although outbreaks occurred throughout the century, a particularly severe outbreak occurred in January of 1873. On the 11th of that month, the Town Board sought to appoint a nurse and guard at the "smallpox hospital" citing the need for "help from all the people near and in the town to stop this fearful disease."[474] No one was found for these positions, but Dr. Luximon Roy agreed to be superintendent of the facility. He was paid $50.00 a month and all supplies needed.

The epidemic appears to have been abating by February 17. The Town Board ordered, "that at the end of 3 days the time of Dr. Luximon Roy as physician at the small pox hospital shall be stopped and that he be ordered to see that the inmates of the hospital disinfect themselves. Ordered that the board supply the inmates of the hospital with 2 bushels of meal and 50 pounds of meat, one load of wood and such disinfectant as they may need and that after these are consumed the town will no longer supply them."[475]

A variety of treatments and "medicines" were employed to combat the epidemics as well as more routine diseases. Physicians favored calomel, (mercurous chloride) for many ailments. A Dr. Johnson wrote in 1840: "I own that Calomel practice is both cheap and easy to the physician, for the whole extent of both theory and practice, is give Calomel, if that will not help, double and treble the dose of Calomel. If the patient recovers, Calomel cured him; if he dies, nothing in the world could have saved him."[476] Physicians did not know that because of the mercury content, calomel was extremely toxic. Repeated use led to a build-up of mercury in the brain, liver and kidneys resulting in memory loss, tremors and, frequently, death.

Another common method of treating patients was to "bleed" them. To bleed a patient a doctor would use a device called a lancet to cut and drain blood from him or her. Leeches were sometimes used in place of the lancet. In theory, this removed the "bad blood" from the patient. Dr. Glen O. Hardeman summarized the standard medical treatment of the period as follows: "We puked and purged, and blistered a patient in the old orthodox antiphlogistic style...."[477] Herbs and assorted drugs were administered to induce vomiting (puking) and diarrhea (purging) and blistering (mustard packs) in an effort to remove toxins from the body. In many cases, the treatment weakened the patients to the point their bodies could no longer fight infection, and they died as a result.

Druggists and hardware stores alike frequently sold medicines. Dr. W. Lewis Boyer was advertised in 1858 as a "Dealer in Drugs, Chemicals, Medicines, Paints, Oils, Dye-Stuffs, Glass, Brushes, perfumery, Soaps, patent Medicines, Cigars, Tobacco, Trusses, Shoulder Braces, and every article usually found in Drug stores...."[478] Jay Marcellus Potter, an Arrow Rock pharmacist, demonstrated the diversity of occupations often held by local merchants. Besides selling medicines, he sold stationery, books, sheet music, cutlery, toys, tobacco and notions in his store. He was also Arrow Rock's postmaster, stagecoach office agent, telegraph operator, and an Aetna insurance agent.[479]

Patent medicines were catchall treatments administered for everything from insomnia, headaches, fevers, female problems, and irritable bowels to purifying the blood. Some of these over-the-counter medicines were called "bitters" obviously due to their taste. Sometimes, they were vainly administered in the face of the deadly epidemics. The primary ingredient of patent medicines was usually alcohol. An 1864 bottle of McLeans patent medicine found under the Tavern was labeled as a *"Cordial, Blood Thinner and Purifier."* Being a "cordial" meant it was suitable for "social imbibing" as well as for medical use. An ad for Dr. Roback's bitters in the *Saline County Progress* tried to assure its readers that the quantity of liquor in its bottle did not supercede its medical qualities:

NOT A BEVERAGE

Unlike most of the bitters of the present day, Dr. Roback's are not intended as a pleasant stimulating whisky beverage, but are per-fectly medicinal, containing only sufficient pure bourbon whisky to hold in solution the medical extractive matter from which they are composed. Sold by Powell & Wilhelm, Arrow Rock, and Chastain & Sappington, Marshall.[480]

The single most common, though not always deadly, disease in the Missouri valley was malaria. Many erroneously believe it to be solely a trop-ical disease. Commonly known as the "shaking ague" or "the intermittent fevers," the disease is marked by cycles of chills, fever and profuse sweat-ing. It was generally thought a fever was a disease rather than a symptom of one. The cause of the disease was believed to be "Marsh miasmata, or the effluvia[481] arising from stagnant water … and one of its great pecu-liarities is its susceptibility of a renewal from very slight causes, such as from the prevalence of an eastern wind…."[482] Transmission of the disease actually was by Anopheles mosquitoes carrying the malaria parasite. The mosquitoes were abundant because of the marshland and quiet backwa-ters along the Missouri River and its tributaries.

Virtually everyone in Arrow Rock was afflicted with "shaking ague" at some time in his or her life. It was such an accepted part of life in the Missouri valley that John Mason Peck wrote in 1831: "The author recol-lects of traveling in an obscure and sickly place in Missouri, and calling on a family that had emigrated, sometime previously, from the low country of South Carolina. Perceiving that nearly all the family were laboring under a paroxysm of the fever and ague, he inquired if they were satisfied with the country and were not disheartened with sickness. The reply was 'Oh no, it is a very healthy country.' 'But are not your family now sick?' 'No, they have only a little brush of the ague.'"[483]

An example of the prevalence of the "shaking ague" and an unusual home remedy were recorded from the Big Bottoms: "In the autumn of 1820, there wasn't a man, woman or child in the entire Bottoms that wasn't laid up with chills and fever. It was known as the sickly year. A prescription for the ague chills and fever in the Bottoms was three lice trapped from the head with a fine tooth comb, and swallowed alive with water before breakfast."[484]

Science, Art, Politics and Tradesmen

Dr. John Sappington and His Anti-Fever Pills

Dr. John Sappington was one of the most prominent physicians in Missouri's frontier history. Born in Havre de Grace, Maryland, May 15, 1776, Sappington spent most of his youth on the Tennessee frontier near Nashville. He spent about five years studying medicine under his father, Dr. Mark Brown Sappington, then set up his own practice in 1799. In 1804, he married Jane Breathitt of Logan County, Kentucky. The Breathitts were a prominent family. Jane's brother, John, became the governor of Kentucky and another brother, Roger, became the private secretary of Andrew Jackson.[485]

The State of Tennessee appointed Dr. Sappington and Thomas Hart Benton to lay out (survey) the town of Franklin, 15 miles south of Nashville. Dr. Sappington practiced medicine in Franklin until 1817, when he emigrated to Missouri. Benton had already moved to St. Louis by 1815 and invited Sappington to come there. Dr. Sappington did not linger in St. Louis but headed west to the rapidly growing Boonslick Country.

Dr. Sappington first located in Howard County near present-day Glasgow. In 1819, he moved his family to Saline County, five miles southwest of the Arrow Rock ferry. He named his home place "Pilot Hickory." The neighborhood became known as the "Sappington Settlement" and was settled by family friends of the Sappingtons such as the Townsends, Brownlees and Finleys.[486] Dr. Sappington was the first doctor in the area; he took on Dr. George Penn as a partner in 1832. As a physician, Sappington's practice took him over a wide area. Records show he billed families in Cooper, Howard, Chariton, Ray and Boone counties, as well as Saline County. After 1836, it seems he had retired from active medical practice or at least limited it to the locality of Arrow Rock. He was reported to have been in ill health then, and again in 1838.[487]

Instead of bleeding patients suffering from malarial fever, Sappington became known for doctoring with "the Peruvian bark." The bark came from the cinchona tree, and Jesuit priests had learned of its use to reduce fever from Peruvian Indians. About 1630, the Jesuits introduced cinchona to Europe. Cinchona was even carried by Lewis and Clark on their exploration of the West. On July 4, 1804, Private Joseph Fields was bitten on the ankle by a rattlesnake, and Captain Lewis applied a poultice of "Peruvian bark" to the bite.[488]

Captain Lewis erroneously thought if Peruvian bark were good internally for fever, it was good externally for snakebite. The bark could be tricky to administer internally. Patients could get too little or too much of its main chemical component. In 1820, two French scientists named Pelletier and Caventou worked with cinchona and successfully "...separated the pure alkaline salt, called quina, from the bulky and inert mass in which Nature had placed it...."[489]

Quina or quinine began to be manufactured in the United States in pure form in 1823. Despite its curative properties, many physicians were reluctant to use quinine. Those who did use it would do so only in conjunction with the old practices of bleeding, purging and puking their patients. Dr. Sappington began attacking these practices, and he advocated that the "essence of the bark" alone was sufficient to treat malarial fever.[490]

Dr. Sappington began the manufacture of "Dr. John Sappington's Anti-Fever Pills" in 1832. Wholesale distribution appears to have begun in November, 1835, when a company called "Sappington and Sons" was formed for pill manufacturing and distribution.[491] Hundreds of pounds of quinine were shipped by steamboat annually from Philadelphia, Pennsylvania, to Arrow Rock. The anti-fever pills contained one grain of quinine, 3/4 grain of licorice, 1/4 grain of myrrh and oil of sassafras for flavoring purposes. Sappington had 25 to 30 agents on horseback distributing the pills. Many of these agents were Sappington relatives, who got their start in Missouri by working for the doctor. Eventually millions of boxes were sold and distributed throughout the southern states and western territories.

The anti-fever pills even traveled on the Santa Fe Trail. Lewis Garrard went on a large wagon train in 1850 and was placed in charge of "medicine" on the trip. A short distance out of Westport he wrote, "...the train was started along the heavy road; dense fogs dampened our clothing and spirits, and but for brandy, and other liquors, fever and ague would have predominated; as it was, Blas and Pierre shook, for which '*cholagogue*' 'quinine' and pills were administered by the 'doctor,' as I was styled."[492]

In 1844, Sappington wrote *The Theory and Treatment of Fevers*, the first known medical treatise published west of the Mississippi. By this time, quinine was becoming accepted in the medical community. Many physicians were still reluctant to give it while the patient actually had a fever. In his book Sappington combated that misguided belief. His family feared that publication of the book would hurt pill sales and lead to duplicate medicines.[493] Dr. Sappington's reply was "... he and they had enough to support them comfortably and that mankind had claims on him as well as his family."[494] The pill business continued to be profitable, but the book was not a financial success.[495] While it is difficult to determine his profit, Dr. Sappington said he "realized considerable sums of money"[496] from the sale of his pills.

Dr. Sappington's views on malaria treatment caused him to be labeled a "quack" by some of the medical authorities of his day. In 1850, Daniel Drake, founder of *The Western Journal of Medical and Physical Sciences*, conducted interviews with physicians along the Missouri River on the treatment of the malaria. He interviewed Dr. William Price, Sappington's son-in-law in Arrow Rock. However, Drake ignored Dr. Sappington, his pills and his book altogether.[497]

Sappington's Anti-Fever Pills had their competitors and imitators as well. One of these was "Moffatt's Life Pills and Phenix Bitters." These were marketed in Boonville, Dr. Sappington's own back yard, so to speak. The advertisements focused on their curative properties as being the only way to successfully treat "fever and ague." Like all patent medicines, they offered cures for all manner of unrelated illnesses and complaints.[498] Despite the critics and competition, the success of quinine in treating malaria cannot be denied. It was the only drug in the world capable of treating malaria until the 1930s.

Dr. Sappington was a farmer as well as a physician. He speculated in land and owned about 4,500 acres in Saline County and more in neighboring counties. He was, of course, a slave owner and had up to 25 slaves valued at $17,750 in 1853. He also rented farm ground, and his tenants and slaves raised wheat, corn, tobacco and hogs. In 1830, he shipped eight kegs and seven boxes of processed tobacco to St. Louis. During the 1820s, he raised cotton and owned a cotton gin, but it appears he gave up the venture by 1830.[499] Wheat became a staple crop, and Sappington had it milled and shipped to St. Louis from Arrow Rock in the 1840s. He even purchased a McCormick reaper in 1849. Even though hemp was the major cash crop of Saline County, there is no evidence the doctor raised it. Oral tradition holds Dr. Sappington introduced Kentucky bluegrass to the area, spreading the seeds along the roadsides wherever he traveled.[500]

The doctor was also a philanthropist. In 1847, he made a proposition that he would give $10,000 worth of land as a site for a manual training school if Saline County would raise $28,000 towards the project within two years. The county failed to raise the needed funds.[501] Dr. Sappington set aside $20,000 in 1853 to be used for the education of "the most necessitous poor children" of Saline County. Since public education is today considered adequate, the Sappington Trust Fund is now used primarily for college students. As of December, 2003, the fund has paid out $495,000 in more than 14,350 individual payments. Prior to establishing the trust fund, he parceled out $55,000 worth of land to his heirs. Additional monies were left to them in his will.

His wife Jane died in 1852 at the age of 69. She was buried in the family cemetery, which had been established in 1831. He died on September 7, 1856. Two stone sarcophagi rest as monuments above the gravesites of Dr. and Mrs. Sappington. The Doctor's inscription reads, "A Truly Honest Man is the Noblest Work of God. He lay like a warrior taking his rest." Mrs. Sappington's inscription simply reads, "Consort to Dr. John Sappington." Oral tradition claims they were buried inside the vaults. This is not true, because the lids have been removed several times for repair work. There is simply no room for a body, let alone a coffin, inside the vaults. In 1859, the Sappington brothers and Claiborne F. Jackson had the cemetery enclosed with a stone wall, topped by an iron railing fence. There are approximately 110 known graves within the plot; all of those buried were related to Doctor Sappington or his wife through blood or marriage.

The Sappington Trust Fund managed the Sappington cemetery from 1904 until 1976. The State of Missouri is mandated to care for the graves of any former governor who is not in a "perpetual care" cemetery. Consequently, ownership passed to the Missouri Department of Natural Resources in 1976 because Governor Marmaduke and Governor Jackson are buried in the cemetery. Sappington Cemetery State Historic Site is administered through Arrow Rock State Historic Site.

Family Affair: Politics and the Sappington Dynasty

Dr. Sappington was a staunch Democrat and a personal friend and supporter of President Andrew Jackson. His close friend Thomas Hart Benton was the second of Missouri's first two federal senators. Sappington never ran for any office himself, but his friendship with President Jackson and Senator Benton meant he had considerable influence in Missouri's Democrat Party. His political influence combined with his wealth from farming, land speculation and pill manufacturing made him a social, economic and political patriarch. His personal library contained nearly three thousand volumes, the largest west of St. Louis.

By 1835, Boonslick men, principally from Howard and Saline counties, gained control of the Democratic Party nomination process. These included Dr. Sappington, Meredith M. Marmaduke, William B. Napton, Dr. George Penn, Dr. John Lowry, Joshua Redman, Owen Rawlins, Chauncey Scott and others who became known as the "Central Clique."[502] For the next 25 years this Clique and their political offspring dominated Missouri's Democratic Party politics. Fayette in Howard County became the base of operations for the Central Clique, and any Democrat seeking office was beholden to them.

Dr. and Mrs. Sappington had nine children: Eliza (Jackson), Lavinia (Marmaduke), Erasmus Darwin, William Breathitt, Jane (Jackson), Louisa (Jackson), Susan (Eddins) and Mary (Price). Sarah Margaret died at the age of thirteen.[503] The Sappington children and their extended families became very prominent in the affairs of Arrow Rock, Saline County and Missouri. In addition, sons Erasmus and William were partners with their father in his many agricultural and business pursuits.

Both sons adhered to the common southern practice of keeping wealth in the family by marrying their first cousins. Erasmus was born in 1809 and married Penelope Caroline Breathitt, the daughter of Kentucky Governor John Breathitt, on November 16, 1838. He operated a mercantile firm in Jonesboro, which supplied some goods to the Santa Fe trade. In 1846, Erasmus ran for a seat in the Missouri legislature, defeating George Caleb Bingham in the recount. He built a mansion named "Mount Airy" about three miles southwest of Arrow Rock. This burned around the turn of the century, but the ruins of the house remained visible until the 1990s. Erasmus died September 30, 1858, and Penelope died November 16, 1904.[504]

William was born in 1811 and married Mary Mildred Breathitt, also the daughter of Governor Breathitt, on September 3, 1844. William studied law but never practiced. Instead, he pursued agriculture and the quinine pill manufacturing business. He was never a candidate for political office, but like his father, wielded considerable influence in Democrat Party politics. William was a delegate to the national convention that nominated James Polk for President and also served in several state conventions and committees. He became president of the Bank of Missouri in 1866, the only bank left in Saline County following the Civil War. For nearly 40 years, he was Chairman of the Board of Trustees for the trust fund established by his father.[505] William died August 16, 1888, and Mary died August 13, 1880.[506]

William B. Sappington's lasting legacy is the magnificent ante-bellum mansion he built three miles southwest of Arrow Rock. In 1844, he started construction of "Prairie Park," a two and one half story brick home in the Greek Revival style. The building project was completed in 1849. Sappington spared no expense. The double parlors and entry hallway present intricate detail molding. The detached summer kitchen is now incorporated into the main home. One of the original slave quarters, also made of brick, remains on the grounds. Recently, it was discovered portions of a large barn on the property contain hand-hewn timbers, forged nails and wooden pegs — an indication it dates to the early period of the house. Tradition says Dr. Sappington spent the last few years of his life in this house; he described the extravagant homes of his sons as "monuments to damn fools." Now a private residence, the owners completely restored "Prairie Park" by 1999, and it is open to tours through the Friends of Arrow Rock, Inc.

Despite the fact William B. Sappington was the wealthiest man in Saline County and had one of the most extravagant homes in Missouri, Thomas Rainey described him as follows: "Personally, he was far from extravagant. He dressed plainly and cared nothing for display." He also remarked Sappington "seemed never to adjust himself to the new order of things after the war." Rainey told a story to remind his readers of the Sappingtons' humble origins. Shortly after they moved to Howard County, Dr. Sappington sent some slaves across the river to prepare his Arrow Rock homestead. He sent young William across the river in a skiff "with a couple of sides of bacon in a sack for the 'hands,' which he had to carry on his shoulder from the river to the farm. Weather was hot, and the boy had stopped to rest by the roadside, when the Rev. Payton Nowlin … came along and had a chat with him." Rev. Nowlin inquired, "What occupation does your father intend for you to follow, when you grow up, my lad?" Sappington replied, "Well sir, so far as I am able to judge, I think he intends to make a horse of me!"[507]

Scandal struck the Sappington family a few years after they arrived in Missouri. Eliza, the eldest daughter, married Alonzo Pearson, a teacher, in 1821. Pearson became a partner with Erasmus in a mercantile firm in Jonesboro, "Pearson and Sappington." In the next eight years, Eliza bore five children to the marriage. In 1830, it was discovered that Pearson had a wife in Alabama whom he had married in Georgia. He deserted her when she was pregnant, and he left her in "a state of absolute want."[508] Pearson's real name was Augustus Parsons, and his jilted wife had tracked him to Missouri and filed for support. Despite Eliza's protests, Dr. Sappington banished Pearson as soon as their fifth child was born. The Doctor's political influence was such the Missouri legislature passed a bill in 1831 declaring Eliza's marriage "null and void from the beginning."[509] She and her five children moved to her parents' home. Dr. Sappington recovered the dowry he had given the couple, then dissolved the Pearson and Sappington Company.

Claiborne Fox Jackson was three times a son-in-law to Dr. and Mrs. Sappington. Jackson was born in Fleming County, Kentucky, April 4, 1804. In June of 1826, Jackson arrived in Franklin, then booming because of the Santa Fe trade. Jackson became a clerk in the firm of Hickman and Lamme, a general store and Santa Fe outfitting firm. Although not formally schooled, Jackson was ambitious and calculating. In 1828, he opened C. F. Jackson & Co. in Franklin. Part of his business was furnishing goods for the Santa Fe trade.[510]

Jackson nearly went bankrupt in 1829 but recovered and opened branch stores in Franklin and New Franklin and in the new town of Philadelphia in Saline County. Jackson soon moved to Philadelphia where he met eighteen-year-old Mary Jane Breathitt Sappington at a Christmas Eve ball in 1830. They were married February 17, 1831, sealing Jackson's entry into the politically influential family. Mary Jane died within five months, and hers became the first grave in the Sappington family cemetery. Family tradition says she died of malaria, the very disease her father was then experimenting against.

Jackson was appointed the first postmaster of Arrow Rock in September of 1832, a reward for his loyalty to the Democrat Party. On September 12, 1833, Jackson married Jane's younger sister, Louisa Catherine Sappington, who had just turned eighteen. He became a partner in Sappington and Sons, the enterprise that was manufacturing and mass-marketing quinine pills. As his involvement in Sappington enterprises grew, he distanced himself from his mercantile business. In 1836, he terminated his partnership in the New Franklin store.

Jackson and other merchants made annual trips to Philadelphia, Pennsylvania, each February to purchase their spring stock of goods. As the rivers were frozen, the trip had to be made by stagecoach. On one such trip, Jackson was with merchants from neighboring Glasgow and Boonville, when a passenger got on in Indiana or Ohio. The stranger began making inquiries about fishing in the Missouri River:

> *Jackson at once began to praise the river for its abundant supply of fish, and remarked that fish weighing two hundred pounds had been caught... The stranger showed that he found it a little hard to swallow a fish story of that size, and Jackson observing it, appealed to his friend from Glasgow. The Glasgow merchant replied, he had lived on the river all his life, and had fished a good deal but had never seen or heard of a fish anything resembling that in size. Of course down at Arrow Rock ... fish might be much larger.*
>
> *Jackson, irritated, appealed to his Boonville friend. Well, he replied, there may have been such fish caught up the river ... at Arrow Rock, but down at Boonville a fish weighing fifteen or twenty pounds was a whopper. It was in vain that Jackson called them liars, and asserted that they knew he was telling the truth ... The stranger left the coach, believing he had met the rival of Jonah, in company with some very conscientious gentlemen from the Missouri river country.*[511]

When Jackson got home, quite a few people had a laugh at his expense. However, in his younger days Jackson was credited as being an "experienced joker himself" and could take one when he was the victim.[512]

Jackson threw his hat into the political ring in 1836, when he was elected state representative of Saline County. Jackson carried the vote in

Arrow Rock by 47 to one, which gave him a six-vote margin countywide. Jackson was soon the protégé of the Central Clique. In 1837, the legislature established the Bank of Missouri in St. Louis and placed its western branch in Fayette. Jackson resigned from the legislature and sold his Arrow Rock store to William Barnes and Jesse McMahan. He moved to Howard County, becoming the bank's first cashier.

Jackson continued to maintain ties to Arrow Rock. He entered into partnership with O. B. Pearson, and they opened a trading company that shipped flour, meat, mules and horses from Arrow Rock to the cotton district of Natchez, Mississippi. Undoubtedly, much of this produce came from the farms of his extended family. Jackson and Louisa also engaged in land speculation, purchasing multiple lots in Arrow Rock, then dividing and reselling them.[513] One of the lots was sold to George Caleb Bingham. Jackson and Louisa had two sons, William and John. Louisa gave birth to a third son, Andrew, in May of 1838. Tragically, she died on May 9 in a runaway accident. Infant Andrew died a month later.

Jackson supposedly approached Dr. Sappington and asked for the third daughter Eliza's hand in marriage. "You can have Eliza," said Dr. John, "but don't come back for the old lady. I want her for myself."[514] Six months after Louisa's death, they were married. Evidence suggests Dr. Sappington, aware of Jackson's ambitions and need to remain connected with his powerful name, actually arranged the marriage. He may have been fearful Eliza would remain unmarried because of the Pearson scandal. There is some indication the story of Jackson asking for Eliza was a joke, told at his expense. Unlike the fish story, Jackson apparently did not take the joke well. He never adopted Eliza's children, and when Dr. Sappington divided his estate prior to his death, he gave part of Jackson's share to his Pearson grandchildren instead.

Jackson farmed 200 acres in Howard County. His log and frame house is one mile north of Fayette on Highway 5 and remains a private residence. In 1844, Jackson was elected to the Missouri House of Representatives and became Speaker, a position he won again in 1846. He failed in a bid to be nominated governor in 1848, but won election as a state senator. During this time, the Central Clique turned against Senator Thomas Hart Benton, who opposed the expansion of slavery into new territories. Senator Jackson, along with William B. Napton, authored the "Jackson Resolutions," which undermined the power of Missouri's senior U.S. Senator. The resulting schism in the Democrat Party allowed the Boonslick Whigs to win several elections, ruining Jackson's political ambitions for nearly a decade. From 1857 to 1860, Jackson served as State Bank Commissioner.

When Dr. Sappington died in 1856, Jackson returned to Saline County and took up residence in the Doctor's old homestead "Pilot Hickory," which he renamed "Fox Castle." Jackson put his energies into the farm and joined the Central Missouri Agricultural Society. He presented himself as a "plain, gentlemen-farmer-looking man, wearing a dry and dusty wig, and a still dustier hat with a broken rim."[515] The image of a common farmer was merely for display; Jackson owned 10 slaves in 1840, but by 1860, he owned 47, far more than any one in his extended family.

Benton was decisively defeated in 1856 and removed from political power. By 1860, state Democratic Party discipline had been restored, and Jackson was nominated for governor. On the national level, the Democratic Party was bitterly divided between the Presidential candidacies of John Breckinridge and Stephen Douglas. Although Jackson leaned towards Douglas, he was careful to position his campaign speeches in neutral terms, as most rural Missourians supported Breckinridge. The *Jefferson Inquirer* criticized him for speaking "in glittering generalities."[516] The paper also declared him ineligible for office because he had temporarily resided in Kansas. He had gone there several times to help influence elections to make Kansas a slave territory.

On August 6, 1860, Jackson was narrowly elected governor, carrying 47 percent of the vote. The remainder was divided between three other candidates. Jackson had little time to savor the pinnacle of his success. Abraham Lincoln was elected President, and within weeks, South Carolina would secede from the Union. With the national crisis deepening, Jackson gave his inaugural speech on January 3, 1861, and clearly sympathized with South Carolina. He defined being "southern" as being in opposition to federal authority. To thunderous applause, he declared that Missouri would "stand by the South."[517]

Jackson and secessionist members of the Legislature fled when federal troops marched on Jefferson City. Jackson was present at the Battles of Boonville, Lexington, and Carthage, Missouri, and Pea Ridge, Arkansas. Maintaining a "government in exile," Jackson continuously petitioned Confederate leaders for the "liberation" of Missouri. One of Jackson's final acts was formally to turn over the remaining Missouri State Guard to the Confederate States in September of 1862. Suffering from stomach cancer and tuberculosis, Jackson died in Little Rock, Arkansas, on December 7, 1862. Eliza died in Little Rock on July 5, 1864, ironically of malarial fever. Both were interred in the Sappington family cemetery in 1871.

In 1826, Lavinia Sappington married Meredith Miles Marmaduke. Tradition says Marmaduke met her when the Santa Fe caravan of 1824 passed the doctor's house. Marmaduke was born in Westmoreland County, Virginia, in 1791. During the War of 1812, he raised a company of volunteers and served as their colonel. Following the war, he was a clerk and marshal in Westmoreland County. Like many Virginians, Marmaduke headed west to the new state of Missouri, arriving in Franklin in 1821. By 1830, Marmaduke got out of the Santa Fe trade and became a business partner with his brother-in-law, Erasmus, filling the position vacated by Alonzo Pearson.

Marmaduke settled on a large farm six miles southwest of Arrow Rock. He was soon elected as a county judge and county surveyor. In addition to surveying the town of Philadelphia (Arrow Rock) in 1829, he helped survey the new county seat of Marshall in 1839. A Democrat, Marmaduke was naturally a member of the Central Clique. In 1840, he was elected lieutenant governor with Thomas Reynolds as governor. Reynolds committed suicide in office, and Marmaduke filled out the remaining nine months of the term. While governor, he made the then novel proposal that the mentally ill should be housed in a special asylum instead of jail. However, the legislature failed to act on his request. Due to a split in the party, Marmaduke did not run for the office in 1844. Instead, he yielded to a candidate who stood a better chance of maintaining party unity.

Marmaduke became a member of the 1845 state constitutional convention. Retiring from politics, he remained active in agricultural and community affairs in Saline County. The Saline County Agricultural and Mechanical Association was formed in 1856, and Marmaduke was named its first president. At the onset of the Civil War, Marmaduke departed from the sentiments of most of his family and neighbors by supporting the Union. His respect in the community was such that he was not personally molested, and little of his property was destroyed. He died on March 26, 1864, and was buried according to the rites of Freemasonry in the Sappington family cemetery.

The Marmadukes had nine children: Vincent, John S., Meredith,

Jr., Darwin W., Henry H., Leslie, Jane (Harwood); Sarah (Yerby), and Lavinia (Bruce). Vincent and John S. became prominent in Missouri state politics.

Vincent was born in 1830 on the Marmaduke estate and at an early age was taught farm work. About 1840, he was sent to Chapel Hill Academy in Lexington, Missouri, for two years. He spent four years at Yale College where he graduated in 1852 or 1853. He studied law and obtained a license to practice, but instead pursued agriculture, establishing a large farm south of Marshall. In 1861, the state legislature called a constitutional convention to consider the question of secession from the Union. Marmaduke attended as a delegate, but surprisingly, none of the delegates advocated secession.[518]

Vincent apparently held to his father's pro-Union views. However, late in 1862 he was suspected of disloyalty and banished to the South. He then joined the Confederate army and rose to the rank of major. After the war, Marmaduke assumed ownership of his father's home place where he again took up farming. A Democrat, Marmaduke was elected state representative from Saline County in 1882. He died on March 25, 1904, and was buried in the Sappington family cemetery.

John Sappington Marmaduke was the last member of the Sappington dynasty to wield extensive political power. John S. was born in 1833 and was highly educated for the time. He attended the local school in Jonesboro, and like his brother, worked on the farm. Marmaduke attended the Chapel Hill Academy for one year. After he turned seventeen, Marmaduke attended Yale College for two years and then Harvard College. However, he cut his school year short to receive an appointment to West Point Military Academy. He graduated as a 2nd Lieutenant in 1856.[519]

John S. Marmaduke's first assignment was the First United States Mounted Riflemen. Soon after, he was transferred to the Seventh U.S. Cavalry under Colonel Albert Sydney Johnston and participated in a conflict in Utah known as the "Mormon War." When the Civil War broke out, Marmaduke, like many officers of southern heritage, questioned where his allegiance should lie. Although his father encouraged him to remain loyal to the Union, John S. chose the South. He resigned his commission and became a member of the Missouri State Guard. His uncle, Governor Jackson, commissioned him a colonel.[520]

John S. was the best-trained military man in Missouri at the outset of the war. After the rout of the State Guard at Boonville, Marmaduke resigned and offered his services to the Confederate government. He was commissioned a Lt. Colonel and placed under the command of now General Albert Sidney Johnston. Marmaduke "took a conspicuous part in the desperate battle of Shiloh, where he was wounded, and made a brigadier-general because of his bravery and unusual ability displayed upon the battlefield."[521] Transferred to Arkansas, Marmaduke was promoted to the rank of Major General. "While commanding the troops in Arkansas, General Marmaduke became involved in a quarrel with General Walker, a superior officer, who challenged him to a duel … In the encounter, General Walker was killed."[522]

John S. fought in multiple engagements in Arkansas and led two cavalry raids into southern Missouri in 1863. He was under the command of General Sterling Price during the invasion of Missouri in the fall of 1864. Price ordered a frontal assault on Fort Davidson on September 27, resulting in 1,200 Confederate casualties in the space of half an hour. This forced Price to cancel his planned attack on St. Louis and turn west. After being defeated at the Battle of Westport on October 23, 1864, Marmaduke's cavalry covered the retreating Confederate army. Marmaduke was captured at the Battle of Mine Creek, Kansas, on October 25, 1864, and was held as a prisoner of war until August of 1865.

After the war, Marmaduke traveled for six months in Europe. He engaged in several business enterprises until 1875, when he was appointed the state railroad commissioner. In 1880, Marmaduke tried, but failed, to get the Democratic nomination for governor of Missouri. In 1884, he won the nomination and served as governor for three years, before dying in office. A major centerpiece of his administrative efforts was railroad reform and breaking a major railroad strike without bloodshed.

The temptation exists to think J. S. Marmaduke's governorship represents a resurgence of Boonslick influence in politics. Unlike during his father and uncle's governorships, there was no longer a Central Clique, and in fact, the unique, regional identity of the Boonslick Country was long dead. Missouri had grown well beyond the region politically, culturally and economically. Once he went away to school, Marmaduke never again resided in the Arrow Rock area. He died of pneumonia on December 28, 1887, and was buried in Jefferson City.

George Caleb Bingham: The Missouri Artist

George Caleb Bingham is Missouri's most famous artist. His works are recognized internationally and are considered an important record of life in early Missouri.

Bingham was born March 20, 1811, in Augusta County, Virginia, to Henry Vest and Mary Amend Bingham. By the time he was twelve, he had developed an interest in drawing. In 1819, his family joined the tide of immigrants to the Boonslick Country, and they settled in Franklin. Henry Bingham opened the Square and Compass Tavern in 1820. He became partners with William Lamme in 1821, opening a tobacco factory and purchasing a 160-acre farm in Arrow Rock Township for growing tobacco.[523]

In December of 1823, Henry died at the age of 38. Mary opened a school for girls in Franklin the following year. The Bingham family eventually lost all their property except for the Arrow Rock farm. Mary sought the assistance of the Masonic Lodge of which her husband had been a member. The Franklin Lodge helped the family secure and move to the Arrow Rock farm in 1827. George was apprenticed to cabinetmaker and Methodist minister, Rev. Jesse Green, who lived nearby.[524]

From 1828 to 1832, Bingham was apprenticed in Boonville to another cabinetmaker and Methodist minister, Rev. Justinian Williams. Bingham expressed an interest in becoming either a lawyer or minister at this time. His friend, James Rollins of Columbia, said, "He frequently preached at the camp meetings common in these days." Bingham began painting signs and was making his early attempts to paint portraits.[525] About 1830, Bingham suffered an attack of measles that left him bald. He wore a wig the remainder of his life.[526]

In 1833, Bingham launched a career as a portrait artist, probably in Arrow Rock. The two earliest surviving portraits from this period are of Dr. and Mrs. Sappington, painted in 1834. Both portraits are now housed in the Arrow Rock State Historic Site visitors' center. Bingham acquired a studio in Columbia, and the *Missouri Intelligencer* noted in 1835 that although "He never saw a portrait painted in his life," he had in his studio a "collection of well finished portraits." He also began traveling extensively seeking portrait commissions. His travels took him to Liberty, St. Louis, Louisville, Kentucky, and Natchez, Mississippi.[527]

Bingham married Elizabeth Hutchinson of Boonville in April of 1836. On July 27, 1837, he purchased Lot 14 of Block 3 in Arrow Rock from

Claiborne Fox Jackson and began construction of a brick Federal-style house. A frame second story was added to the brick first story. There was also an ell to the house, a dogtrot porch connecting the house to a detached kitchen. The Works Progress Administration (WPA) removed the second story and the ell in a 1936 restoration project.[528] Some authorities believed the second story and the ell were not original, and dated to the 1870s or later.[529] Repair work undertaken by the Department of Natural Resources in 1998 discovered the foundation of the house extended three to four feet below ground level and was resting on massive stone piers spaced about three feet apart. The foundation was far more substantial than what was needed to support a single story brick house, or even a brick house with a frame second story.

Bingham Turley, a lifelong Arrow Rock resident and distant cousin of the artist, related family oral history concerning the house's construction. His great-grandfather was a carpenter and a first cousin to Bingham. Bingham had intended to build a two-story brick house, but the expense was too great. His cousin suggested they finish the second story as frame to save money.[530] The ell was original to the house, and the Missouri State Park Board conducted an archaeological excavation and reconstruction of it in 1964–1965.[531] Although there is still debate on the originality of the second story, this author believes Mr. Turley's account is correct. Unfortunately, the physical evidence to prove or disprove the date of construction is gone.

Bingham also purchased a small part of a lot on Main Street across from the Tavern. While there is no conclusive evidence, it seems probable he maintained a small studio there. As Bingham developed his art career, he was often on the move. Between 1837 and 1840, he traveled extensively to Fayette, Glasgow, Boonville, Rocheport, St. Louis, Philadelphia, Baltimore and New York City. From 1841 to 1844, he was in Washington, D.C. painting portraits. In 1843, he wrote Elizabeth from Washington, D.C. saying, "I can be nothing else but a painter and as a painter, how much so ever I might desire it, I cannot live at Arrow Rock."[532] Bingham sold his Arrow Rock house in 1845, but the deed was not filed until January 12, 1857, probably pending payment.[533]

Bingham was very interested in politics despite his assertion he could only be a painter. In the spring of 1840, he was active in the Whig Party presidential convention held in Rocheport. On August 1 of that year, he was an election judge in Arrow Rock's first election.[534] Bingham also continued to maintain his residence in Arrow Rock after he sold the house. In 1846, he was elected as the Saline County representative to the Missouri State Legislature. His opponent, Erasmus D. Sappington, contested the election and won, and was thus seated instead of Bingham. Bingham was elected to the Arrow Rock Board of Trustees on April 24, 1847. The board members voted him in as chairman.[535] In May of 1848, Bingham was again nominated as the Whig candidate to the State House of Representatives, but he declined the nomination. In June, he accepted the nomination and this time defeated Erasmus Sappington for the office.

Personal tragedies, fairly typical of 19th century Missouri, visited the Bingham family. Bingham's first son, Newton, was born in March of 1837, but died in March of 1841. Horace, his second son, was born that same month. A daughter, Clara, was born in 1845, but Elizabeth died on November 29, 1848, after giving birth to another son, Joseph. Joseph died the following month. It appears his mother and his surviving children continued to occupy the Arrow Rock house. Bingham's sister, Amanda, wrote to their brother, Henry, on January 1, 1849, "We are at this time staying at George's with Mother and his dear motherless children."[536] At the same time, there was an application for renting the house, but Bingham refused because he expected Henry to occupy it in the spring. On December 2, 1849, Bingham married his second wife, Eliza K. Thomas of Columbia. Her parents, Rev. Dr. Robert Stewart Thomas and Elvira (Johnston) Thomas, were co-founders of William Jewell College in Liberty, Missouri.[537]

From 1844 to 1851, Bingham painted many of the genre scenes for which he is famous: *Fur Traders Descending the Missouri, The Concealed Enemy, The Jolly Flatboatmen, Raftsmen Playing Cards, Lighter Relieving a Steamer Aground, The Squatters, Fishing on the Mississippi* and *Shooting for the Beef.* The scenes captured images of the river men, pioneers and Indians in Missouri in an age before the popularization of the camera. Inspired by his political experiences, he painted a series depicting the political processes of Missouri. In 1851, he was in Columbia working on *The County Election* and *Canvassing for a Vote.* He briefly returned to Arrow Rock when his mother died. In 1853, he began painting *Stump Speaking.* From these paintings, one can discern the election practices of the time.[538]

Over the years, there have been speculations and claims that the subjects in these paintings represent specific people and buildings in Arrow Rock.

Near the end of his life, Dr. Oscar Potter produced a key for *The County Election* and *Stump Speaking*, identifying residents of Arrow Rock.[539] Despite Potter's friendship with Bingham, some scholars doubted the authenticity of his identification key. There is evidence, however, that Bingham modeled his figures on real people. On April 10, 1854, Bingham wrote to his friend, James Rollins:

> *I have already commenced thinking for another large composition, which I will entitle 'Verdict of the People.' I intend it to be a representation of the scene that takes place at the close of an exciting political contest, just when the final result of the ballot is proclaimed from the stand of judges. The subject will doubtless strike you as one well calculated to furnish that contrast and variety of expression, which confers the chief value upon pictures of this class. I might very properly introduce into it some of those comically long faces which were seen about Fayette, Missouri, when our friend Claib [Claiborne Fox Jackson] was so genteelly whipped last summer...It is much larger and will contain more striking points than either of its predecessors [Stump Speaking and County Election]. I desire it to cap the climax.*[540]

Bingham's art was an expression of his political views and a way of tweaking the nose of opposition members in the Democratic Party. The December 9, 1858, edition of the Marshall *Weekly Democrat* seems to further confirm Dr. Potter's assertion the images were based on real people.

> *Daily Expected. — Mr. Geo. C. Bingham of this place, the distinguished "Missouri Artist," is daily expected at home from a long professional tour in Europe, during which he completed full length portraits of Washington and Jefferson for the State. These are to be suspended in the Capitol at Jefferson City, and it is said are master pieces of art, securing immortal fame to the artist. — [Columbia Statesman]*
>
> *Mr. Bingham is, we believe, a native of this county, and represented it one term in the Legislature several years ago, The portraits in his painting of the County Election, are many of them if not all from the faces of some of our worthiest citizens, and no one acquainted with the originals would fail to recognize them in the picture. Mr. B.'s relatives still reside in Saline county.*[541]

In both *The County Election* and *Stump Speaking* there is a rotund man conspicuously seated on a platform. Mr. C. B. Rollins, the son of James Rollins, said the portly man was former Governor Meredith M. Marmaduke. Rollins recalled, "Marmaduke ... was so insulted when even his friends recognized him as this figure that he threatened a libel suit and went so far as to challenge Bingham to a duel."[542]

Perhaps Bingham did not intend this figure to be Marmaduke or anyone else. Using actual people as models, however, would certainly impart a sense of realism to the painting. It seems safe to say these figures were at least patterned after people Bingham regularly saw. It seems less likely the street scenes are specific representations of Arrow Rock or any other community. The paintings represent artistic compositions rather than a "photographic" image. The architecture of the buildings he painted was so commonplace the pictures could easily represent any Missouri town of the period. However, it can be said the activities depicted in Bingham's works actually occurred in the streets and along the waterfront of Arrow Rock.

Bingham went to France to pursue his study of art in August of 1856. After living in Paris a few months, he moved to Dusseldorf, Prussia (Germany), where he remained until January of 1859. When he came back to visit family in Arrow Rock, his reputation preceded him:

> *George C. Bingham. — Wednesday's Herald has the following: We understand this gentleman, who has earned a world wide reputation as an artist, who has been a long time absent in Europe, is now in Jefferson City, and expects soon to visit Saline county, his former home, and the scene of his early triumphs. We think the citizens of Saline county should receive him with some public expression of regard, not as a politician, but as a great man, a fellow-citizen, and one of the most distinguished artists of the age.*

Weekly Democrat, Marshall, Missouri, Feb. 4, 1859.[543]

In May, Bingham again departed for Dusseldorf, but returned in September due to the death of his father-in-law. This was his last visit overseas, and he returned to Columbia, Missouri. Eliza taught music at Stephens College. Daughter Clara presented to the legislature an embroidered likeness of President Washington, hailed for its realism.[544]

By 1861, the family had moved to Independence, Missouri. Bingham was distressed as the threat of civil war loomed over the nation. He wrote to his friend James Rollins that there was no portrait work to be obtained. In the summer of 1861, he was appointed a captain of the United States Volunteer Reserve Corps in Kansas City. He found military duty unpleasant and resigned in January of 1862. He was subsequently appointed State Treasurer.

In August of 1863, General Thomas Ewing ordered the evacuation and destruction of farms and homes in the Missouri counties bordering Kansas. His objective was to retaliate for William Quantrill's raid on Lawrence, Kansas, and deprive the Confederate guerrillas of food and sanctuary. Bingham was outraged and confronted Ewing, declaring, "If you persist in executing that order, I will make you infamous with pen and brush as far as I am able."[545] Union and Confederate supporters suffered alike under the order, and no compensation or provision was made for the resulting refugees. After the war, as he promised, Bingham painted *Order No. 11* depicting the excesses of General Ewing.

In 1866, Bingham was a candidate for Congress but was defeated in the nomination process. In 1869, he was elected school director in Independence. He moved to Kansas City in 1870 and traveled extensively for almost three years. In 1874, he was elected to the Kansas City Board of Police Commissioners. In January of 1875, Governor Charles Hardin appointed him Adjutant General of Missouri.

Personal tragedy continued to follow Bingham. In October of 1876, Eliza became mentally deranged and was institutionalized in Fulton, Missouri, until her death on November 3. Bingham himself became ill and was given leave from state office. After recovering his health somewhat, he was appointed Professor of Art at the University of Missouri-Columbia in 1877. In June of 1878, Bingham married his third wife, Mrs. Martha "Mattie" Lykins of Kansas City. Shortly thereafter, he was appointed a commissioner to select a design for the Robert E. Lee Monument Association, and accordingly, he traveled to Richmond, Virginia. When he returned to Missouri, he was ill with pneumonia. Bingham died of *cholera morbus* on July 7, 1879, and was buried in Union Cemetery of Kansas City.

In the midst of his political and public service endeavors, Bingham continued painting portraits and genre scenes of life in Missouri as he had experienced it. Bingham was always, first and foremost, the "Missouri Artist." In 1940, Albert Christ-Janer, an early Bingham biographer, summarized his contributions to the nation: "We are indebted to him for his lasting representations of the scenes which surrounded him, scenes which have kept alive for us today part of the seething, rugged and vigorous life which bequeathed to us the social and economic structure that is our own."[546]

George Caleb Bingham remains Arrow Rock's most famous resident. The Department of the Interior, National Park Service, designated his home, located in Arrow Rock State Historic Site, a National Historic Landmark on December 21, 1965.[547] Although it no longer has its second story, it has been restored and furnished as a small Federal-style house of the period. Each year, hundreds of Missouri elementary school children are introduced to the life of George Caleb Bingham and early 19th century life through interpretive programs held in the house.

Bingham led a very active life. He moved frequently and demonstrated just how mobile people in the 19th century could be. Because of his many cultural and political contributions, it is easier to follow the events of his life through a chronology:

- 1811 Born in Augusta County, Virginia.
- 1819 Family moves to Franklin, Missouri.
- 1820 Reportedly observes Chester Harding completing a portrait of Daniel Boone.
- 1823 Father dies.
- 1824 Mother opens school for girls.
- 1827 Family moves to farm near Arrow Rock. Apprenticed to cabinetmaker and Methodist minister Jesse Green. Studies religion and law and preaches.
- 1828 Apprenticed to cabinetmaker and Methodist minister Justinian Williams in Boonville.
- 1830 Contracts measles. Begins painting portraits.
- 1834 Paints portraits of Dr. and Mrs. Sappington. Meets James Rollins of Columbia, becoming fast friends.
- 1835 Paints self-portrait. Travels to St. Louis seeking portrait commissions.
- 1836 Marries Sarah Elizabeth Hutchison of Boonville in April.
- 1837 Son, Newton, is born. Bingham purchases lot 14 of block 3 in Arrow Rock on July 27 for $50 from Claiborne Fox Jackson and begins building a brick home.

- 1838 Lives in Philadelphia four months, travels to New York and exhibits a painting *Western Boatmen Ashore*.
- 1838 – 1840 Returns to Arrow Rock, painting portraits and sketches life in the country and on the Missouri River.
- 1840 Attends Whig Convention in Rocheport, Missouri. Serves as election judge of first election for Town Trustees held in Arrow Rock.
- 1840 –1844 Lives with his family in Washington, D.C.
- 1841 Newton dies in March; another son, Horace, is born the same month.
- 1844 Completes *The Jolly Flatboatmen* then returns to Missouri, participates in Whig Convention in Boonville.
- 1845 Daughter, Clara, is born. Submits four paintings to the American Art Union: *Fur Traders Descending the Missouri; The Concealed Enemy; Cottage Scenery; Landscape*. Sells Arrow Rock home, but deed is not filed.
- 1846 Runs for state representative from Saline County. Narrowly defeats Erasmus Sappington, who contests, then wins the election.
- 1847 Elected to Arrow Rock Board of Trustees and is made chairman. Completes *Lighter Relieving a Steamer Aground; Raftsmen Playing Cards*.
- 1848 Attends Whig Convention in Boonville. Defeats Erasmus Sappington in election for state representative from Saline County. Sarah dies in Arrow Rock in November; infant son, Joseph, dies in December. Completes *Captured by Indians* and *Stump Orator*.
- 1849 Marries Eliza Thomas of Columbia.
- 1850 – 1851 Exhibits *Shooting for the Beef* in St. Louis. Moves to New York. Completes *Fishing on the Mississippi; The Squatters; The Wood Boat; Trapper's Return; Checker Players*.
- 1851 Mother dies in Arrow Rock, and he returns to Missouri. Begins painting *The Emigration of Daniel Boone*. Opens a studio in Columbia, Missouri.

- 1852 Attends Whig convention in Baltimore.
- 1853 Travels to New Orleans, Lexington, Kentucky, and New York. In Philadelphia supervising engraving of *The County Election*. Begins painting *Stump Speaking*.
- 1854 In Philadelphia and New York, returns briefly to St. Louis.
- 1855 Completes *Verdict of the People*, the third and final installment of his "election series."
- 1856 Missouri legislature commissions full-length portraits of George Washington and Thomas Jefferson. Travels to Paris, France, then on to Dusseldorf, Germany.
- 1857 Deed to house in Arrow Rock is finally filed.
- 1859 Returns to Missouri with finished portraits and installs them in capitol building.
- 1860 Residing in Independence, Missouri.
- 1861 Becomes captain in the U.S. Volunteer Reserve Corps in Kansas City. Son, James Rollins, is born.
- 1862 – 1865 Resigns as captain. Appointed treasurer of the state of Missouri.
- 1863 Confronts Union General Thomas Ewing over his "scorched earth" policy. Threatens to make Ewing infamous.
- 1865 Begins painting *Order No. 11* in response to General Thomas Ewing's decree of August, 1863. Residing at Bingham-Waggoner House in Independence.
- 1870 Moves to Kansas City, Missouri.
- 1871 – 1873 Travels to Philadelphia, Colorado, Texas and Kentucky.
- 1874 Appointed Kansas City Police Commissioner.
- 1875 Appointed Adjutant General of Missouri.
- 1876 Eliza suffers from mental disorder and dies while institutionalized in Fulton, Missouri.
- 1877 Appointed professor of art at the University of Missouri.
- 1878 Marries Mrs. Martha "Mattie" Lykins in Kansas City. Travels to Virginia.
- 1879 Ill with pneumonia. Dies of *cholera morbus* on July 7 and is buried in Union Cemetery in Kansas City.[548]

John Sites, Gunsmith

A wide variety of skilled tradesmen lived in Arrow Rock. These included blacksmiths, wagon wrights, saddle makers, coopers, carpenters, boat builders, stonemasons and potters. One such tradesman, gunsmith John P. Sites, Jr., left his mark on the history of Arrow Rock. An examination of his life also provides a contrast of the life of middle-class merchants and tradesmen with those of the farmers and wealthy plantation owners.[549]

Sites, popularly known as "Uncle Johnnie" later in life, was born in Rockingham County, Virginia, on May 31, 1821. His father, John Sites, Sr., was a skilled gunsmith when he moved his family to Marion in Cole County, Missouri, in 1834. The following year, he established a gunsmith shop in Boonville, which thrived until his death in 1853. John, Jr. worked as an apprentice for his father until 1841. On September 23rd of that year, he married Nancy "Nannie" Jane Tool (sometimes spelled Toole) of Madison County, Kentucky.[550] Nancy was born on April 3, 1825.

Shortly after their marriage, John Jr. established a gunsmith shop in Clifton, Cooper County, Missouri. In 1844, the couple relocated to Arrow Rock where John set up another gunsmith shop. Their only son, Charles, was born October 22 of that year, but died on July 31, 1855. John and Nannie lived at various locations in Arrow Rock and reportedly opened their home to orphans. For example, they raised a grandnephew, Ernest Randolph. In 1866, they purchased a small brick home on the corner of 5th and High Streets for $600. Records indicate this house had been built by 1837.[551]

Sites' first shop was located on Main Street, across from the Tavern and approximately where a large interpretive sign now stands. Unfortunately, there is little information about his business in these early years. Sites' arrival in Arrow Rock coincided with the boom period of the town. The Santa Fe trade through Arrow Rock was in its last days, but the great migrations to California and Oregon were soon to begin. Guns made by John Sites, Jr. have been found in California, Oregon, Montana and New Mexico, evidence that he supplied some of the westward bound immigrants and traders. Sites could build an entire gun "lock, stock and barrel" although much of his work probably involved repairs and converting rifles from flintlock to the more efficient percussion lock.[552]

Thomas C. Rainey knew John Sites well and reported he never lost faith in Arrow Rock. He must have come close, however, because he put his shop and home up for sale in January of 1868, "being desirous of closing out and winding up business."[553] Although he sold the shop building, he had no takers for the little house on 5th and High Streets. In March of that year, he purchased part of lot 92 in back of the Masonic Hall. He continued his gun business at the location where the restored gunsmith shop now stands.[554]

In 1872, the Sites began enlarging their home. They rented a house from merchant Ben F. Townsend for $6.00 a month from November, 1872, until September, 1875, while the improvements were underway. This work included raising the roof, adding two rooms, a stairway, storeroom and a Victorian style porch. Although the house seems very elegant, by Victorian standards it is still considered modest. While working on the house in 1875, Sites fell from a ladder and broke his collarbone.

Sites also bought merchandise from Ben Townsend but did not always pay his bills promptly. He began paying interest on his account and settled his debt by bartering gunpowder, shot, gun wads and work on "John T. gun." This was probably a gun belonging to John Townsend, Ben's son.[555] Bartering was still a common practice among merchants and their customers for settling accounts. Sites also owned some property along the Boonville-Arrow Rock road, now within the state historic site. He became rather well known locally for the peach orchard he maintained there.[556]

Thomas Rainey described John Sites as, "... good natured; stammered badly and when he was using his mouthpiece as a gateway for profanity, he smoked." John was not a religious man, but Nannie was a Campbellite. Since that denomination did not have a church in Arrow Rock, once a year he took Nannie to church services in Cooper County. At one of these meetings, he repented, was baptized and joined the church. Rainey said, "We did not believe it was possible for John to quit both smoking and swearing, as he proposed to do. We thought if he did not smoke he would swear on account of it, and if he did not swear he would have to smoke to console himself.... But we were mistaken. I never knew such another change in a man. He stopped swearing; he stopped smoking, and became an active, zealous, missionary Christian to the end of his life. He was largely instrumental in building and supporting the Christian church in Arrow Rock."[557]

Rainey further stated John could not read or write, and this was also noted in the 1880 census. Nannie would read to him from the Bible, and he would memorize the verses. Some descendants dispute he was entirely illiterate.[558] Sites liked to argue church doctrine and would quote the scriptures he knew. If his opponent quoted a verse John did not know, he would end the debate by raising his voice, citing a verse he knew, then would tuck his cane under his arm and walk off laughing.[559]

Rainey described Nannie as very delicate, "though she looked well." He wrote, "They lived only a short block and half from my store, but often Nannie positively could not walk to it. John would hitch his gentle old horse to a buggy, and Nannie would ride down. She was a handsome, tidy lady, but also very timid, so that John would have to lead the horse, to be sure of the safety of his precious freight. She would be all dressed up, and here they would come, John leading and looking admiringly around as if Nannie were a great pound cake with icing all over.

A more gallant and devoted husband never lived, and Nannie knew it. She kept his house neatly, did the domestic work which John did not voluntarily take off her hands, fed him a diet well prepared and was a faithful, good wife."[560]

By the latter half of the 19th century, economically priced, mass manufactured guns became available through mail order. Gunsmiths like Sites went through a transition. They still dealt in guns and repaired them, but they seldom built them. Thomas Rainey described Sites as "handy" with tools and a "… healer of the infirmities of old guns, clocks, pocket-knives and women's scissors."[561] The Arrow Rock *Enterprise* in 1891 carried the following ad under the heading "Sporting Goods:" "If you want anything in the line of Guns, Ammunition, Fishing Tackle or anything of the kind, call on J. P. Sites." The Arrow Rock *Statesmen* carried this front-page ad on January 8, 1897:

> *"HUNTERS*
> *If you want Anything in the Sporting Line*
> *CALL ON J. P. Sites*
> *He carries a general stock of*
> *Guns, Pistols, Ammunition*
> *Fishing Tackle*
> *He Makes a Specialty of*
> *Lock and Gun Repairing"*[562]

Nannie Sites passed away on November 26, 1900, and was buried in the Arrow Rock cemetery. John went to live in Cooper County with his nephew Captain Tom Sites, who operated the steamboat *Nadine* on the Lamine and Missouri rivers. John passed away on April 9, 1904, and was buried in Arrow Rock. His property, assessed at $800 in 1877, sold for $595 after his death, an indication of the economic decline that had gripped Arrow Rock.[563]

The Friends of Arrow Rock, Inc. have restored the Sites home to a circa 1875 appearance. The gun shop has been restored and furnished to an 1850 – 1870 appearance. During restoration, the floor under the building underwent archaeological investigation, and the interior was restored according to the findings. Elderly residents who remembered the building in their youth corroborated architectural details, such as placement of windows. The shop is fully furnished with the tools for repairing or building a gun "lock, stock and barrel."

Wallace Gusler, master gunsmith at Colonial Williamsburg, visited Arrow Rock in September of 2000. He confirmed, to his knowledge, the Sites shop is the only historic gunsmith shop restoration in the original (not reconstructed) building and on its original location.[564] The Sites house and gun shop are open on guided tours and for school programs. Periodically, special demonstrations of 19th century gunsmith techniques are given in the shop.

The Calaboose and Godsey's Diggings

One of the most popular buildings with tourists in Arrow Rock is the stone jail known as the calaboose. It has an arch vault style of construction. Visitors squint through the heavy forged bars of the door into the dank single cell. At one time, the town board equipped it with a potbellied stove so prisoners could stay warm. The first calaboose was built in 1866 of hewn logs about 8-by-12 feet in size with a plank floor. On June 2, 1873, the Town Board discussed the cost of building a stone calaboose and sent out an invitation for bids. On June 9th, the bid was awarded to a "Mr. Ryan" although the amount is not recorded.

Some early tourist literature has been published indicating the jail is still awaiting its first prisoner. Although records are sparse, this is incorrect. The *Saline County Progress* carried a humorous remark from its Arrow Rock "correspondent" in the February 28, 1868 edition: "We have a calaboose or jail that is usually empty probably because we have neither Editor or Lawyer."[565] According to the Arrow Rock *Enterprise* newspaper, the Town Board ordered repairs to the structure in March of 1892. The remark "usually empty" and the fact the board was still maintaining the jail indicates it had at least some use on occasion.

Tom White was described as a jolly African American resident who had a distinctive laugh that "could be heard two blocks away." White also had a reputation for enjoying brandy, and when drinking he would laugh even louder. One night around 1920, Constable Robert Stith locked Tom in the jail after he had too much brandy. There were still several houses near the jail at that time. Tom hollered so loudly he woke everyone up. The residents got Constable Stith to let him out so they could sleep. He said the reason he hollered was because of the snakes in the cell. It is unknown whether the snakes were real or the result of an alcoholic delirium. In later years, Tom took great delight in telling people he was the last person ever to be locked up in the old Calaboose.[566] Another tradition says it was Ed Fizer, a white resident, who was locked in the calaboose.

The Board of Trustees devoted a considerable amount of time and expense to maintaining access to the Missouri River. Through the years they expended funds to build "bridges" in the intervening hollows between the riverfront and Main Street. Some of these "bridges" may have actually been embankments and rock walls, remnants of which may be seen along First and Van Buren and the approach to the river landing.

On March 2, 1848, the Board of Trustees officially opened "first street beginning from Main street and following said street until it intersects the street running from the river between Joseph Huston and J. A. J. Adertons Warehouses...."[567] Undoubtedly this route had long been in use, but now the town would pay for improvements. This was a long distance and an arduous grade for the wagon teamsters carrying commodities between the business district and the river landing.

The Town Board appropriated three hundred dollars on June 1, 1842, "for the grading and clearing out of that part of Main street lying nearest the Missouri river, as expressed in contract between (Burton) Godsey, Town, Trustees & Citizens."[568] This is possibly the earliest reference to what became known as "Godsey's Diggings," a rather well known and visible landmark in town.

The board sought to shorten the commercial route between the wharf and the business district by linking Main Street directly to the river landing. A committee was appointed on April 14, 1857, "to examine the practicability of opening the street through Godsey's diggings...."[569] The diggings became the butt of satire in the July 14, 1858 edition of the *Weekly Democrat* newspaper: "The work at Godsey's diggings goes on slowly. The contractors have ordered a ship load of boys from the Emerald Isle to finish the work, and we hear it hinted that our city fathers have ordered from the Novelty Works a double back-action steam engine to hoist freight and passengers from the landing. From a plan of the apparatus and machinery it presents quite a complete appearance. Engineers report that there will be power enough to raise 213 pounds of freight and two and a half passengers per day; and with careful handling the machinery will last just twenty-three days."[570]

The project was never completed, and it is not known how much money the town spent on it. Even if it had been completed, the degree of angle from the end of Main Street to the riverbank would have been too steep for it to be usable. The long route of First Street remained in use. Today, Godsey's Diggings remains as a ravine overgrown with trees and brush. The rock bluff at the east end of excavation still bears the marks of attempts to dig through it.

Store of Jay Marcellus Potter, #2 Public Square, across Main Street from the Tavern, c. 1870. Jay Potter is on the far right with the moustache and cane. Part of his inventory of books, school supplies, medicine bottles, and toys can be seen in the window. *Photo courtesy Dr. Thomas B. Hall III*

Main Street, looking east, c. 1890. Although they were muddy, macadam prevented the streets from becoming deeply rutted. *MDNR*

Samuel McMahan's dry goods store, c. 1898. This building was completely destroyed in the fire of 1901. *MDNR*

Ben Townsend's Livery Stable, c. 1890. The stable was located on the northwest corner of Main and Second Street. *FAR*

Thomas C. Rainey, the early chronicler of Arrow Rock history, 1914. *FAR*

Pharmacist Will Hubbard in his drug store on Main Street, c. 1900. *FAR*

T. B. Morris' "Cash Supply House" on Main Street, c. 1890. *FAR*

Hudson's hog train, c. 1910. On Main Street looking west toward the Masonic Lodge Hall. *FAR*

Group looking at new National Trails directional sign at the corner of 3rd and Main, c. 1912. The building was the African American Odd Fellows lodge hall, later moved to the north part of town and no longer standing. *MDNR*

Group of young men in Arrow Rock, c. 1898. Their attire indicates Arrow Rock still had something of a "western flavor" at this date. *MDNR*

Building a riverboat in the Moehle boatyard at the Arrow Rock landing, c. 1890. *FAR*

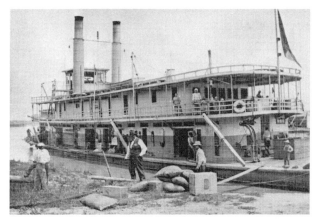

The *A. M. Scott*, loading cargo at the Arrow Rock landing, c. 1915. *MDNR*

Snagboat *Horatio Wright* c. 1900. Snag boats improved navigation by pulling up
dangerous snags and sawyers that accumulated in the river bed. *FAR*

Class of 1890, of the McMahan Institute. Anna (Reid) McMahan is on the left, and her husband Templeton McMahan stands behind her. Jesse Kibler, sister of "Miss Anna," is on the right. *MDNR*

A group of young men gathered in front of the Tavern, 1898. *MDNR*

Cutting hay with Deering farm equipment, c. 1898. Photo taken by George H. Bingham, a professional photographer in Arrow Rock. *MDNR*

Plowing corn rows in Diggs' field in the river bottoms, 1896. *MDNR*

Putting up hay on the Lawless farm in the Arrow Rock bottoms, c. 1900. *FAR*

Bascom Diggs, editor of the Arrow Rock *Statesman* newspaper, 1898. His growth had been stunted due to an accident as a child. *MDNR*

The Arrow Rock *Statesman* office and pressroom in the lower floor of the I.O.O.F. Lodge Hall, c. 1898. *MDNR*

The Big Spring, c. 1900. The spring was enclosed in what appears to be part of a steamboat boiler. *MDNR*

The Big Spring, c. 1933. *MDNR*

"The Boardwalk," looking east, pre-1901 fire. *MDNR*

Main Street business district after the 1901 fire, looking west. Right forefront is present-day boardwalk area with original two-story buildings. *MDNR*

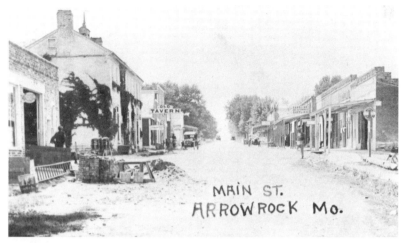

Main Street business district, 1916, looking west. On right, two-story buildings were rebuilt as one-story following 1901 fire. On left, note that additional buildings were on each side of the Tavern. *MDNR*

Main Street, c. 1930, looking east. Buildings in left forefront are now replaced by homes. Building on right no longer standing. *MDNR*

Main Street, c. 1940. *MDNR*

A view from the jail to the north, c. 1935. This photograph indicates how open the area around Arrow Rock once was. Trees were sparse in the prairie environment, and the larger ones had been cut down in the 19th century for lumber and steamboat fuel. *MDNR*

Shroyer gravesite, c. 1936. The picnic shelter in the recreation area is to the right, and the Missouri River can be seen to the left. Today, this panoramic view is obscured by thick forest growth. *MDNR*

Tavern, 1912. The building adjacent to it apparently dates from the mid-19th century, and may have been the two-story brick Academy building. *MDNR*

Tavern, 1926. The first restoration of the building had been completed the previous year. *MDNR*

The Tavern Rest Room, c. 1912. Established as "a means of teaching Missouri history to the passerby." It was from this beginning that the preservation of Arrow Rock began. Today, the room depicts the Huston Store as it may have appeared in 1840. *MDNR*

Rena Brown and her family, c. 1915. They were all employed as cooks, maids or waiters at the Tavern. *MDNR*

Georgia Willy (*left*) and her staff in the Tavern kitchen, c. 1956. Georgia was renowned for her pan-fried chicken. African Americans comprised the majority of the Tavern staff up through the early 1960s. *MDNR*

Congregation standing in front of Brown's Chapel Free Will Baptist Church, c. 1940s. *MDNR*

The African American School, c. 1940s. This is probably the third school built on the same location on Morgan Street. *MDNR*

Students at the Arrow Rock African School, c. 1943. *MDNR*

Dennis Banks, historian of Arrow Rock's African American churches. *FAR*

The Tavern, c.1914, looking west. *MDNR*

Dan Kuhn's steam sawmill behind the Tavern, 1907. The building in the background is the Academy Boarding House. *MDNR*

Students at the Arrow Rock Public School, 1889. *MDNR*

The Arrow Rock Public School, 1915. *MDNR*

The Arrow Rock Public School, after it burned in 1928. *MDNR*

View toward the "Courthouse" and Main Street, c. 1955. This gives an indication of the deteriorated condition of the town. The store building past the Courthouse was lost to fire in the 1960s. *MDNR*

Tavern, c. 1920, rear view before restoration. *MDNR*

Lucia Argubright, c. 1965.
Mrs. Argubright was a leader among
Arrow Rock residents in restoring their
historic homes. The Dr. Price house is
in the background. *FAR*

Sallie Hailey, Friends of Arrow Rock founding member, examines the Courthouse as it
undergoes restoration. c. 1960. *MDNR*

Firemen's Benefit Pig Supper on the Tavern lawn, c. 1970. On the left are Cora Lee
Miller, Marianne and Dr. John Lawrence, and on the right is Bill Miller. They were
instrumental in advancing historic preservation in the community. *Patricia McDaniel*

The 1872 Baptist Church was restored in 1960 as the Arrow Rock Lyceum Theatre. *MDNR*

No longer thought to be the 1839 courthouse, this early log building was the first restoration project of the Friends of Arrow Rock in 1960, and upon completion was deeded to the State of Missouri. *MDNR*

The John P. Sites House, 1907. The Edwards family then occupied it. *FAR*

J. P. Sites gun shop, before 1967 restoration. *FAR*

War and Its Aftermath

The Gathering Storm: Abolitionism and Judge Lynch

"It was resolved that Benjamin Hawpe be appointed Captain of Patrol and that William Parks, E. K. Chase & William H. McCowan be and are hereby appointed patrols for the Town of Arrow Rock for six months from date whose duty it shall be to guard the Town and prevent the unlawful meeting of Negroes and see that no Negro is out from home after nine o'clock at night without a pass and if so found shall be dealt with as the Law directs."[571] With this ordinance, the Board of Trustees reauthorized the slave patrols it established three years earlier. In the mind of the Southerners, the fears of a slave insurrection were increasing due to abolitionist activity.

The number of religious and civil organizations in the North calling for the abolition of slavery increased after 1833. These groups were generally labeled "free-soilers." Most Missourians found them repugnant, and few within the state dared challenge the "peculiar institution" of slavery. Senator Thomas Hart Benton did not support the free-soilers, but he did oppose the expansion of slavery into new territories.[572] This put him at odds with the "Central Clique" and his old ally, Claiborne Fox Jackson. Jackson, with the aid of William B. Napton, Sr., set about to undermine the political power of Benton. Together they drafted a set of resolutions that encompassed five main points:

> *1) Any attempt by Congress to pass legislation on slavery in the states was a violation of the Constitution.*
> *2) The organization of federal territories that excluded slavery was an insult to slave-holding states.*
> *3) The principles of the Missouri Compromise of 1821 were to be upheld.*
> *4) Only the people residing in a territory at the time they framed*

a constitution for state government could prohibit slavery. Thus, slavery could not be brought to a vote by later generations.

5) If Congress passed an act contrary to these principles, Missouri would "cooperate with other slaveholding states in taking such measures as may be deemed necessary for their mutual protection against northern fanaticism."[573]

The "Jackson Resolutions," as they became known, were passed in both houses of the Missouri legislature by an overwhelming majority and signed by Governor Austin King on March 10, 1849.[574] At that time, senators were elected by their state legislatures, not by popular vote. Consequently, Benton was out of office by 1851. He was elected to the Missouri House of Representatives and continued to fight to resume his federal senatorial career. However, he never regained his power and prestige in Missouri politics.

The ambitions of both sides of the slavery question soon focused on the Kansas Territory. Kansas was going to be the death of slavery or the preservation of it as far as Missourians were concerned. Free-soilers were moving into Kansas with the aid of the "New England Emigrant Aid Society." Pro-slavery Missourians were actively encouraged to go to Kansas to offset those numbers. But not all the Missourians who went to Kansas were pro-slavery.

British born George Howe Furse had joined a western fur trapping expedition under the Sublette brothers in 1832. On the way out from St. Louis and back, the expedition passed through Arrow Rock. Furse decided to settle in Arrow Rock, and in 1836, he married Martha Fall. Furse became a bookkeeper for Meredith Miles Marmaduke and tutored Marmaduke's children at their home. Furse resented the way slaves were treated, especially after witnessing one man literally wear his fingers to the bone cutting hemp. He argued against slavery on an "intellectual plane to avoid arousing the hostility of the violent sect."[575] Word began to spread Furse was an abolitionist. In mid-1856 after the birth of their fourth child, the Furse family left Arrow Rock. They moved to Kansas to join with other abolitionists.

Prominent men from Saline County aided the pro-slavery Kansas faction in 1855. The evening before the March 30 election for the Kansas legislature, pro-slavery leaders gathered at Lawrence and met at the tent of Claiborne Fox Jackson to receive voting instructions. As a result of this conference, the pro-slavery men carried the election. Returns showed 6,307 votes had been cast although the territory had only half that number of legal voters.[576] Anger and bitterness erupted into violence between the two sides.

Violence escalated into open warfare by May 21. "From time to time, provisions such as bacon, flour, potatoes, etc. together with arms and ammunition, were sent into Kansas from Saline [County]."[577] "Visiting statesmen" from Saline County such as Claiborne F. Jackson, W. B. Crews, William H. Letcher, and Frank Mitchell made trips to encourage the pro-slavery camps. Captain John Reid, who commanded Company D during the Mexican War, led a contingent of Saline County men to Kansas. Owing to subsequent events, few seemed willing to admit to their role in the violence. They fought against the free-soilers at Leavenworth and Osawatomie. At Marais de Cygne "... twenty-two free state men were captured, tied to stakes or trees and shot."[578] The violence between Missouri "border ruffians" and Kansas "Jayhawkers" continued right through the Civil War. Some authorities consider "Bleeding Kansas" to be the beginning of the Civil War.

By 1856, the Whig Party had collapsed nationally. Frank Blair of St. Louis was a leader of the Democratic faction that still backed Thomas Hart Benton. Blair, like Benton, supported limitations on the expansion of slavery. He attempted to build a coalition with the old-line Whigs and the Know-Nothing party. At the 1857 Democratic Party convention in Jefferson City, Benton's men nominated him for governor while the anti-Benton men nominated Trusten Polk. Slavery became a key issue, and Benton trailed far behind the other gubernatorial candidates in the election. Blair's coalition eventually fell apart, and Benton was out of politics.

In 1858, a large and festive barbecue was held in Arrow Rock to celebrate the final defeat of Blair and the Benton Democrats. A correspondent calling himself "ANTI-BLAIR" gave this report in the Sept. 3, 1858 edition of the Marshall *Weekly Democrat*:

> *When I arrived, I soon discovered that there was a large concourse of men of all political creeds; for this was no partisan meeting — they had met here for one purpose; to exult over the downfall of Blair and his satellites ... Dinner being over, there followed a 'feast of reason and flow of soul.' It being announced that Mr. C.F. Jackson would address the eager crowd, we all repaired to the rustic stand erected for the occasion, where Mr. J spoke in his usual*

able manner, for an hour and a half, to the great delight of his auditors....Our fellow townsman J. W. Bryant was then called for... to address the audience... He struck telling blows, It was a glorious day for Saline and the people of the whole of our proud State when Emancipation was repudiated, and Blair and Gardenshire driven to the wall...The dinner did credit to the hospitality of the citizens of Arrow Rock, and we, feeling 'good all over' concluded it was glory enough for one day and returned home.[579]

The slavery issue was rapidly coming to a head in the nation as well. Anti-abolition and anti-black fervor now reached its peak in Arrow Rock and Saline County. As a result, the spring and summer of 1859 saw tragic events, which mocked the judicial system and plunged Arrow Rock and Saline County into mob fury fueled by racism.

On May 13th, Benjamin Hinton of Waverly was found in his cabin, his skull crushed from a bludgeon. Robbery was clearly the motive as his possessions had been ransacked. John, a slave at a nearby farm, was arrested for the murder after he was allegedly found in the possession of blood-stained money he used to pay a debt. John confessed to a part in the crime, but said he had a white accomplice who had actually committed the murder. He was taken to Boonville for safekeeping as he was threatened with lynching in Marshall.

As Judge Russell Hicks of the Sixth Circuit Court in Lexington prepared for a July 19th trial, he received disturbing news from Arrow Rock:

While holding the Lafayette circuit court, a petition, signed by a large number of citizens of Saline, was presented to me, requesting a special term of the trial of the negro (John) as soon as convenient...Some days before the special term was held a Negro, named Holman, committed an assault upon a young man, named Durrett, inflicting a wound on one of his arms which greatly endangered his life, and will, it is thought, make him a cripple for life. This occurred in the neighborhood of Arrow Rock. Again a short time before the special term, a negro, named Jim, was charged with attempted rape on a white lady in the vicinity of Marshall. Both of these negroes were in jail. And yet again, on the day preceding the special term, a negro, belonging to Dr. Price, at Arrow Rock, had attempted rape upon a white girl,

*some twelve years of age. The girl was severely injured, and the
negro on Monday night was hung.*[580]

In the case of the twelve-year-old Arrow Rock girl, a "committee" of
Arrow Rock citizens was convened who "examined" the unnamed black
man and pronounced him guilty. Dr. Price, "being satisfied of his guilt,
delivered him up to the citizens...."[581]

On the day of John's trial, a large crowd of citizens, mainly from Arrow
Rock and Waverly, filled the courtroom and Public Square in Marshall.
Judge Hicks sternly warned the crowd against taking the law into their
own hands. John was tried and found guilty, but Judge Hicks told his
attorneys they would have time to prepare motions for a new trial, if they
so desired. Judge Hicks wrote, "At this time I saw, as I thought, signs of
impatience on the countenances of some, for the expected sentence. The
thought flashed across my mind that if the prisoner was publicly ordered
back to jail, he would never reach there."[582]

Court was recessed for the dinner hour, but John and Jim were ordered
to remain in the courthouse. Privately, the sheriff was told to convey John
back to jail once the crowd dispersed. Jim remained in the courthouse
under the guard of deputies and the jury. Judge Hicks walked with the
sheriff to insure John's arrival to the jail. When they reached the gate of the
courthouse, Judge Hicks saw a mob coming over the courthouse fence and
another coming down the street towards the jail. Judge Hicks had a limp
and could not keep up, but the sheriff and his prisoner reached the jail
before the mob.

James Shackelford of Arrow Rock Township stood on the jail steps and
harangued the crowd to action. The jailer was overpowered, and John and
Holman were taken out. The mob wrested Jim away from the deputies and
jury after threatening them with pistols. The three hapless black men were
taken to a walnut grove 200 yards north of the courthouse where Jim and
Holman were hanged, and John was burned to death at the stake. For
nearly ten minutes, he screamed out to those he knew in the crowd, begging
for help.

*"Judge Hicks was so much chagrined, mortified, and indignant at
the lawlessness of the people and the contempt they showed for his
court that he declared he would never again hold a term of court in
Saline County. Accordingly, he tendered his resignation which
was accepted."*[583]

Shackelford vigorously defended the lynching in several letters to the Marshall *Weekly Democrat* and sought to cast the blame for the horrible events elsewhere: "Abolitionists and Negro sympathizers have a great deal to do in creating a spirit of insubordination amongst our Negro population. Every abolitionist ought to be driven out of the country; every free Negro should be sold into slavery or go out of the state; no more emancipation without sending the Negroes out of the state."[584]

The raid on the federal arsenal at Harper's Ferry, Virginia, by abolitionist John Brown and his followers in October of 1859, sought to spark a nationwide slave revolt. Emotions in Saline County still ran high over the summer lynching, and news of Brown's raid further inflamed passions. Meetings were held at Arrow Rock and other communities in which speeches were made and resolutions adopted condemning the raiders and "their sympathizers, aiders and abettors."[585] William B. Sappington, Dr. Legrand Atwood and Thomas Harvey were appointed to deliver a memorial to the state legislature relative to the issue of emancipation of the slaves:

> *First, Pledging the State of Missouri to other southern states in such measures as may be necessary for the maintenance of their rights under the constitution.*
>
> *Second, To revive the militia laws.*
>
> *Third, To make void negro testimony received in the courts against the citizens of those states where negroes are permitted to testify against white persons.*
>
> *Fourth, To amend the constitution so that Negroes convicted of rape or other high crimes should suffer death.*[586]

James Shackelford, firebrand of the Marshall lynching, offered a fifth resolution which was also adopted by the committee: "That in the event of the election of a black-republican president in 1860, that a convention of the southern states be called to take such measures as will conduce to the great interests of the south."[587] This, of course, was a direct attack on the Republican Party and their Presidential candidate, Abraham Lincoln.

In December of 1859, a barn belonging to George Neff about six miles northwest of Arrow Rock burned. There was little of value in it, and the total loss was around $300. Automatically, a black man was accused. "A negro man was tried in Arrow Rock... on a charge of having set fire to it, but no proof being adduced of his guilt, he was acquitted."[588] It is interesting to note, he was "tried" in Arrow Rock even though the court did not meet there. Given the atmosphere at the time, it is remarkable the man survived. Perhaps the minimal property loss, combined with cold weather, dampened enthusiasm for another lynching. Perhaps the citizens realized they had overplayed their hand earlier in the summer. For example, James Shackelford placed his farm "near the Arrow Rock road"[589] up for sale on December 2, and eventually left the county.

In 1860, enslaved persons only made up 9.7% of Missouri's population and about 3% of the total in the United States. In contrast, the total population of Saline County was 14,699, and one third, or 4,876, were slaves. There was only a handful of free blacks in the county, and their freedom was constantly in jeopardy. They were in danger of being abducted by slave traders and "sold south." As the election of 1860 approached, the property rights of slave owners were a key political issue for the citizens of Arrow Rock and the Missouri River counties where slavery was concentrated.

Arrow Rock resident Claiborne Fox Jackson carried the 1860 election as governor. John Bell of Kentucky carried the vote for President in Saline County. Abraham Lincoln, "the black Republican," though elected President, failed to get a single vote in Saline County. Upon assuming office, Governor Jackson issued a call for volunteers for the Missouri State Guard, and the men of Arrow Rock and Saline County swelled its ranks.

Civil War

The sectionalism and border warfare that divided America in the 1850s erupted into full-scale war with the bombardment of Fort Sumter, South Carolina, on April 14, 1861. Arrow Rock was not to be the scene of any major battles. However, events in the community are indicative of conditions experienced in Missouri: the imposition of martial law, the cruelty of guerrilla raids and the pitting of family and friends against each other.

Former Governor Meredith Miles Marmaduke remained a staunch Union supporter. His son, John S., torn over which side to choose, "...took a furlough, came home, and talked the matter over with his father before making a final decision."[590] A family member related his father told him, "John, there can be but one result. You will sacrifice your profession. Secession will fail. Slavery will be abolished. But you must decide for yourself following your own convictions."[591] Governor Marmaduke took this message to his fellow Saline citizens but to no avail.

John S. resigned his commission in the U.S. Army and joined the Missouri State Guard. Governor Jackson's son, William, also resigned his commission in the Army and formed a unit known as the Saline Jackson Guards. As the war intensified, they acted as partisan guerrillas.

When news of the war came, there were public meetings and a general consternation over what to do. Abraham Lincoln issued a call to the states on April 15 for 75,000 troops to "put down the rebellion." Secretary of War Simon Cameron informed Jackson Missouri's quota was to be 3,120 men. Jackson's reply was short and terse, "June 16, 1861, Honorable Simon Cameron, Secretary of War — Sir, your requisition is unconstitutional, and in its object inhuman and diabolical. Not one man will Missouri provide to carry on any such unholy crusade against her southern sisters."[592]

Jackson assembled the pro-secessionist Missouri State Guard at Camp Jackson near St. Louis. On May 10th, U.S. Army Captain Nathaniel Lyon captured the camp and most of the guardsmen without firing a shot. Rioting then commenced in the streets of St. Louis, and was subdued by force by Lyon. With this element of the State Guard neutralized, Lyon was promoted to general and on June 14 captured Jefferson City and placed the capital under martial law. Jackson and the pro-secessionist members of the legislature had fled to Boonville at Lyon's approach. Seventeen hundred troops under Lyon prepared to advance on Boonville by steamboat.[593]

Jackson, against the advice of his nephew Colonel John S. Marmaduke, decided to make a stand at Boonville. Although he had 1,800 men under his command, only 500 to 600 were armed well enough to participate in a battle. Most of them were just farmers and laborers armed with shotguns and small caliber hunting rifles. Arrow Rock members of the State Guard experienced their first battle on June 17, 1861. The armies met just east of Boonville. Before the guardsmen could get in range with their weapons, the Federal troops fired a cannon barrage. After the dreadful cannonading, the inexperienced guardsmen "… left in about the order they came — every man for himself."[594] The First Battle of Boonville was derisively known thereafter as the "Boonville Races" because of the speed with which the guardsmen fled and the Federals pursued them.

Will H. Wood, the Arrow Rock merchant, was present at the battle as were two of his brothers. Wood related to Thomas Rainey in later years,

"...he came away, bringing his armor from the field, and as he was moving along pretty lively, by the time he came to the LaMine River he was hot, tired and very thirsty. He crossed the river, stopped at a cabin near the road, and asked a lady for a drink of water. She came out with a large gourd full...Then she inquired 'What is your name?' 'My name is Wood.' Waving her gourd up the road, the disgusted woman said, 'Go on! Go on! You are running stock! Two more of your name have just passed on!'"[595] This was the end of Wood's military career.

On July 22, a state convention was convened in Jefferson City. The major executive offices and seats in the general assembly were declared "vacated," and the convention itself filled the empty positions. Hamilton R. Gamble, a former resident of the Big Bottoms, was elected governor by the convention. Jackson attempted to maintain a government in exile: first in Neosho, Missouri, then Little Rock, Arkansas, and finally in Marshall, Texas. Despite Jackson's efforts, Missouri was officially secured for the Union.

Secessionists began shooting at passing riverboats from the heights of the Arrow Rock bluffs. The Federal response forced the Arrow Rock Masonic Lodge to cancel its August 9, 1861, meeting. "On the night for our regular meeting in August, 1861, our town was cannonaded by Federal troops descending the river in steamboats, and nearly every person in town fled to the country, hence there was no meeting, and this is the first time we have had no meeting on the regular night since our lodge was first organized."[596] The damage must have been minimal for little information survives of this bombardment. However, it was a harbinger of worse things to come.

As Arrow Rock had been a crossroads for Indians, explorers and settlers, it now became a crossroads for military forces. State Guard troops under General Sterling Price were moving north towards the Union strong point of Lexington. General Martin Green in northeast Missouri began moving southwest to join him. On September 13, U.S. Colonel Jefferson Davis hoped to prevent Green from crossing the river and dispatched "... a regiment on the (steamboat) *War Eagle*, with some cannon, to Arrow Rock and Glasgow."[597] He was too late for he wired General Fremont later that same day, "Green has crossed at Arrow Rock and is marching on Booneville."[598] On September 18, the Battle of Lexington was underway, and Col. Davis "...sent two regiments to Arrow Rock, with orders to take a post in a day or two opposite Glasgow."[599] His objective was to relieve the besieged Federal garrison in Lexington. However, he first had to secure the river crossings to prevent any reinforcements from reaching Price.

Price captured Lexington on the 23rd, and shortly thereafter the St. Louis Conference of the Methodist Church opened at Arrow Rock with thirty ministers present. Rev. Dr. William Prottsman made the motion the convention should remove to Waverly in order to be nearer the protection of pro-Confederate forces. After some ridicule, the motion was tabled. A short time later a steamboat ascended the river, and panic ensued as the populace expected Federal troops to either shell the town or disembark momentarily. "A motion to adjourn was quickly passed. In a very few minutes all the preachers were in buggies or on horseback, racing to Waverly. It was reported that all you could see was flying coat-tails!"[600]

On December 2, 1861, Major General Henry Halleck sent the following orders to Colonel Frederick Steele at Sedalia, "It is proposed that you send a cavalry force of, say 400 to Marshall to seize all secessionists in arms or who have been in arms, then move on to Arrow Rock or to Grand Pass and Waverly...."[601] Steele replied to Halleck that 400 men of Merrill's Horse Cavalry were already heading towards Marshall and had captured a supply train bound for Price's army. The force then turned east towards Arrow Rock, and Steele gave the following report:

> *December 5, marched about 15 miles; took several prisoners, some horses and mules, and encamped on the farm of the notorious Claiborne F. Jackson, and raised the stars and stripes over the traitor's house.*
>
> *December 6, marched north about 18 miles through Arrow Rock, where we found several kegs of powder concealed in warehouses; destroyed the ferry-boat, and while doing it our men were fired upon by a few men from across the river; the fire having been returned, the enemy ran. Leaving Arrow Rock, we marched north through Saline City, where we captured some arms and powder; encamped on Judge Robert Field's farm.*[602]

The activities of Merrill's cavalry led to the closing of the Arrow Rock post office on December 7. It was not reopened until January 25, 1862.[603]

During 1862, many of the Missouri State Guard units were disbanded or turned over to regular Confederate army units. Many family names associated with Arrow Rock and vicinity appear on the muster rolls of Companies G and H, Second Missouri Cavalry, Company E, First Missouri Cavalry, and a scattering of other Confederate units operating in the trans-Mississippi west. There are too many to enumerate here. Some of these men fought at Shiloh and Vicksburg. Colonel Stephen Cooper, later an Arrow Rock merchant, led his regiment at the Battle of Franklin, Tennessee, "coming out of it with one arm shot away and half his men killed."[604] Still others joined the "irregular troops," the bands of partisan guerrillas commonly known as "bushwhackers" that roamed the countryside.

At the beginning of the war, Federal troops stationed in Missouri were primarily from Illinois, Indiana and Iowa. These regular army troops were sent east of the Mississippi River as fighting intensified in that theater. Thereafter, most of the Union troops stationed in Missouri belonged to one of three types of units. The Missouri State Militia (M.S.M) was armed, equipped and paid by the U. S. government, and they ranged throughout the state combating guerrillas and Confederate raiders. The Enrolled Missouri Militia (E.M.M.) was usually active within a specific locality and often did garrison duty in towns or at strategic points such as bridges and ferry crossings. They were raised, paid and equipped by the state of Missouri although they took orders from regular army commanders. Their level of training and arms was generally inferior to the M.S.M. The Provisional Militia was perhaps more similar to the old-time militia, when local farmers and laborers were called up by the state for special emergencies or for specified short periods of time. They were probably the least equipped and disciplined of the three forces.

Records of the E.M.M. are incomplete. Reminiscences about the local units conflict in details. Company H, 71st Regiment of the E. M. M., was probably mustered into service in August of 1862. Most of its members were from Arrow Rock Township and nearby. George Caleb Bingham was commissioned captain. Captain Bingham was a younger cousin of his namesake, the artist. On August 20, 1862, Dr. Glen O. Hardeman was commissioned Surgeon of the Seventy-First.[605] Dr. Hardeman lived at "Lo Mismo" farm, four miles west of Arrow Rock. A loyal Unionist, he had informed Federal authorities as to the identity of some local bushwhackers. Consequently, he was a marked man.

Permelia (Townsend) Hardeman wrote to her husband about a visit by the bushwhackers to "Lo Mismo:"

October 17th, 1862 — My Dear Husband, We were visited last night about two O clock by the bushwhackers. I was up with the baby when they came. They first surrounded the house when three or four of them ran up on the Portico and ordered you to open the door. I told them you was not at home … They then said if I did not open it they would break it open … young Odonnel came into my room and called for a candle, said they wanted to search for arms. They got both of the guns and then went up stair, took some of my bed blankets, three pair of coarse sox … They even took as small a thing as comb and brush.[606]

There were few loyal Union men in Arrow Rock and Saline County, and their lives were in danger as Mrs. Hardeman's letters illustrate. Generally, it was much safer for Union men to serve in the army than to be at home with their families. For much of its service, Company H of the 71st E. M. M. was garrisoned in Marshall or Lexington, and this duty station probably saved Dr. Hardeman's life. While the bushwhackers would be savage to men, they generally adhered to a strict code that prevented them from molesting the women and children. Since most of the men were in military service on one side or the other, women such as Mrs. Hardeman found themselves in a new situation. They had to oversee the operations of the farms and businesses that their husbands normally ran.

On October 12, 1862, General Richard C. Vaughn, local commander of the E. M. M., took direct action to relieve the plight of the Union men:

… On Wednesday last I came down to Miami with 150 men of Colonel Neil's command in consequence of learning from Colonel Wilson that he was menaced.

On yesterday we sent a scout into the neighborhood of Arrow Rock. They were attacked from the brush and had 1 man killed and 4 wounded, 1 mortally I fear by Jackson's guerrillas. I shall not hereafter attempt to wage war against these men; it is an idle sacrifice of men. Hereafter I shall direct operations exclusively against their wealthy sympathizers and abettors. I suggest that I be permitted to appoint commissioners to levy an assessment of $15,000 on the disloyal men of this county for the benefit of the militia whose families I learn are in a state of deplorable destitution.

I have brought the matter of clothing to the notice of the county
court, and they have agreed to issue county bonds to the amount of
$3,500, and I have notified the bank at Arrow Rock that it will
have to cash these bonds immediately....[607]

Vaughn's action does not seem to have had the desired effect. Guerrilla activity continued with the support of many Arrow Rock citizens.

The Provisional Government of Missouri held a state convention on October 16, 1862. The new constitution drafted at the convention required all public officials swear an oath of loyalty to the United States. Although not dated, this oath appeared in the Records of the Town of Arrow Rock:

We the undersigned Trustees of the Town of Arrow Rock do
solemnly swear that we will uphold the institutions of the United
States and the State of Missouri, and that we will not take up
arms against the Government of the United States, nor the
Provisional Government of the State of Missouri, nor give aid
or comfort to the enemies of either during the present Civil War
so help me God

H. S. Mills   B. Sappington
H. S. Wilhelm   Chas. W. Parsons[608]
L. Noble

Conditions were so unsettled that in 1861, the Arrow Rock Board of Trustees conducted little business except to pay some debts. During the years 1863 and 1864, the Town Board did not convene at all. The county court continued to issue directives. According to the June, 1862, proceedings: "It is ordered by the court, that Vincent Marmaduke, Capt. James Boyer, Robert Nowlin, W. B. Sappington, John Durrett, James Neff, Willis Piper, D. W. Marmaduke, and Wm. Durrett be, and are hereby appointed a patrol for Arrow Rock township, to serve for one year from this date...."[609] The patrol did not complete the term of their commission. On February 4, 1865, the Masonic Lodge recorded, "Owing to the troubles of the times and the absence of the members, there was no regular meeting of Arrow Rock Lodge No. 55 from the July meeting 1864 to February 1865."[610]

The first casualty in Arrow Rock was James A. Boyer. There are conflicting accounts, and what follows is an attempt to reconcile those discrepancies. James was the son of Dr. W. Lewis Boyer, a town pharmacist.

James was also a former chairman of the Arrow Rock Board of Trustees. In 1860, he was appointed Town Constable; he may have still held that office when the war broke out.[611] On November 30, 1862,[612] Boyer was killed on the river wharf. Private William Chase, E.M.M., "...discharged the contents of one chamber of his pistol into the forehead of the unfortunate Boyer. The report of the pistol was heard by persons in the village... A negro boy ran up town and reported that a man was killed at the landing. The boy was soon followed by Chase, who deliberately told what he had done, and surrendered, voluntarily, to Captain Bingham...."[613]

William Chase was the man appointed as the town's public nurse in 1850. Undoubtedly, Chase and Boyer knew each other well. The Boyer family owned a warehouse on the wharf, accounting for his presence there. The reason for the shooting remains unknown. Possibly the two had argued over the sides they had chosen in the war. Boyer was buried in the Sappington family cemetery. Chase was taken to Boonville for a military trial, but was freed by the unit of German "home guards" stationed there.[614] After that, Chase seems to have dropped out of sight.

Federal troops of the E.M.M. or M.S.M. constantly garrisoned Arrow Rock from 1862 to 1865. Troop movements on the Missouri River and the roads between Arrow Rock and Glasgow, Marshall and Boonville were routine occurrences, but little appears to have happened in the town itself. Skirmishes occurred in the surrounding countryside, but most only amounted to a soldier killed here, and a guerrilla there. However, the plundering and pillaging of the rural population became truly unbearable. Old Santa Fe trader, Philip W. Thompson, summed up the situation in an appeal to General William Rosecrans for help:

> *Chestnut Hill, Saline County*
> *June 20, 1864*
> *General Rosecrans:*
>
> *Dear Sir: Permit me to say to you that the home guard is an entire failure. Men are called from their farms to guard the little villages whilst their homes are plundered by the bushwhackers, and no effort made to rid the country of these scoundrels. A Mr. Keaton, a good loyal citizen, is now at my house. He was in the Enrolled State Militia last summer, and had been called on by Captain Potter, of the home guards, to watch Arrow Rock. Last Friday he was released and returned home. That night 10*

*bushwhackers came and robbed his house. He shot 1 of them
through his neck tie, which was left on the floor with much blood.
He returned to Arrow Rock, but could not get any assistance to go
with him in hunt the scoundrels. I am seventy-three years old and
offered to go if they would turn out, but none would turn out.*

*We are in a bad state of affairs. Our county have bands
committing depredations. The cry was that if the soldiers would
leave we would protect the county. The truth is, Saline has but
few strictly loyal men, not sufficient to protect themselves. If we
cannot get protection, not one Union man will escape those
scoundrels. I have suffered the two last years, and do not expect
to escape this season. I have a faithful man living with me, who
will assist in defending our rights to the last. Men are afraid
to write the true situation of things as they exist, for fear of the
rebels. I am willing to hazard all for the good of my country.
Please consider our situation.*

Most respectfully, your most obedient and humble servant

P. W. THOMPSON[615]

Three days later, Captain Jay Marcellus Potter of the Arrow Rock "home
guards" received a letter from his immediate commander addressing some
of the concerns outlined by Thompson. Potter, like most members of the
Provisional Militia was not very well trained in military tactics or in the
duties of an officer. He was still, first and foremost, a pharmacist and merchant. It appears, even at army headquarters, the purpose and duties of
the home guard remained somewhat confusing:

Capt. J. M. Potter,
   Citizen Guards, Arrow Rock MO.:
*Captain: Some complaints are made by the members of your
company that the citizens of your county are detailed to stand
guard in the town. The commanding general directs me to say
that he is of the opinion that the object of the organization is to
have the members' duties so divided that they will be on duty as
near their residences as practicable, and that the protection of the
agricultural interest is of primary importance ... the people of
the towns, being congregated together, are amply able to protect
themselves, and that they should be sent to the country adjoining*

on patrol and guard duty, as in this way both will be guarded
and the farmers enabled to pursue their business ... the several
members of the citizen guard should have their arms always with
them, so that they will be prepared for defense or attack without
first meeting at the point of rendezvous. Endeavor if you please,
to harmonize the differences in your company, and make all feel that
they are under a mutual protection. I have ordered a few troops to your
place, so that the people of the town will be relieved from guard duty.

J. H. STEGER,
Assistant Adjutant General[616]

The troops dispatched to Arrow Rock by Steger were First M.S.M. cavalry under Lt. J. M. Woodruff. These men were better trained and had actual combat experience. Woodruff's company was quartered in an unnamed brick building on Main Street down the street from Wood and Huston's large mercantile house. As an act of precaution, Lt. Woodruff placed his unit flag on the Wood & Huston building. The closest thing to an actual battle in Arrow Rock then occurred on the night of July 20, 1864.

A band of guerrillas rode into town just after 10 p.m. bent on exterminating the M.S.M. "They fired several volleys at the store and finally set it on fire, expecting to dislodge the enemy."[617] Lt. Woodruff's ruse had worked, and by the time the bushwhackers discovered their mistake, the Federals were awake and prepared for the guerrillas inside their "brick fortress." The fight lasted nearly 45 minutes, and the guerrillas set fire to other buildings in the block in an attempt to drive out the Federals. In the confusion and darkness the Federals slipped out the back door of the building and into the countryside.

Major Henry Suess gave Brigadier General E. B. Brown this after-action report: "July 22, 1864 — I arrived at Arrow Rock at 7:30 last night. Found the three missing soldiers of the First Missouri State Militia here. The rebels were under Todd and Yeager, about 150 strong. Yeager was mortally wounded in the head. They took about 40 horses and $20,000 worth of goods. One woman was wounded by the rebels. Todd left at 11 p.m. taking Yeager in an ambulance, and traveled twenty-two miles that night, camping about seven miles from Miami."[618]

George Todd and Dick Yeager had participated in William Quantrill's infamous raid on Lawrence, Kansas, in August of 1863. They were also comrades-in-arms of William "Bloody Bill" Anderson, the most notorious of all the Missouri guerrillas. The three had recently raided Fayette but were repulsed by the local militia. After that, Todd and Yeager separated from Anderson when they scattered in the countryside. Dr. J. N. Dunlap was summoned to dress Yeager's mortal wounds. This placed the doctor in grave danger of arrest and execution. Jennie Flannery, who assisted Dr. Dunlap, later "...rode into Marshall, admitted to the Federal commandant that she, and only she, was the one that had nursed the outlaw."[619] Dr. Dunlap was thus spared, but Miss Flannery was promptly arrested and held prisoner. Other accounts identify the endangered man whom Miss Flannery saved as "old Mr. Gilliam" to whose farm the guerrillas had retreated after the raid. Perhaps the incident involved both parties.

The slow death of Yeager was not enough for Federal soldiers who scoured Saline and neighboring Lafayette counties looking for Todd. The threat of retaliation became so pronounced after this episode that Dr. Dunlap "...went to Canada, and Joseph Huston [Jr.] and family accompanied him, the two families spending the winter in a small house in Ingersoll, Canada...."[620] Their mercantile house destroyed by the raid, Huston's partner, Will H. Wood, retreated to St. Louis. They buried what was left of their capital on the farm of Wood's father, hoping to return when conditions were more settled.[621]

On August 5, 1864, guerrillas burned the courthouse in Marshall after "plundering some of the inhabitants and shooting five negroes in town and four a short distance from town."[622] Lt. Colonel Bazil Lazear of the 1st Cavalry M.S.M. arrived in Marshall on the 7th and marched towards Arrow Rock. In two skirmishes, three guerrillas were killed and several others wounded. Near Arrow Rock the soldiers found another black man who had been killed by guerrillas. Lt. Col. Lazear wrote, "This is certainly the most rebellious county I have been in. I have arrested several women that I will send in due time, and have arrested several of the worst rebels that I am holding hostage for the lives of Union men... This county needs rough handling, and as the guerrillas have threatened what they will do, I have warned and notified their friends that I would hold them responsible for the acts of the guerrillas, and will retaliate for any violence done the Union men either in person or property."[623]

The women he arrested included Sue Bryant of Marshall, Bennie Elliott and Sallie Pearson of Arrow Rock, and Amanda and Missouri

Jackson of Saline City, and of course, Jennie Flannery who had aided Yeager. The charges against these ladies were generally for "harboring, feeding, and furnishing information to the bushwhackers."[624] Sue Bryant was taken to a female prison in St. Louis. Jennie Flannery, Sallie Pearson and the Jackson sisters eventually took the oath of allegiance and were released after spending several weeks in jail. Bennie Elliott remained recalcitrant and was placed in the state penitentiary at Jefferson City.[625]

According to the 1881 Saline County history, Lt. Colonel Lazear arrested Marshall Durrett Piper along with about sixteen of his neighbors, placed them on parole and ordered them to report to Arrow Rock regularly each morning. On the 8th of August 1864, Piper rode the short distance into town accompanied by Esquire Davidson, a Union man. Colonel Lazear assembled the parolees and delivered a speech reproaching them for past conduct. "Closing, he pointed to Piper, saying, 'As for that fellow, he will be shot today at two o'clock.'" Despite the protests of Davidson and others, Piper was led out at two, and shot by a firing squad of ten men.[626] Supposedly, eleven bullets were found in Piper's body. Years later, it was said an unnamed neighbor with a grudge against Piper fired out the window of his house the same time the firing squad discharged their weapons.[627]

Lazear paints a differing picture of the circumstances. "A party of twenty (guerrillas) camped within eight miles of camp the night of the 7th on the premises of one Marshall Piper, who gave us no notice of the fact, and being a notorious rebel and under bond was shot… when they allow them (guerrillas) to feed and camp upon their property day after day and give no information but deny that they know anything of them, it is as good evidence of their guilt as I want … the removal of 100 families to the South would do more good to quiet this county than to hunt guerrillas one year and leave the families here.[628]

Supposedly, Piper's 11-year-old son, Alonzo (Lon), swore vengeance on Lt. Col. Lazear. Several days after Piper was shot, Mason Brown told Lon he had heard he (Brown) was to be the next example made by Lazear. Lon Piper concealed himself in the bushes on the route to the Brown farm outside of Arrow Rock where he shot Lazear with his father's pistol. The colonel's body lay in the road several days before being discovered. Lon Piper, who lived until 1949, repeated this story prior to his death.[629] However, Lt. Col. Lazear turns up in military reports up to the end of the war. If Lon Piper shot anyone, it was another soldier in Lazear's command. The account has other flaws. It seems unlikely any sane soldier would be traveling alone, let alone try to arrest someone by himself. This is especially true given the guerrilla activity in the area.

The bushwhackers continued paying visits to "Lo Mismo" farm in 1864. Many were boys from Arrow Rock, obviously well known to the Hardeman family as this letter from Permelia to Dr. Hardeman reveals:

> *August 7th 1864 — My Dear Husband ... I have had two visits from them since you left. The first company came Wednesday evening, about sixteen of them. They did not take a great deal, but searched every room in the house and broke open all the trunks ... The[y] asked where [you] was and said you was the G-d-d-m rascal that went to Lexington and brought the Feds down here ... I did not recognize any of them, but heard afterwards that Dick Pearson, Will Stean and Bill Durriett was with them. Will Stean said he was in the house, but did not take any thing.*
>
> *There were five here Friday morning but they did not come in the house. They were hunting Fudge Brown Negroes, and searching the cabins for arms and asked what Dr. Hardiman harbored negroes here for. I told him you did not and was as clear of it as him or any body else, and he said these darned Union men were harboring the negroes. It was that William threatened to shoot you last summer for reporting on him. Tom Dysart and Tom Woodson was with him. I did not know the other two.*
>
> *I have heard of six joining them: Tom Dysart, Finas Dysart, Dick Pearson, Will Stean, John Will Piper and I am sorry to say Willie Jones....*[630]

In late August, guerrillas in William S. Jackson's command were at a church service at the Concord Church northwest of Arrow Rock when a company of M.S.M. attempted to capture them. Another account says the church was in Blackwater Township. Both accounts were cited in the 1881 Saline County History. Regardless of where it happened, all escaped except "Lieutenant Durrett" who was shot through the ankle and fell from his horse. He was quickly taken to Arrow Rock, tried by military tribunal and found guilty of burning the Saline County courthouse and "of being a bushwhacker generally." He was sentenced to be shot, and the order was carried out almost immediately. His last words were, "Tell the boys to keep on fighting."[631] Unable to stand, he was propped against a fence and then riddled with musket balls. It is possible this "Lt. Durrett" is the same person as "Bill Durriet" who Mrs. Hardeman wrote about when her home was ransacked. Certainly, they were related, if not the same man.

In late September of 1864, regular Confederate forces under Major General Sterling Price made one last push into Missouri. On the 13th of October, his forces were bivouacked in Boonville. Price heard 5,000 stands of arms were stored in Glasgow. On the 14th, nearly 2,000 Confederates under General John Clark moved to Arrow Rock where they began crossing the river. Another 125 men with artillery under Colonel Jo Shelby moved directly north and took position across the river from Glasgow. At 5:00 a.m. the following day, Shelby's artillery opened fire, but Clark's troops were not in position as they had been delayed in making the crossing. Possibly the ferry had not been replaced after it was burned in December of 1861. Clark captured Glasgow and its 500-man garrison by early afternoon, but they found only 1,500 stands of arms. Among those captured were Captain George Caleb Bingham and members of the 71st E.M.M.[632]

General Robert E. Lee's surrender at Appomattox Courthouse, on April 14, 1865, signaled the final end of the Confederacy. However, the guerrilla war in Missouri continued. On May 1, 1865, Captain James Eads wrote Captain C. G. Laurant: "I have today about 100 men in the brush, and will keep every efficient or available man in the brush until we kill or drive out every bushwhacker and murderer who infests this country. The men are out on the trail of twelve bushwhackers, and I hear of fifteen within three miles of Arrow Rock who took dinner at a Mrs. Scripture's, and her son went off with them. I shall endeavor to call on her soon."[633]

While the Civil War disrupted life in Arrow Rock, the war was occasionally punctuated by light moments. William Barnes was one of the old settlers from Virginia and by the time of the war was an old man. A jovial and friendly man, he was fondly referred to as "Uncle Billy." His daughter-in-law, Amanda, was the artist George Caleb Bingham's sister. He was an outspoken Southern sympathizer, which kept him under close surveillance by Federal authorities. On one occasion a company of M.S.M. decided to camp near his house. "Seeing some fat steers grazing in a nearby pasture, they told Uncle 'Billy' they were in need of fresh meat and were going to kill one of his best. He consented to it readily, and was so jolly and cheerful over his loss that when they left the next morning, they gave him a hind quarter, which they had left over. He assured them they were perfectly welcome to come around and kill another whenever they pleased."[634] George Baker, a Union man, owned the steers and had pastured them adjacent to Uncle Billy's house. When he went to check on them, Uncle Billy told him about the incident with "great glee" and offered him a part of his own beef. Baker took the joke in stride, and the two remained steadfast friends in spite of the war.

Humor aside, Anthony O'Sullivan eloquently summed up the true picture of the Civil War and its aftermath. "We mourn the unhappy condition of our country and the amount of human suffering we have witnessed. Our imagination carries us to the homes of our fellow citizens — seats around the domestic hearth are vacant. Thousands of maimed and emaciated, with no means for future support, fill our soul with agony, and we are ready to exclaim — My God, my God why hast Thou forsaken us?"[635]

In response to the tragedy of the war, Thomas Rainey said, "During the winter of 1865–66, the ladies of the town and vicinity decided to get up an entertainment for the benefit of Southern sufferers in hospitals…They presented a series of tableaux, in groups, classic and historical, which were planned and well staged. All the personages in the tableaux were ladies, and their costumes and poses were in exceeding good taste…they met the enthusiastic approval of a very large audience, and …they raised several hundred dollars."[636]

Reconstruction

Pockets of Confederate resistance held out as late as June of 1865. Real peace was even slower in coming to Missouri. "The war was just over, and returned soldiers from both armies were back home. There was no cordiality between them, particularly between those, on both sides, who had skirmished around without doing much fighting. The actual soldiers fraternized better," Thomas C. Rainey wrote.[637] No state in or out of the Union witnessed more "bushwhacking" than the state of Missouri.[638] The spirit of lawlessness still pervaded the state, and in Saline County, crimes actually seemed to be on the increase.

Local law officers and the Federal soldiers in the county seemed to have little control. The citizens often did not trust them. On April 21, 1866, a large group of citizens representing all political parties and including ex-Confederate and ex-Union soldiers convened at the Methodist Episcopal Church in Marshall. A vigilante group was formed called the "Honest Men's League" with their goal being to "...repress all lawlessness in the county, and bring to a swift and severe punishment all offenders against justice and law."[639] Branches of the Honest Men's League were formed in many Saline County communities, including Arrow Rock.

Later that spring, a gang of former bushwhackers led by James Marshall rented a brick house about two and a half miles out of town, not far from the old Sappington neighborhood. They frequently rode into Arrow Rock with pistols in their belts, and when they got drunk in the saloons, "they boasted of their bloody careers in the war." At one point they "shot up" the town causing considerable alarm. The gang was also suspected of fencing stolen horses in the county. The Honest Men's League requested assistance from Sheriff John Wall, who sent his deputy, Frank M. Sappington, to Arrow Rock with an arrest warrant for the gang.[640]

Deputy Sappington formed a posse of about thirty men from the Honest Men's League, which included Thomas Rainey, Captain George C. Bingham, ex-Federal, and Colonel William S. Jackson, ex-Confederate. "The posse was armed with pistols and the usual fowling pieces, and started at nightfall."[641] The house was surrounded, and one of the men stepped up on the porch and knocked on the front door. A woman cried out, and a shot was fired from an upper window. During the exchange of gunfire, two or three gang members got out of the house and fled into the darkness. The unnamed woman received some buckshot in the arm.

Rainey reported the episode had a healing effect on the town. "Arrow Rock was strongly Southern, but this little episode convinced the riff-raff that 'Secesh' wouldn't tolerate thieves and bullies. It caused both sides to realize that it was best to work in harmony and let bygones go."[642] A day or two after the event, Marshall's gang rode up to the residence of a Mr. Goode on the Cooper County line, killing him and his son Jerry. Another son, twelve-year-old Finis seized a gun and shot one of the murderers as they were riding away. Papers on the body identified him as Marion Claybrook of the 10th Missouri Confederate Cavalry.[643] For Arrow Rock, the war was finally over.

As town government was shut down for over two years, a special election was held for the Board of Trustees on September 23, 1865. Michael Dickey and Perry Crews were elected to the board and took the required loyalty oath. Dickey was also appointed Town Constable, the first civilian law officer in town since the war broke out. Only four votes were cast in the election, probably because most of the voters refused to take the loyalty oath. Another election was held April 1, 1866, but to no gain. There were seven candidates for five vacancies on the board. Again, there were only four votes. "None of the new officers could qualify according to law. Consequently the old Trustees were held over."[644] The new officers probably refused to take the loyalty oath.

Economic recovery was slow. In the summer of 1865, Will H. Wood and Joseph Huston, Jr. met in St. Louis and determined to reopen their Arrow Rock business. Huston went to Arrow Rock to retrieve their hidden capital, and Wood began purchasing goods in St. Louis. Wood arrived in Arrow Rock several days later and found Huston in despair. He had been unable to find their small cache of gold coins in the field where they hid it. Wood tried to remain optimistic. "They took with them 'John' and 'Nelse' two trusty old servants, well-known in Arrow Rock. They worked till noon with no reward. A stop was made for lunch…The two workmen ate a hearty meal, and 'Nelse' closing his [jack] knife with a bang, said: 'Now I'se had my dinner I'm g'wine to find that money,' and almost at the first stroke he touched a solid substance which proved to be the pot of gold."[645] Wood and Huston opened their salesroom over the ruins of their old store. The determination of two loyal African American men had helped make the resurrection of the firm possible. Foreseeing the decline of the river towns, Wood and Huston sold their business to Dr. F. R. Durrett in 1870. Wood became connected with the Bank of Arrow Rock. In 1874 Wood and Huston established the Wood & Huston Bank in Marshall, which continues today.

The Arrow Rock bank was the only one remaining in the county, but had only $5,000 in capital and less than $50,000 in deposits.[646] Despite this, it appeared the pre-war prosperity of Arrow Rock would return. Steamboats were running again on the river, and once abandoned farms began producing crops again. With town government reconstituted, new construction and even street improvements were underway. The *Saline County Progress* printed this optimistic assessment in February of 1868:

Editor of Progress: We wish to call your attention to conditions in

Arrow Rock. We have over one hundred dwelling houses, nine of which are built of brick, fourteen stores, eleven of brick — ten dry good and grocery stores, two drug stores, one boot and variety store, one jewelry store, one Odd Fellows' hall, one Masonic Hall, two churches, two schools (one African), one sash and blind factory, three blacksmith shops, two wagon maker shops, one boot and shoe store, one bakery, one cooper shop, one dentist, four physicians, one express office, one furniture store, one dress making and millinery shop, one gunsmith shop, two hotels, one insurance office, one livery stable, two saddlery shops, one lumber yard, one steam saw mill, two flowering mills, one paint shop, one carding machine, one woolen factory, one shingle and steam planing mill, one billiard hall, one bank, one broker and exchange dealer, one art gallery, one stage and post office, one large brick yard, four warehouses on the river.

Several buildings will be erected here in the spring, amongst which will be a large Masonic Hall to be built of brick, one Odd Fellows' Hall, a large male and female seminary to be built of brick. Each of three buildings will be quite an ornament to our town. Wood, Huston & Co. will also build another large warehouse of brick, which will be one of the largest and best in this upper country. We have a calaboose or jail, which, however, is almost always tenantless, probably because we are blessed with neither editors or lawyers.

Our sidewalks are well paved, and our main street is macadamized, a thing no other town in our county can boast of. Our corporation laws are rigidly enforced, and law and order prevails. Taking all things into consideration, Arrow Rock is one of the most quiet, orderly and well regulated towns on the Missouri River.[647]

Despite this glowing report, economic and transportation conditions had in fact changed. Arrow Rock, as well as the entire Boonslick Country, was edging towards decline, even if imperceptibly. Much of the pre-war economy had been based on the local production of hemp and tobacco. Both crops were labor intensive and thus dependent on slave labor. By extension, slaves were the primary source of labor in many other endeavors and civil improvement projects. With emancipation, that pool of forced labor was gone.

Whereas hemp had been the king crop of Saline County in 1860, it was virtually worthless after the war. Although cotton was still abundantly grown in the south, hemp rope was no longer necessary. Cheaper jute rope, imported from India, and reusable steel hoops began to be used for holding the cotton bales together. The need for rope rigging on the masts of sailing ships was rapidly passing as well. Shipping fleets were rapidly converting to steam power. Only limited production of hemp and manufacture of hemp ropes continued, primarily for local use. Thomas Rainey described the era by saying: "The old Missouri ... was passing out; the new Missouri was at the threshold, requiring new methods."[648]

The next jarring impact on Arrow Rock came in the form of transportation. Railroads began to supplant the river commerce on which Arrow Rock and many of the Boonslick towns were so dependent. The Columbia, Missouri *Statesman* offered what seemed like a prophecy in 1853: "What will be the fate of your river towns [with the coming of the railroad]? Will not the flourishing town of Rocheport be ruined?"[649] Few railroads were in the state in the 1850s, but in the 1870s, they crisscrossed the entire state. Freight and passengers could be moved in greater volume more quickly and cheaply than by steamboat or wagon. Furthermore, the railroad could run year round whereas steamboats were limited by seasonal river conditions. New areas of land far removed from the rivers were opened to settlement and agricultural and manufacturing production by railroads. Just as the boomtowns had appeared along the Missouri River in the 1820s, they now appeared along the railroad lines.

Arrow Rock appeared destined to capitalize on the railroad bonanza. As early as 1860, the town made a half-hearted attempt to gain a rail line, but steamboat commerce was thriving so no one really believed editorials such as those in the Columbia *Statesman*. However, with the explosion of rail service after the Civil War, the town made a serious effort to get a line. The November 6, 1868, edition of the *Saline County Progress* carried this ad:

> *"Clear the Track!*
> *The Cars are Coming!*
> *Order for an Election in Arrow Rock Township for a Township*
> *subscription of $100,000 to the Arrow Rock and Boonville*
> *Railroad.*

> *Saline County Court, November Term, November 2, 1868*
> *IN THE COUNTY COURT of Saline county, Mo. ss*
> *WHEREAS, A petition in due form and subscribed by at least*
> *twenty-five tax payers and residents of Arrow Rock township,*
> *Saline county, Missouri has been presented to this Court, asking*
> *a special election in said township with a view to subscribing*
> *one hundred thousand dollars to the Arrow Rock and Boonville*
> *Railroad Company, in conformity to an act entitled 'An act to*
> *facilitate the construction of rail roads in the State of Missouri,'*
> *approved March 23rd, 1868....*"[650]

The January 29, 1869, edition of the *Saline County Progress* reported "... connection by rail with the Pacific Road via Boonville, has, it seems, fallen through, but nothing daunted, they seem now in a fair way to obtain Railroad connections still more desirable than was the Boonville and Arrow Rock Railroad...The people of Arrow Rock Township, we are pleased to see, are at work in earnest in this matter."[651]

Railroad bonds were sold as "subscriptions" solicited from citizens to help fund the rail line. For the next year and a half, there were innumerable committee meetings, meetings with railroad officials, and even court hearings in an attempt to resolve the Arrow Rock railroad proposal. For a time it appeared the Louisiana and Missouri River Railroad would indeed have a route through Arrow Rock. On December 30, 1870, the *Saline County Progress* reported Saline City was competing with Arrow Rock for the proposed rail route. But finally, in July of 1872, the Missouri Supreme Court voided $400,000 in Louisiana and Missouri River Railroad bonds, "creating much demonstration and rejoicing throughout the county."[652] Some realized what the loss of rail service would mean, while others felt the railroads had taken advantage of farmers. For both Arrow Rock and Saline City, the court decision was the final blow for a chance at lasting economic recovery.

While the pre-war growth of Arrow Rock and the Boonslick Country seemed staggering for the time, it was absolutely dwarfed by the post-war growth of Kansas City and St. Louis. Manufactured products in St. Louis rose from $27 million in value in 1870 to $114 million in 1880, and then doubled again to $228 million by 1890. St. Louis was linked by rail to the vast urban markets of the East after the completion of the Eads Bridge over the Mississippi in 1874. Kansas City grew even more spectacularly from a population of 3,500 in 1865 to more than 32,000 in 1870. Kansas City became a railhead for Texas cattle drovers shipping their beef by train to eastern markets. Wheat shipped from Kansas City grew from 678,000 bushels in 1871 to 9 million bushels by 1878.[653] Once again, transportation and communication affected the economic development of communities. Arrow Rock and much of the Boonslick Country did not fit into the new economic equation.

Even in the face of such overwhelming economic competition and its own declining population, some in Arrow Rock continued to hold to the hope of the town returning to its former glory. The July 29, 1870 edition of the *Saline County Progress* offered this report:

> *ARROW ROCK — Upon a recent visit to Arrow Rock, we were pleased to notice the evidence of thrift and life in the town. Although not putting on the airs of Marshall in the way of improvements, nor yet aspiring to be the "hub" of the universe, or the metropolis of Missouri, Arrow Rock has her full share of trade, and her merchants look happy and contented. As a shipping point Arrow Rock is no "small fry," in fact, does a larger river shipping than any point on the river between St. Louis and Kansas City. Her merchants handle about as much of the 'substantial' as an equal number of retail dealers anywhere. At this season of the year trade is always brisk, from the fact that the farmers are delivering their wheat and other grain for shipment, and while in town purchase their dry goods, groceries, hardware, &c. So long as the Missouri river flows by her, Arrow Rock has no reason to fear for her safety.[654]*

But almost symbolically, the channel of the Missouri was indeed steadily moving away from the town. In another 30 plus years, the river would be nearly a mile away. Economic power translated into political power, and as Kansas City and St. Louis ascended, Arrow Rock and the Boonslick Country descended. Also, the Boonslick citizens had chosen the wrong side in the war. "Central Clique" Democrats, in the mold of the Jacksons, Marmadukes and Sappingtons, no longer dominated party politics. Political dominance in the state shifted irrevocably to the new urban centers, and much of government was in the hands of the Republican Party, often referred to as "the Radicals."

The new state constitution required citizens to take an "oath of allegiance" to the Union in order to vote, something many of the former Confederates refused to do. The Voter Board of Registration is frequently vilified in Saline County newspaper editorials. Words like "treachery," "villainous outrages" and "inquisitors" are used to describe the board. The Arrow Rock southerners saw voting as a racial problem as well. "Radical clique wishes the negro to vote and nine-tenths of the old farmers and taxpayers to be ... politically beneath the negro."[655] Voting by African Americans was a bitter pill many of the southerners refused to swallow. They were outraged at the election of Ulysses S. Grant as President in 1868, and again in 1872, and they blamed African American voters. On April 2, 1872, the Town Board noted without much comment in its minutes this was the "first time Negroes voted in Arrow Rock."[656] Proposals were soon made to give women the right to vote as "a remedy against negro voters precipitated upon us."[657]

"By 1873 the population of Arrow Rock had shrunk to 600, with about twenty business firms and two steam flour mills still operating."[658] A real turning point for Arrow Rock occurred on December 28, 1872. About 1:00 a.m., the town experienced what was then, "the most destructive fire that has ever been known in Central Missouri."[659] The January 1, 1873 edition of the *Saline County Progress* reported: "The fire originated in the upper room of John Gilpin's saloon...."[660] This was located on the corner of Fourth and Main, now the site of the Arrow Rock Country Store. An entire row of buildings on Fourth Street and the half block of Main Street and several residences were destroyed.

Volunteer firefighters had little water available to them. "Blankets and rolls of cloth were placed on the roof of Sutherlin & Durritt's store, and by vigilant work, the fire was kept from crossing the street...."[661] The *Saline County Progress* published a list (with spelling errors) of those who distinguished themselves at the fire: "'Captain' Ish, Elisha Ancell, Dr. Dickinson, Lucius Ainsbury, Mr. Clark, D. J. Hervey and son, Clark Coiner, I. P. Davis, T. C. McMahan, Givens Horn, Griff Dickinson, Jimmy Ancell, R. J. McMahan, Dr. McClelland, William Jones, 'and three colored men Nelson, Spencer, and Sack.'"[662]

A lack of wind and heavy snow cover probably prevented the total loss of the business district. Following the disaster, the mood of the community quickly turned from grief to anger: "We learn that this house was frequented at night by a crowd of cardplayers and whisky drinkers, and that on Sunday night their revels and maudling shouting were heard by all in the neighborhood till within a short time of the fire. We hope that hereafter every man in Arrow Rock may find some more creditable means of making a living than by keeping a saloon, and if our young men can find no better place to spend their time and their money, they will confer a favor on the community and their friends by going to the river and drowning themselves."[663]

The anger soon gave way to vengeance. The Boonville *Weekly Eagle* reported on January 31: "The dreadful news reached us yesterday that our Neighboring town Arrow Rock, had just begun undergoing the terrors of lynch law. This awful state of affairs seems to have grown out of the late firing of that place. It was then thought that the terrible misfortune was caused by incinderism."[664] The newspaper reported another attempt was made on January 28 to set fire to the town. An "infuriated mob" arrested three young men, John Sweeney, Clark Coiner (possibly the son of former Constable Coiner) and Rueben Elder, a black man.[665] Ironically, Clark Coiner had been cited in the *Saline County Progress* as one of the heroes of the December 28 fire.

Sweeney was hanged from a tree that night. The Marshall stage driver "saw the body of the unfortunate man still swinging from a limb by the roadside"[666] as he drove into town the following day. Jesse McMahan reported to the *Weekly Eagle* that the other two men were lynched the following night.[667] However, *The Peoples Tribune*, a Jefferson City newspaper, gave a different account in its February 12 edition. It reported four fires were discovered on January 13, but were suppressed before getting out of control. "A detective was engaged, and he discovered that three men caused the first fire, and attempted those of the 13th — this Sweeney, negro, and Coiner, white, and Elder, negro. The two last have been sent to jail in Lexington."[668] This was the only account that identified Sweeney as African American. These widely differing newspaper accounts serve as a reminder how difficult it can be to ascertain and interpret historical "facts."

The fire practically accomplished what the temperance movement could not. On April 21, 1873, the Board of Trustees increased license fees for "dram shops" from $75 to $400 annually. A committee was also appointed to draft an ordinance to regulate "Tippling Houses" and enforce the Sunday liquor law.[669] A "dram shop" served liquor, but it was often just one component of a larger business, the Tavern being an example. A "tippling house" on the other hand, was a place where liquor was the only business. Undoubtedly, these high fees were intended to discourage liquor consumption altogether.

Most of the structures lost in the fire were two and three story buildings. While many were at least partially rebuilt, the fire delivered a blow the town could ill-afford. From this point on, Arrow Rock's economic fortunes were clearly and irrevocably in decline.

Freedmen: The African American Experience

Slavery had been a cornerstone for much of the economic and social life of Saline County and the Boonslick district. This region had supported the Napton-Jackson Resolutions of the 1850s, tying their destiny to slavery. They opposed those who supported either abolition or limiting the expansion of slavery into new territories. President Lincoln's Emancipation Proclamation in 1863 had not affected slaves in the border states of Missouri, Kentucky and Maryland because those states had not seceded from the Union. Though Missouri slavery had been declining as a result of the war, the emancipation of Missouri slaves on January 22, 1865, suddenly and irrevocably ended this component of Arrow Rock's economy.

As freedmen, African Americans remained a vital and vibrant part of Arrow Rock. More than ever, they were indispensable in maintaining the prosperity and infrastructure of the town. Without the African American community, Arrow Rock's slide towards economic oblivion probably would have occurred more quickly.

Thomas C. Rainey acknowledged the benefit the area had reaped from its black residents.

> *In spite of opinions to the contrary, I believe the colored race in Missouri is advancing in intelligence and good morals. The whole body of them should not be condemned because some of their number are brutal and worthless. On the contrary, I think it is the duty of every true Southern man to speak an encouraging word to every worthy colored man he meets. The forefathers of many of them helped to fence and clear the fields, open the roadways, and make Saline a pleasant place to live in. Although they now lie in nameless graves, we owe respect to their memory. They were also pioneers.*[670]

Aspects of his remarks are condescending by today's standards. However, for Missouri in 1914, these remarks were a revolutionary departure from the prevailing attitude.

By 1870, the black population of Saline County had declined by a thousand as the freedmen set off to find their fortunes elsewhere. The result was a dramatic reduction in the availability of blacks for laborers, which gave farm owners two options: grow less labor-intensive crops or hire laborers at a competitive wage and borrow money to pay for laborsaving equipment. *Colman's Rural World*, a popular farming magazine noted in 1879, "With improved implements and machines we now have, a farmer with one hired man can carry on farming on a larger scale than he could a generation ago with half a dozen hired men."[671] Black and white farm laborers were being pushed from the land by these labor-saving implements, and moving to larger towns.

Arrow Rock Township's black population declined 36% between 1860 and 1870 while the white population grew 7%. The over 700 blacks living in the township continued to provide a labor pool for farmers, merchants and business people. In 1880, 60% of Arrow Rock's blacks still worked and lived in white households as laborers or domestic servants. They had no definite starting or quitting time, and wages were meager or "room and board" could be considered payment for their services. It was difficult for blacks who "lived in" to fulfill family responsibilities since their first responsibility was to the white head of household. In effect, African Americans in Arrow Rock as well as most of rural Missouri were trapped in a state of what President Lincoln had termed after emancipation, "a hazy realm between bondage and freedom."

Arrow Rock blacks were evidently frustrated as well and seemed to make a conscious effort to end the situation of "living in" by establishing their own households, separate and away from the control of the white population. By 1900, there was not a single black person living in a white residence in Arrow Rock. All African Americans were living in a household headed by a black person, usually a male. Blacks continued to be employed as farm laborers and domestics, but at the end of the day, they had their own homes and families to go to. At the same time, African American social and religious institutions, which had been squelched or marginalized, came into full bloom. The area north of Morgan Street, especially, developed into a "black community"[672] constituting nearly 50%

of Arrow Rock's population.

Another phenomenon occurring during this time was the establishment of freedmen hamlets. In 1871, Joe Penny, a freedman from Kentucky, paid $160 for 8 acres of land in Saline County. This was the first of eleven purchases to be made in the next eight years by Penny and other black families in the area. By 1879, the land acquisitions constituted 64 acres known as Pennytown, the largest of Saline County's black hamlets. Pennytown was about 12 miles southwest of Arrow Rock. Like their Arrow Rock counterparts, with whom they interacted and were often related to, Pennytown residents were successful in their vision of self-reliance.[673] Some local whites resented this independence and prosperity. At one point, Penny feigned leaving the county to bring some relief to the black community. By the turn of the century, "pennytown" was used in slang to describe an African American enclave.

In 1886, a white landowner permitted Pennytown residents to erect a frame house of worship on his land. Church trustees purchased the land for ten dollars in 1894. The building burned, but a new one was erected on the same spot by 1926.[674] By the 1940s, Pennytown was dying out as the population moved to urban areas. The church was in a state of decay in 1988 but was added to the National Register of Historic Places. Through efforts initiated by Pennytown resident and historian Josephine Lawrence, the church was completely restored in 1998. Pennytown descendants periodically hold reunions and worship services there. It is the only structure remaining of the once-thriving community.

Whites evidently became more frustrated as they lost their hold over the black population. Southern traditions, rooted in the old slave code mentality, died hard. Traditionally, the South had defined "Negroes" in one of two stereotypes: "the Sambo or as the devil."[675] The Sambo stereotype described the Negro as innately childlike, dependent, and irresponsible, fun-loving and given to petty thievery. The devil stereotype described the Negro male as the ruthless murderer, arsonist, and rapist.[676]

In the generation before the Civil War, the devil stereotype seems to have prevailed in Arrow Rock. Undoubtedly, some of this stereotype was a backlash against abolitionism. This stereotype was a primary reason for the appointment of the various "town patrols" throughout the 1840s and 1850s. The horrible lynchings of 1859 were its ultimate fruit. But, there were no slave insurrections after Nat Turner's revolt in Virginia in 1831. During the Civil War itself, there was little aggression against white families by slaves even though most of the men were away in military service.

The resentment against blacks increased with emancipation, and the idea of blacks voting in elections pushed many to violence. The *Saline County Progress* carried an editorial on the formation of the Ku Klux Klan in its February 28, 1868 edition:

> *This is, beyond doubt, the most ridiculous political organization that has come to light for many a day. It is a secret order lately established in Middle Tennessee, and has for its object the intimidation of the blacks ... It is to work upon the fears of the colored people, and intimidate them to such an extent as to keep them from the ballot-box. The members of the society, clad in winding-sheets, and carefully masked, visit the quarters of the freedmen, where, in hollow, sepulchral tones, they represent themselves as rebel soldiers who have come forth from their graves. All this, of course, works deeply upon the superstitious natures of the freedmen, and no wonder that they feel an ominous dread. It is a fact, that wherever the society exists, the colored people venture forth after night-fall with extreme reluctance, and never, when they can avoid it.*
>
> *We admit this is rather small business for white men to be engaged in; but we wonder what the founders of our government would think could they only see in what hands the liberties of the people are entrusted — to ignorant, half-witted blacks, who can be frightened from the polls by the nightly appearance of a squad of persons arrayed in white....*[677]

Thus, while the editorial generally condemned the activities of the Klan, it simply could not pass up the chance to make demeaning remarks about African Americans. Bitter letters by Arrow Rock citizens periodically appear in newspapers of the time. Freedom for African Americans was very hard for the whites to accept. The bitterness led to even more violence against blacks, and lynching during the reconstruction period became a frequent occurrence throughout Missouri.

As slaves, African Americans were forced to develop separate social and religious activities as a means of promoting solidarity. Even with freedom and property ownership, Arrow Rock blacks had to continue to maintain their separate social, religious and educational institutions. There were no "official" laws enforcing segregation in Missouri, except for public schools. However, African Americans understood if they violated "their place" as perceived by Anglo-American society, they could suffer for it.

Documentation regarding the African American component of Arrow Rock history is scarce. Blacks seldom entrusted their records to white officials for obvious reasons. Consequently, county records regarding African American-owned properties and households are difficult to trace. Also, many early historians simply did not see any significance or value to what blacks did in their community. Fortunately, these attitudes have been steadily changing since the 1970s. The Friends of Arrow Rock, Inc. and the University of Missouri at St. Louis and William Woods College in cooperation with the Missouri Humanities Council and the Missouri Department of Natural Resources have conducted joint projects to recover Arrow Rock's African American heritage. Descendants of Arrow Rock's black residents have been instrumental in providing information about their ancestors.

What has increasingly emerged from these projects is a picture of African Americans as a vibrant, vital part of Arrow Rock's history and economic well-being. They overcame discrimination and segregation to maintain personal dignity and even pride in their community. Their presence left an indelible mark on the white residents. As Mrs. Mary Rinne, a long time white resident, said in a 1997 interview, "I think Arrow Rock was a lot more exciting and interesting when the colored people were here."[678] Theresa Habernal, one of the last African Americans to attend school in Arrow Rock, often comes back to the place that shaped her early life. Asked why in a 1997 interview, she responded, "Because that's where my roots are."[679]

Historic Preservation

A New Beginning

Following the Civil War, the plantations were broken up into smaller yeoman farms. For example, the Murrell plantation, "Oak Grove," decreased in size from 640 acres to 308 acres. The area saw a new wave of immigrants taking up residence. Their names were German in origin, such as Moehle, Kuhn, Goetz, Zimmerman, Putsch, Fritz, Topel, Eilers and Junkerman. They were primarily yeoman farmers or middle-class merchants. Although many of the old families from the upper South remained, few retained the wealth and prominence they had known before the war.

By the turn of the century, Arrow Rock was spoken of as "an ancient village."[680] Most of the buildings including the old Tavern had become shabby relics of their former selves. On July 11, 1901, a falling lantern in J. W. Wheeler's drug store on Main Street caused a second disastrous fire. This time, all the buildings on the north side of Main Street were destroyed. The Arrow Rock bank was gutted and had to set up temporary quarters in the Hotel (Tavern).

The brick walls of many of the buildings remained. Most of them had been two and three story structures. However, the economic decline had reached such a point that only the first floors were rebuilt. Even the buildings that had not been destroyed in the fire were now threatened with destruction by neglect. The population had declined to about 300. Arrow Rock was on the verge of becoming a ghost town.

In 1912, several local residents realized that Arrow Rock and its remaining buildings formed an important legacy of Missouri's history. That year the local chapter of the National Old Trails Road Association furnished a room in the old Tavern with local artifacts and relics, "as a means of teaching Missouri history to the passerby."[681] The Old Trails Association, in which the Daughters of the American Revolution (D.A.R.)

played an active role, sought to establish a national highway system by connecting the old Indian and pioneer trails across the nation. The Arrow Rock ferry crossing and its associations with the Santa Fe Trail made the town a point of interest.

The community held a huge street fair on August 30 and 31 of that same year. The Arrow Rock *Statesman* advertised, "Prizes of $12.00 and $5.00 for the best and second best outfit representing the original Santa Fe Trailers. Fix you up an old time movers outfit, ox-teams, mule teams, or any and come down and camp at the Big Spring...."[682] The editor of the Boonville *Republican* assured readers of the *Statesman,* that "Boonville will be there en masse unless roads are hub deep in mud — and in that event they will charter a boat for they intend to show Arrow Rock and her enthusiastic people that Boonville never forgets a friend."[683]

Thomas C. Rainey made several speaking appearances, and in 1914, published *Along the Old Trail, Pioneer Sketches of Arrow Rock and Vicinity*. This was a collection of anecdotes about his experiences as a storekeeper in Arrow Rock from 1865 through 1879. Also in 1914, John Percy Huston, Sr., published a small booklet, *The Old Tavern At Arrow Rock*. Huston went into more detail about the founding of Arrow Rock and his grand-father's construction of the Tavern. Paul Biggs published his booklet on the Tavern in 1927. Although it does contain some factual errors, it was the first publication to promote the Tavern as an attraction to tourists. As automobile travel and road building spread through Missouri, Arrow Rock became a popular spot for mid-Missouri tourism.

The D.A.R. took the bold step of persuading the Missouri State Leg-islature to set aside the Tavern as a historic shrine. Women from the Arrow Rock, Marshall and Boonville chapters in particular took the lead to have the old building made into a historic shrine. In September of 1923, the legislature purchased the old brick building for $5,000. The Tavern became the first building in Missouri set aside for historic preser-vation purposes using public funds. The D.A.R. was named "permanent custodian" of the building, and they took over its management. Restora-tion and repair work of the structure was undertaken in 1925. The D.A.R. continued the tradition of serving meals and providing lodging. D.A.R. chapters from around the state furnished each room of the building.

In 1926, the Arrow Rock State Park was created on acreage surrounding the Tavern. Over the course of the years, the size of the facility was increased. Primarily, the focus of the state park was on recreation, such as camping and picnicking. The D.A.R. was allowed to handle interpretation, and they published several small pamphlets about Arrow Rock and gave tours of the Tavern. The state acquired significant properties, including the Academy Boarding House, the Calaboose and the Big Spring valley, amounting to a total of 33.93 acres. At this time, the old Fish and Game Commission managed the state park system. The commission quite naturally was more interested in sport hunting and fishing. Except for the efforts of the D.A.R., little was done in the areas of historic preservation and interpretation.

Ironically, it was during the Great Depression that the Missouri State Park system underwent one of its most phenomenal periods of growth. Two federal programs, the Civilian Conservation Corps (CCC) and the Works Progress Administration (WPA) were implemented to give unemployed men work. State park facilities were prime locations for projects. There were no CCC projects at Arrow Rock, but there were several WPA projects. Four structures remain from the WPA era; the gazebo located at the end of High Street, and in Arrow Rock State Historic Site there is the Shroyer grave shelter at the edge of town, the stone arch bridge in the Big Spring valley, and the stone picnic shelter. Citizens in Arrow Rock were often willing sellers of their property because of the need for cash. Consequently, the state was able to purchase the acreage in the town fronting Main Street. The most significant acquisition at this time was the George Caleb Bingham House.

During the Depression, citizens of Missouri voted on a change in the state constitution that would have a dramatic impact on the future of Arrow Rock. In 1934, the Fish and Game Commission was changed into the Department of Conservation, broadening its duty to protect and restore the wildlife and natural resources of the state. The task of managing state parks was moved to a new body, the State Park Board. Acreage south of town was added to Arrow Rock State Park, and the WPA was employed to develop this area into a campground and picnic area.

Visitation records for the early period of Arrow Rock as a tourist destination are scant. However, the Report of the Board of Managers of Arrow Rock Tavern dated October 5, 1937, provides some indication of the amount of visitation occurring. "It is gratifying to report that our citizens are awakening to the interest and value of our State history, which is demonstrated in the attendance at our Old Arrow Rock Tavern. There have been 1,482 who have gone through the Tavern enjoying the relics and history, in addition to those who have taken meals there. There were 1,834 meals served since December (1936)."[684] In more recent years, there have been more people than that who have eaten a meal or taken a tour in a single month.

The Report of the Board of Managers went on optimistically to report a new venture that would revitalize Arrow Rock. "The Bridge to be placed over the river near Arrow Rock seems to be assured. Congress has passed and sent to President Roosevelt [a bill] granting permission to the County Court of Saline County."[685] Of course, the bridge over the river eluded Arrow Rock just as the railroad line had. Arrow Rock was not destined to experience economic revival based on transportation, agriculture or manufacturing. Arrow Rock's revival was to come from its history.

The Friends of Arrow Rock, Inc.

Despite the efforts of the D.A.R. and the State Park Board, it became apparent in the 1950s that the task of preserving many Arrow Rock structures was beyond the scope and capability of either group. "On June 14, 1959, a group of people met here in the Old Tavern and heartily endorsed the establishment of an organization devoted solely to the preservation and restoration of the village of Arrow Rock."[686] The Friends of Arrow Rock, Inc. entered the scene as a dynamic force in the preservation of the town. Dues of one dollar were collected at that first meeting.

The first president was Mrs. David Eads who suggested the organization's logo and banner, "Guarding Missouri's Heritage." The Marshall *Democrat News* carried a report from John Hall in its December 9, 1959 edition, "The president [Mrs. Eads] recalled that the Friends of Arrow Rock was organized in June 1959, with five officers, 50 charter members and dreams of restoring Arrow Rock as a village of the 1880s. She said the organization now has 400 members and also had the endorsements of its work from many organizations."[687]

A number of citizens prominent in Saline County and Missouri were affiliated with the formation of the Friends of Arrow Rock. Officers were Mrs. Louise Perry Eads, Columbia, President; Hugh Stephens, Jefferson City, First Vice-President; Dr. John Lawrence, Arrow Rock, Second Vice-President; Mrs. Sallie Hailey, Arrow Rock, Secretary; Leonard Van

Dyke, Marshall, Treasurer; Mrs. C. Wayne Elsea, Marshall, Recorder. Arrow Rock resident Sallie Hailey, a descendant of the Wood family, was also the first woman in Missouri to be appointed to a state cabinet-level position, under the administration of Governor John Dalton. Mrs. Elsea was a Sappington descendant.

The Trustees also included some very distinguished members: John P. Huston, Jr., Marshall, great-grandson of Joseph Huston, Jr.; Frank C. Barnhill, Marshall, an avid local historian; Mrs. Frederick Groves, National Society of the D.A.R.; Charles van Ravenswaay, Director of the Missouri Historical Society, and President Harry S. Truman. Governor Frank Dalton was an honorary board member.[688] The publication of the Arrow Rock Cookbook in 1965 evidenced that the Friends had a statewide and even national vision from its inception. Edited by Mrs. John Percy Huston, the cookbook was designed to be a "collection of elegant recipes from distinguished hostesses." Those who contributed recipes were virtually a "who's who" of local, state and national D.A.R. and political leaders of the 1960s, including Bess Truman, Patricia Nixon, and Jacqueline Kennedy. The cookbook has been reprinted five times and is still for sale. The drive for the preservation of Arrow Rock as a whole accelerated at this point.

The first project undertaken by the Friends was the restoration of the building known as the log courthouse. Not knowing if the fledgling organization could handle continued maintenance, upon completion of restoration, the Friends deeded the structure and adjacent lots to the State of Missouri. Although this building is no longer thought to be the courthouse, it is one of the earliest surviving buildings in town. This project also marked the beginning of an era of cooperation between the Friends and the Missouri State Park Board and its successor agency. The Friends quickly learned they could indeed both restore and maintain historic properties, as their current holdings show.

The town of Arrow Rock was declared a National Historic Landmark in 1963 by the United States Department of the Interior. The Friends served as hosts for the dedication ceremony held in 1964. In 1965, they instituted a program of walking tours of the town and historic buildings in cooperation with the State of Missouri. Since 1976, the Friends have assumed full responsibility for funding guides used for tours. That year, they also participated in an exhibit of George Caleb Bingham sketches. Governor Kit Bond and his wife spearheaded an effort to keep Bingham's sketches in Missouri. The Arrow Rock show raised $12,500, enough for Bingham Sketches, Inc. to purchase one sketch to remain in Missouri.

In 1984, the Friends, in conjunction with the Arrow Rock State Historic Site, instituted the Spring Children's Education Programs. Every April and May, approximately 1,500 elementary students from within a 75 miles radius of Arrow Rock participate in interactive programs to learn about Arrow Rock's history. In recent years, the program has extended into June to accommodate summer schools. Biennially in September, the Friends and the Historic Site host the Children's Craft Festival. This program draws up to 2,000 students and adults for a single day to view demonstrations of 19th century crafts.

The Friends have been leaders in efforts to recover and preserve Arrow Rock's African American heritage. In the 1970s, Friends members began taking oral histories of African American residents and their descendants. The Friends sponsor the Juneteenth Celebration every other year. Juneteenth is said to have originated in Texas where slaves did not hear about the January 1, 1863 Emancipation Proclamation until June 19, 1865. In 1996, the Friends began working with multiple agencies and institutions to undertake archaeological excavations of the Black Lodge site and additional sites in Arrow Rock.

The Friends have over 550 members from nearly every state in the Union. They own, lease and manage 13 historic properties in the community. They have published seven books (including this volume) and reprinted five other publications. Grants and awards have been received from the National Endowment for the Humanities, the American Association for State and Local History, the Santa Fe Trail Association, the Missouri Alliance for Historic Preservation, The State Historical Society of Missouri and the Missouri Humanities Council. They remain a vital force in the preservation and promotion of Arrow Rock. Following is a list of their completed projects:

> 1962 *Log Courthouse purchased and restored. Subsequently deeded to the State of Missouri.*
>
> 1963 *Secured two Main Street store buildings. One became the Friends Information Center and the other the Loom House, a weaving shop.*
>
> 1964 *Christian Church restored to c. 1876 appearance in cooperation with Arrow Rock Craft Club. The Friends*

have a 99-year lease on the building.

1966 I.O.O.F. Lodge Hall acquired and furnished as a museum.

1967 J. P. Sites Gun Shop acquired and underwent restoration.

1973 J. P. Sites House acquired and restored.

1974 Constructed Sappington Memorial Building as a museum adjacent to Lyceum Theater.

1976 Moved log cabin from southeast Saline County to Main Street Arrow Rock. Used as a pioneer doctor's museum until 1998.

1987 Purchased lot at entrance of town and removed a modern building, the Black Sheep Inn.

1989 Bill and Cora Lee Miller announce gift of the Dr. Bradford House and their antique business.

1990 Gift of Christopher Collection of Early Missouri Firearms from Byron Christopher Shutz.

1993 Arrow Rock Post Office is moved into the newly-restored former Loom House.

1994 Friends moved office to former post office building, which has been restored to a turn-of-the-century appearance.

1998 Brown's Chapel Free Will Baptist Church undergoes restoration.

2000 Black Lodge Hall acquired from Ted and Virginia Fisher; undergoes restoration.

2003 Restoration of the Lawless House, leased from the Missouri Department of Natural Resources. Located on the west edge of town, this 1903 farmstead demonstrates changes in technology and lifestyles.

2004 Renovation of Sappington Memorial Building and creation of exhibits to interpret the life and medical contributions of Dr. Sappington.

2004 Received gift of house on Block 29 from Sue Stubbs as rental property.

Heritage Tourism: The Modern Crossroads

Concurrently with activities of the Friends of Arrow Rock, the community began to see economic revival in other areas. In 1960, the Arrow Rock Lyceum Theater was founded by several individuals when the Baptist

Church building was sold at auction. Missouri's oldest repertory theater produces professional plays and musicals each summer and fall. In 1993, the theater expanded into a new 408-seat auditorium, and the portion that was the old Baptist Church now serves as the theater lobby and box office. Approximately 30,000 people now view performances every season.

The 1960s saw the creation of the Arrow Rock Craft Club, a cooperative of local artisans who continue the tradition of producing quality hand-crafted items, and the Country Store and Miller's Antiques became popular destinations along with the Old Tavern. Private individuals had begun restorations of some of the major properties in the area: "Prairie Park," 3.5 miles west of Arrow Rock, and the Price House and Bradford House on Main Street. Private restorations in the surrounding area contin-ued in the 1980s and 1990s. Restored homes include the Sanders A. H. Townsend house, a second restoration of William B. Sappington's home, "Prairie Park," the George A. Murrell home, "Oak Grove," and currently "Lo Mismo," the home of John Locke Hardeman, is being restored.

Arrow Rock briefly became the town of Hannibal, Missouri, in 1972. A film production of *Tom Sawyer* was shot in town. The movie starred Johnny Whitaker as Tom; Celeste Holm as Aunt Polly; Warren Oates as Muff Potter; and Jodie Foster, in her third movie role, as Becky Thatcher. For several weeks, the residents of Arrow Rock played the parts of 19th century townspeople. Tom and Huck's funeral took place in the Christian Church. The graveyard scene took place in the Sappington cemetery. The court scene was held in the I.O.O.F. Hall, and a special window was installed for "Injun Joe" to jump through in his escape. The blacksmith shop, constructed as a set, remains in use as a small business near the town entrance on Main Street. Unfortunately, the two-story Greek Revival house on Main Street that served as "Aunt Polly's" home burned shortly after filming was completed.

In 1976, Missouri state government underwent reorganization. The Missouri State Park Board was dissolved, and its functions were placed under the Missouri Department of Natural Resources, Division of State Parks. Arrow Rock State Park was re-designated Arrow Rock State His-toric Site to accurately reflect its rich cultural history. Additional acreage was purchased south of town, and this was converted into a modern recre-ation area. In 1984, Missouri voters approved the Third State Building Fund for capital improvements and the first round of the 1/10th of 1%

Parks and Soils Sales Tax (PSST). The tax provided a stable source of funding for the state park and historic site system.

In Arrow Rock State Historic Site, major restorations of the Tavern, Hall House, Bingham House, Academy Boarding House and Courthouse were completed between 1984 and 1991. One of the most significant undertakings occurred in 1991, when the State Historic Site Visitors' Center was completed. State Representative Martha Jarman and State Senator James Mathewson were instrumental in securing the support of Governor John Ashcroft and the State Legislature for the project. This million-dollar facility provided, for the first time, centralized archival storage for thousands of artifacts and manuscripts pertaining to Arrow Rock history. In 1993, the exhibits were completed and visitors had a place where they could become oriented to the community and its history before beginning to explore it. The Visitors' Center also serves as a major point of education for thousands of Missouri school children and teacher education workshops.

Other projects completed at Arrow Rock with PSST funding included campground improvements such as the electrification of campsites and construction of new shower facilities. The old Barger stock pond was renovated and christened Big Soldier Lake after the Little Osage chief who negotiated with George Sibley at Arrow Rock. It is managed in cooperation with the Missouri Department of Conservation and stocked with bass, bluegill, and channel catfish. A one-and-a-half-mile-hiking trail, beginning in the visitors' center parking lot, follows the circumference of the site boundary. By 1991, the historic site encompassed 169 acres, nine historic structures and multiple archaeological sites ranging from prehistoric through Arrow Rock's heyday. Continued support of the PSST by Missouri citizens is vital to ensure the continued operation and preservation of Arrow Rock State Historic Site and the Missouri State Park system.

The Historic Arrow Rock Council (HARC) acts as an umbrella organization for the town, sponsoring many cultural events such as Bluegrass Festivals, and Hanging of the Greens, kicking off the Christmas season in town. Every second full weekend of October, the town holds a Heritage Crafts Festival, drawing several thousand people. HARC was founded in 1979. The Arrow Rock Area Merchants Association, formed in 1986, promotes the viability of the town's gift and antique shops and numerous bed and breakfast establishments.

As a community, the village of Arrow Rock maintains a town government in the form of the Board of Trustees, whose existence dates back to Arrow Rock's first town election, August 1, 1840. The Arrow Rock Volunteer Fire Department, formed in 1954, helps protect the structures of the community and now handles local medical emergencies through its First Responder program. In the 1970s, the town established a water department purchasing water from Slater, Missouri, instead of using local wells. The town voted in a historic zoning ordinance in the 1970s. A Board of Architectural Review studies proposals for future development and home renovations to ensure the town keeps its historic ambiance. In 2003, a sewer was installed using individual septic tanks but creating a community lateral field in the bottoms below Arrow Rock. This project took more than ten years to negotiate.

Visitors make the common mistake of assuming that the town of Arrow Rock is entirely controlled as a state-owned historic site. In reality, most of the community is privately owned. However, all of Arrow Rock's civic and historical organizations, public and private, work together to preserve the historic resource that Arrow Rock represents, and to welcome the modern day traveler to this crossroads of the Missouri frontier. Ultimately, it is the people of Missouri who will decide if Arrow Rock is worthy of continued preservation for future generations. With its unique and colorful history, now dating back in records almost 300 years, Arrow Rock's many friends hope that the answer will be a resounding "Yes!"

About the Author

MICHAEL DICKEY IS ORIGINALLY FROM INDEPENDENCE, MISSOURI, and graduated from Central Missouri State University in 1976, with a B.S. in Art (emphasis in art history). He has always had an interest in Missouri's natural and cultural resources.

Mike has an extensive background in historical reenactments starting as a "mountain man" in high school. He has since been involved with the First Regiment, First Brigade, Missouri Militia (1830s militia), 10th Missouri Infantry, Holmes' Brigade (Union soldier), and the Macon Silver-Grays (Missouri State Guardsman). Currently he is active with the First U.S. Infantry, Boone's Company Missouri Rangers (War of 1812). This organization also promotes research into Missouri's territorial history and conducts symposiums each year.

Mike has been employed by the Missouri Department of Natural Resources, Division of State Parks, since 1985. He became the administrator of Arrow Rock State Historic Site, Sappington Cemetery and Boone's Lick State Historic Site in 1995. His articles have appeared in various historical publications, and he is a frequent speaker at workshops and public forums.

Endnotes

1 1881 *History of Saline County, Missouri*, p. 471.
2 Biggs, p. 6.
3 March, Vol. I, p.4.
4 Read, p. 269.
5 American Indian History from Prehistory to the Nineteenth Century Relating to Regional St. Louis. Website.
6 D'Anville's "Carte de la Louisiane" was drawn in 1732 and published in 1752. Some sources erroneously transcribed the date as 1723.
7 Benson, p. 74.
8 Thwaites, p. 244.
9 Rainey, p. 11.
10 *Ibid.*, pp. 11–12.
11 Biggs.
12 1881 *History of Saline County, Missouri*, pp. 474–475.
13 *Ibid.*
14 Bradbury, p. 11.
15 Burns, *Osage Indian Bands & Clans*, pp. 1, 33.
16 Mathews, p. 98–99.
17 Moulton, p. 296.
18 Burns, *History of the Osage People*.
19 Louis Burns to Michael Dickey, personal communication September, 2003.
20 Mathews, pp. 454–455.
21 Benson, pp. 74–75.
22 1881 *History of Saline County, Missouri*, p. 164.
23 March, Vol. I, p. 15.
24 Norall, p. 116.
25 Plattner Collection, Arrow Rock State Historic Site.
26 Rainey, pp. 10–11.
27 1881 *History of Saline County, Missouri*, pp. 167–168.
28 March, Vol. 1, p. 19.
29 *Ibid.*, p. 23.
30 Mathews, p. 211.
31 Long knife was a reference to the bayonet used by soldiers or knives carried by American woodsmen.
32 Mathews, pp. 224–225.
33 *Ibid.*, "Wah-kon" Mystery or "Wah-kon-dah" Great Mystery was analogous to the "Great Spirit" or the Osage version of God.
34 *Ibid.*
35 March, Vol. I, p. 64.
36 Mathews, p. 951.
37 Brackenridge.

38   Moulton, p. 296.
39   Moulton, p. 303.
40   *Ibid.*, p. 302.
41   Mathews, p. 277.
42   Lewis & Clark Across Missouri web site, Survey No. 3004. lewisclark.geog.missouri.edu/index.shtml.
43   *Ibid.*, Survey No. 3328.
44   Boone's Lick State Historic Site Interpretive Text, 2000.
45   *Lewis & Clark National Historic Trail*, National Park Service Pamphlet, 2002.
46   Moulton, p. 286.
47   *Ibid.*, p. 287.
48   *Ibid.*, p. 288.
49   Coues, p. 18.
50   Moulton, pp. 288–289.
51   Coues, p. 18.
52   Boone's Lick State Historic Site Interpretive File, Arrow Rock SHS.
53   *Ibid.*
54   Crock jug from spring operation in ARSHS collection.
55   Benson, pp. 74–75.
56   1881 *History of Saline County, Missouri*, p. 507.
57   Napton, pp. 350–351.
58   *The Western Emigrant*, Boonville, MO, July 18, 1839, Collection of Friends of Historic Boonville.
59   1881 *History of Saline County, Missouri*, p. 493.
60   *Ibid.* p. 193.
61   Bradbury.
62   Lay, *Early Boone's Lick Indian Events.*
63   Gregg, *Westward with Dragoons*, pp. 7–8,15.
64   *Ibid.*, p. 28.
65   *Ibid.*, p. 34.
66   *Ibid.*, pp. 67–68.
67   *Ibid.*, p. 65.
68   Mathews, pp. 388–389.
69   Gregg, *Westward With Dragoons*, p. 46.
70   Jones, p. 103.
71   Gregg, *Westward With Dragoons*, p. 27.
72   *Ibid.*, p. 28.
73   von Sachsen-Altenburg and Dyer, p. 67.
74   *Ibid.*, p. 69.
75   Franklin *Missouri Intelligencer*, April 1, 1820, MSHS.
76   Gregg, *Westward With Dragoons*, p. 27.
77   Lay, *Early Boone's Lick Indian Events.*
78   Rathbone, p. 132.
79   1881 *History of Saline County, Missouri*, p. 184.
80   *Ibid.*, p. 187.
81   *Ibid.*, pp. 185–186.
82   *Ibid.*
83   *Ibid.*
84   *Ibid.*
85   Kennedy, *Arrow Rock, Missouri, and Thereabouts.*
86   1881 *History of Saline County, Missouri*, p. 183, and Rainey, p. 38.
87   Kennedy, *Arrow Rock News.*
88   U.S. Fish and Wildlife Service News Release.
89   Norrall, p. 117.

90   1881 *History of Saline County, Missouri*, pp. 468–469.
91   von Sachsen-Altenburg and Dyer, p. 68.
92   Thwaites, p. 244.
93   Benson, p. 74.
94   Thwaites, p. 244.
95   1881 *History of Saline County, Missouri*, p. 474.
96   Lay, *Early Boone's Lick Indian Events*.
97   Bryan, p. 469, Reprint of the *Life of Black Hawk*, October, 1833.
98   *Ibid.*
99   Hagin, p. 46.
100 March, Vol. I, p. 284.
101 McDaniel, p. 19.
102 Dickey, 1998.
103 *Ibid.*
104 Sibley to William Clark, Nov. 28, 1813, Territorial Papers.
105 Dickey, 1998.
106 Coyner, p. 125.
107 *Ibid*, p. 126.
108 *Ibid*, p. 127.
109 Gregg, "War of 1812 on the Missouri Frontier," Part III, pp. 330–331.
110 Dickey, 1998.
111 *Missouri Historical Review*, Vol. 32:122–123.
112 Thorp.
113 *Ibid.*
114 Lay, *Early Boone's Lick Indian Events*.
115 *Ibid.*
116 *Ibid.*
117 Thorp.
118 Hamilton, *Arrow Rock: Where Wheels Started West*, p. 10.
119 Babcock, p. 137.
120 Lay, *Early Boone's Lick Indian Events*.
121 *Ibid.*
122 *Missouri Gazette*, August 13, 1814, SHSM, Columbia, MO.
123 *St. Louis Missouri Gazette & Illinois Advertiser*, Sept. 24, 1814,
     Missouri Historical Review Vol. 32, No. 1.
124 Lay, *Early Boone's Lick Indian Events*.
125 *Ibid.*
126 *Ibid.*
127 *Ibid.*
128 *Ibid.*
129 1881 *History of Saline County, Missouri*, p. 159.
130 Lay, *Early Boone's Lick Indian Events*.
131 March, Vol. I, pp. 296–297.
132 Lay, *Early Boone's Lick Indian Events*.
133 1881 *History of Saline County, Missouri*, p. 146.
134 Rainey, p. 24.
135 Lay, *Early Boone's Lick Indian Events*.
136 *Ibid.*
137 Thorp.
138 March, Vol. I, p. 304.
139 "Memorial of the State of Missouri in Relation to Indian Depredations Upon the Citizens
     of That State, Washington, D.C., 1825," Missouri Historical Society, St. Louis, MO.
140 *Ibid.*

141 *Ibid.*
142 *Ibid.*
143 Lay, *Early Boone's Lick Indian Events.*
144 Babcock, p. 137.
145 Franklin *Missouri Intelligencer*, June 18, 1825, SHSM.
146 Babcock, p. 146.
147 March, Vol. I, p. 311.
148 *Ibid.*, p. 313.
149 *Ibid.*, p. 314.
150 *Ibid.*, p. 315.
151 Napton, p. 367.
152 Gregg, Kate, *The Road to Santa Fe*, p. 55.
153 1881 *History of Saline County, Missouri*, p. 147.
154 Rainey, p. 26.
155 *Ibid.*, pp. 26-27.
156 1881 *History of Saline County, Missouri*, p. 147.
157 *Ibid.*
158 Lewis & Clark Across Missouri web site, Survey No. 2520. lewisclark.geog.missouri.edu/index.shtml.
159 1881 *History of Saline County, Missouri*, pp. 151–152.
160 *Ibid.*
161 1881 *History of Saline County, Missouri*, p. 164.
162 Franklin *Missouri Intelligencer*, August 17, 1829, State Historical Society of Missouri, Columbia, MO.
163 *Ibid.*, p. 319.
164 March, Vol. I, p. 318.
165 *Ibid.*
166 *Ibid.*, p. 375.
167 1881 *History of Saline County, Missouri*, p. 475.
168 *Ibid.*, p. 166.
169 Saline County Court Records, August 9, 1830.
170 Hardeman, *Wilderness Calling*, p. 97.
171 Busby helped Sibley build the Osage Trading House. He was killed in February, 1815.
172 Osman to Ferrill, September 9, 1817, Missouri Historical Society, St. Louis, MO.
173 van Ravenswaay, p. 4.
174 Biggs, p. 2.
175 Benson, p. 74.
176 *Ibid.*
177 von Sachsen-Altenburg and Dyer, pp. 67–68.
178 *Ibid.* p. 69.
179 Windell, pp. 192–193.
180 Hamilton, *Arrow Rock: Where Wheels Started West*, p. 13.
181 Napton, *Past & Present of Saline County*, p. 83.
182 1881 *History of Saline County, Missouri*, p. 194.
183 *Missouri Historical Review*, Vol. 43:99.
184 Rainey, p. 19.
185 Kennedy, Items from the Glasgow *Weekly Times.*
186 Boonville Ferry Broadside, ARSHS.
187 Hamilton, *Arrow Rock: Where Wheels Started West*, pp. 13–14.
188 Lay, *Notes on the Santa Fe Trail.*
189 *Ibid.*
190 Lay, *Notes on the Santa Fe Trail.* Becknell published the story of his 1821 and 1822 expeditions in the April 23, 1823 edition of the *Missouri Intelligencer.*
191 *Ibid.*
192 Duffus, pp. 68–69.

193 Lay, *Notes on the Santa Fe Trail.*
194 March, Vol. I, p. 482.
195 Lay, *Notes on the Santa Fe Trail.*
196 March, Vol. I, p. 485.
197 Gregg, Josiah, *On the Road to Santa Fe*, pp. 52–53.
198 *Ibid.*
199 Lay, *Notes on the Santa Fe Trail.*
200 Dickey, 2003.
201 Lay, *Notes on the Santa Fe Trail.*
202 Gregg, Josiah, p. 332.
203 *Ibid.*
204 Napton, p. 359.
205 Napton, pp. 107–108.
206 Lay, *Notes on the Santa Fe Trail.*
207 Gregg, Josiah, *On the Road to Santa Fe.* pp. 54–55.
208 Letter of Agreement; Marmaduke, Sappington & McMahan, October 30, 1827, WHMC-SHSM.
209 Hardeman, *Wilderness Calling*, pp. 110–114.
210 *Ibid.*, pp. 114–115.
211 Napton, *Past and Present of Saline County*, p. 804.
212 Manual Alvarez Papers, New Mexico State Records & Archives, Santa Fe, NM.
213 Barnhill, p. 32.
214 Forry, Joseph Huston Chronology, 1985.
215 Robert W. Thompson personal communication to Michael Dickey, June, 2003.
216 Napton, *Past and Present of Saline County*, p. 804.
217 *Ibid.*
218 Hafen, p. 303.
219 *Ibid.* p. 307.
220 *Ibid.* p. 308.
221 Turley Family Records, by Beth Mitchell, Lester F. Turley et al, Turley Family Historical Research Association, 1981.
222 *Ibid.*
223 *Ibid.*
224 Rainey, p. 45.
225 *Ibid.*, p. 18.
226 Parkman, p. 2.
227 Napton, *Past and Present of Saline County*, p. 109.
228 Leopard and Shoemaker, Vol. I, p. 137.
229 Hamilton, Records of the Town of Arrow Rock.
230 *Ibid.*
231 van Ravenswaay, p. 6.
232 Fayette *Missouri Intelligencer*, July 3, 1829, State Historical Society of Missouri, Columbia, MO.
233 Saline County Court Records, transcript in Arrow Rock State Historic Site files.
234 *Ibid.*
235 Thwaites, p. 244.
236 Territorial Law Vol. II, p. 370, Missouri Secretary of State's Office.
237 van Ravenswaay, p. 9.
238 Hamilton, Records of the Town of Arrow Rock.
239 *Ibid.*
240 *Ibid.*
241 Missouri State Archives web site.
242 Gilliam *Globe*, Sept. 29, 1916, Arrow Rock SHS file copy.
243 1881 *History of Saline County, Missouri*, p. 195.
244 *Ibid.*, p. 196.

245 *Ibid.*, p. 206.
246 *Ibid.*, pp. 207–208.
247 *Ibid.*, p. 203.
248 *Ibid.*, pp. 203–204.
249 *Ibid.*, p. 204.
250 *Ibid.*, p. 230.
251 *Ibid.*, pp. 478–479.
252 Missouri State Archives web site.
253 Saline County Court Records, November 12, 1839.
254 1881 *History of Saline County, Missouri*, p. 227.
255 van Ravenswaay, p. 13.
256 Wilson.
257 *Ibid.*
258 Griffith, p. 49.
259 1881 *History of Saline County, Missouri*, p. 399.
260 *Ibid.*
261 Jean Hamilton identifies him as William Becknell's brother. However, this may be an error in the historical account. "Captain Becknell" appears to actually be William Becknell.
262 *Ibid.*
263 *Ibid.*, p. 217.
264 *Ibid.*
265 1881 *History of Saline County, Missouri*, p. 223.
266 *Ibid.*, p. 224.
267 Beeding to Lackland, June 1, 1847, Missouri Historical Society, St. Louis, MO.
268 Magoffin, pp. 228-229.
269 1881 *History of Saline County, Missouri*, p. 248.
270 *Ibid.*, p. 249.
271 March, Vol. I., p. 578.
272 Lay, *Notes on Missouri River Steamboats.*
273 *Ibid.*
274 1881 *History of Saline County, Missouri*, p. 208.
275 Dyer, p. 8.
276 *Ibid.*
277 Notes on Waterway Travel, ARSHS.
278 Dyer, p. 10.
279 1881 *History of Saline County, Missouri*, p. 554.
280 Dyer, p. 1.
281 *Ibid.*
282 "The Missouri River and Its Victims," Missouri Historical Review, Volume 21, No. 4.
283 van Ravenswaay, p. 19.
284 Notes on Waterways Travel, ARSHS.
285 Arrow Rock *Enterprise* Notes, FAR archives.
286 Kennedy, *Arrow Rock News Commerce & Comments.*
287 *Ibid.*, March 19, 1858.
288 *Ibid.*, January 29, 1858.
289 *Ibid.*, April 9, 1858.
290 Hamilton, Records of the Town of Arrow Rock.
291 *Ibid.*
292 *Ibid.*
293 Rainey, p. 18.
294 1881 *History of Saline County, Missouri*, p. 775.
295 Dyer, p. 13.
296 Museum Exhibits Plan, ARSHS.

297 *Ibid.*
298 Kennedy, *Arrow Rock News Commerce & Comments*, Marshall *Weekly Democrat*, February 18, 1859.
299 *Ibid.*, February 14, 1859.
300 Franklin *Missouri Intelligencer*, October 2, 1824, State Historical Society of Missouri, Columbia, MO.
301 Handwritten Bill of Sale, Joseph Huston to Benjamin Huston, ARSHS.
302 Lenoir Letter, 1835, SHSM – WMC (transcript at ARSHS).
303 Notes/Letters written by J. Locke Hardeman, Arrow Rock, to Nathaniel B. Tucker, Williamsburg, Va., Dec. 15, 1845 WMC – SHSM.
304 Baumann, Rogers, & Miller. p. 4.
305 *Ibid.*, pp. 4–5.
306 *Ibid.*, pp. 8–9.
307 Beeding to Lackland, June 1, 1847, MSH.
308 Harper & Forry.
309 Phillips, p. 216.
310 Hamilton, Records of the Town of Arrow Rock.
311 Kennedy, *Arrow Rock News Commerce & Comments*, October 1, 1858.
312 *Ibid.*
313 *Ibid.*
314 *Ibid.*, February 1, 1860.
315 Baumann, p. 81.
316 *Ibid.*, pp. 81–82.
317 Kennedy, *Arrow Rock, Missouri, and Thereabouts.*
318 *Ibid.*
319 Hamilton, Records of the Town of Arrow Rock.
320 *Ibid.*
321 *Ibid.*
322 von Sachsen-Altenburg and Dyer, p. 112.
323 Sunder, p. 50.
324 Hamilton, Records of the Town of Arrow Rock.
325 Mo. Society D.A.R., 1963, and Hall family tradition.
326 Hamilton, Records of the Town of Arrow Rock.
327 Kennedy, *Arrow Rock News Commerce & Comments*, March 4, 1858.
328 Hamilton, Records of the Town of Arrow Rock.
329 *Ibid.*
330 *Ibid.*
331 *Ibid.*
332 *Ibid.*
333 *Ibid.*
334 Kennedy, *Arrow News Commerce & Comments*, May 13, 1859.
335 Hamilton, Records of the Town of Arrow Rock.
336 *Ibid.*
337 *Ibid.*
338 *Ibid.*
339 *Ibid.*
340 *Ibid.*
341 *Ibid.*
342 *Ibid.*
343 Bill Lovin, Arrow Rock Lodge 55, personal communication to Michael Dickey, December, 2003.
344 Kennedy, *Arrow Rock News Commerce & Comments.*
345 Friends of Arrow Rock, Newspapers File.
346 Burge.
347 Bryan and Rose, pp. 81–82.
348 Burge.

349 Bryan and Rose, p. 83.
350 1881 *History of Saline County, Missouri*, p. 176.
351 *Ibid.*, p. 217.
352 *Ibid.*, p. 218.
353 *Ibid.*
354 Burge.
355 *Ibid.*
356 1881 *History of Saline County, Missouri*, pp. 175–176.
357 Burge.
358 *Ibid.*
359 Rainey, pp. 48–49.
360 *Ibid.*
361 Burge.
362 *Ibid.*
363 Burge.
364 *Ibid.*
365 Baumann, p. 64.
366 Burge.
367 *Ibid.*
368 Burge.
369 Parsons & Habernal.
370 Burge.
371 *Ibid.*
372 Baumann, p. 69.
373 Burge.
374 *Ibid.*
375 *Ibid.*
376 Burge.
377 Parsons & Habernal.
378 Rathbone, p. 190.
379 *The Western Emigrant*, Boonville, MO, August 1, 1839, Collection of Friends of Historic Boonville.
380 Kennedy, *Arrow Rock News Commerce & Comments.*
381 Bowen.
382 *Ibid.*
383 *Ibid.*
384 Hamilton, Records of the Town of Arrow Rock.
385 van Ravenswaay, p. 15.
386 Kennedy, *Arrow Rock, Missouri, and Thereabouts*, p. 27.
387 van Ravenswaay, p. 15.
388 Kennedy, *Arrow Rock News Commerce & Commerce, Weekly Democrat*, March 5, 1858.
389 Rainey, p. 63.
390 *Ibid.*, p. 60.
391 Hamilton, Records of the Town of Arrow Rock.
392 Rainey, p. 61.
393 Baumann p. 71
394 Barnhill, pp. 13–15.
395 *Ibid.*, p. 16.
396 *Ibid.*, p. 15.
397 Barnhill, p. 18.
398 1881 *History of Saline County, Missouri*, p. 478.
399 *Ibid.*
400 *Ibid.*
401 Baumann, p. 70.

402 *Ibid.*, pp. 71–72.
403 Kremer and Hoaglin, p. 13.
404 Baumann, p. 71.
405 *Ibid.*, p. 85.
406 Baumann, p. 87.
407 *Ibid.*
408 Rainey, p. 17.
409 A 19th century term for an establishment where liquor consumption is its main purpose.
410 van Ravenswaay, p. 10.
411 *Ibid.*, p. 11.
412 Rainey, p. 90.
413 Case Family Papers, MHS, St. Louis, MO.
414 Rainey, p. 32.
415 Tavern invitation, December 13, 1841, ARSHS.
416 Invitation to Arrow Rock Hotel, December 27, 1870, ARSHS.
417 van Ravenswaay, p. 11.
418 *Ibid.*, pp. 11–12.
419 *Ibid.* p. 12.
420 Hamilton, Records of the Town of Arrow Rock.
421 Thomas Cobb ledger, ARSHS.
422 Van Ravenswaay, p. 12.
423 Eastham.
424 Kennedy, *Arrow Rock, Missouri, and Thereabouts, Saline County Progress*, March 6, 1868.
425 *Ibid.*, January 3, 1868.
426 *Ibid.*, August 27, 1869.
427 Barnhill, p. 15.
428 *Ibid.*
429 Forry, Chronology of Joseph Huston.
430 Kennedy, *Arrow Rock News Commerce & Comments.*
431 Hamilton, *Arrow Rock: Where Wheels Started West.*
432 van Ravenswaay to Pointer, November 13, 1938, WMC – SHSM.
433 Baumann, pp. 104–105.
434 Hamilton, Records of the Town of Arrow Rock.
435 Laws of Missouri, Vol. 5, 1842–1843, Missouri Secretary of State.
436 Hamilton, Records of Town of Arrow Rock.
437 van Ravenswaay, p. 13.
438 Kennedy, *Arrow Rock News Commerce & Comments*, Marshall *Weekly Democrat*, February 11, 1859.
439 *Ibid.*, March 19, 1858.
440 Kremer, James Milton Turner, p. 33.
441 *Ibid.*
442 Arrow Rock *Enterprise*, August 5, 1892.
443 Kremer and Hoaglin, p. 6.
444 As identified on the Arrow Rock plat map of 1896.
445 Arrow Rock *Enterprise*, month and day unknown, 1891 (FAR).
446 Rainey, pp. 69–70.
447 *Ibid.*
448 Kennedy, *Arrow Rock News Commerce & Comments,* Marshall *Weekly Democrat*, September 30, 1859.
449 *Ibid.*, October 10, 1860.
450 Kennedy, *Arrow Rock, Missouri, and Thereabouts.*
451 Arrow Rock *Enterprise*, no date, Friends of Arrow Rock Newspaper Excerpts.
452 Kennedy, *Arrow Rock News Commerce and Comments.*
453 Hamilton, Records of the Town of Arrow Rock.
454 William Ashley Burial Ground web site.

455 Sappington Negro Cemetery, Friends of Arrow Rock, Inc., 2001.
456 *Ibid.*
457 Kennedy, *Arrow Rock News Commerce & Comments*. Marshall *Weekly Democrat*, October 7, 1859.
458 *The Western Emigrant*, August 1, 1839, Friends of Historic Boonville.
459 March, Vol. I, p. 703.
460 Letter of Beeding to Lackland, June 1, 1847, Missouri Historical Society, St. Louis, MO.
461 Sappington, p. 208.
462 *Ibid.*, p. 212.
463 *A Treatise on Cholera*, Library of Congress web site.
464 *Ibid.*
465 Sappington, p. 213.
466 *Ibid.*, p. 215.
467 Dr. Tom Hall, personal communication to Michael Dickey, October, 2003.
468 1881 *History of Saline County, Missouri*, p. 254.
469 Hamilton, Records of the Town of Arrow Rock.
470 Thompson Medical Diploma, Arrow Rock SHS artifacts collection.
471 Robert Thompson, personal communication to Michael Dickey, June 2003.
472 Kennedy, Glasgow *Weekly Times*, July 12, 1849.
473 Hamilton, Records of the Town of Arrow Rock.
474 *Ibid.*
475 *Ibid.*
476 March, Vol. I, p. 715.
477 Rainey, p. 90.
478 Kennedy, *Arrow Rock News Commerce & Comments*, Marshall *Weekly Democrat*, Feb. 5, 1858.
479 Dr. Tom Hall, personal communication to Michael Dickey, September, 2003.
480 Kennedy, *Arrow Rock, Missouri, and Thereabouts, Saline County Progress*, January 8, 1869.
481 Vapors or gases from decomposing marsh vegetation.
482 *The Western Emigrant*, August 1, 1839.
483 Babcock, *Forty Years of Pioneer Life: Memoir of John Mason Peck, D.D.*, pp. 6–7.
484 1881 *History of Saline County, Missouri*, p. 409.
485 Riley, pp. 1–2.
486 *Ibid.*, p. 7.
487 *Ibid.*, pp. 25–27.
488 Moulton, p. 347.
489 Sappington, p. 26.
490 RPH Laboratory Medicine.
491 Phillips, p. 72.
492 Garrard, p. 13.
493 Riley, pp. 42–43.
494 Napton, p. 387.
495 Riley, p. 45.
496 Sappington, p. 79.
497 Riley, p. 34.
498 *The Western Emigrant*, August 1, 1839, Friends of Historic Boonville.
499 Fuenfhausen.
500 Rainey, p. 80.
501 Riley, pp. 91–96.
502 Phillips, pp. 81, 174.
503 Napton, p. 387.
504 Bloch, pp. 168–169.
505 Rainey, p. 77.
506 Bloch, pp. 168–169.
507 Rainey, pp. 77–78.

508 Phillips, p. 70.
509 Riley, p. 9.
510 Phillips, pp. 60–61.
511 Rainey, pp. 38–39.
512 *Ibid.*
513 Phillips, p. 87.
514 *Life* Magazine, March 2, 1942, and Riley, p. 5.
515 Phillips, p. 216.
516 *Ibid.*, p. 229.
517 Phillips, p. 236.
518 Napton, pp. 344–345.
519 *Ibid.*, pp. 393–396.
520 *Ibid.*
521 Guitar and Shoemaker, p. 4.
522 Napton, pp. 394–395.
523 Bloch, p. 272.
524 *Ibid.*
525 *Ibid.*
526 Dickey, "George Caleb Bingham, A Synopsis."
527 Bloch, p. 272.
528 Caldwell, p. 14.
529 Caldwell, p. 12.
530 Bingham Turley, personal communication to Michael Dickey, December, 1998.
531 Caldwell, p. 14.
532 Caldwell, p. 12.
533 *Ibid.*
534 Hamilton, Records of the Town of Arrow Rock.
535 *Ibid.*
536 Caldwell, p. 12.
537 Bloch. p. 185.
538 Dickey, "George Caleb Bingham, A Synopsis."
539 *Ibid.*
540 Rathbone, p. 194.
541 Kennedy, *Arrow Rock News Commerce & Comments.*
542 Christ-Janer, p. 79.
543 Kennedy, *Arrow Rock News Commerce & Comments.*
544 Dickey, "George Caleb Bingham, A Synopsis."
545 Christ-Janer, p. 102.
546 *Ibid.*, pp. 1–2.
547 National Historic Landmarks Program, George Caleb Bingham House.
548 Compiled from *The Paintings of George Caleb Bingham* by E. Maurice Bloch, *George Caleb Bingham of Missouri*, by Albert Christ-Janer, *George Caleb Bingham*, by Michael Shapiro, *Missouri's National Historic Landmarks: Village of Arrow Rock and George Caleb Bingham Home* by Dorothy J. Caldwell and *George Caleb Bingham: the Missouri Artist* by Fern Helen Rusk.
549 Stubbs.
550 *Ibid.*
551 *Ibid.*
552 *Ibid.*
553 *Ibid.*
554 *Ibid.*
555 *Ibid.*
556 *Ibid.*
557 Rainey, pp. 43–44.

558 Tommy Sites to Michael Dickey, personal communication, September, 1990.
559 Rainey, p. 43.
560 *Ibid.*, p. 44.
561 Rainey, p. 42.
562 Stubbs.
563 *Ibid.*
564 Hall, "Wallace Gusler on the Development of the American Long Rifle."
565 Kennedy, *Arrow Rock, Missouri, and Thereabouts.*
566 Robert Thompson, personal communication to Michael Dickey, June 2003.
567 Hamilton, Records of the Town of Arrow Rock.
568 *Ibid.*
569 *Ibid.*
570 Kennedy, *Arrow Rock News Commerce & Comments*, Marshall *Weekly Democrat*, July 14, 1858.
571 Hamilton, Records of the Town of Arrow Rock.
572 March, Vol. I, p. 827.
573 *Ibid.*, p. 829.
574 *Ibid.*
575 Furse, p. 10.
576 March, Vol. II, p. 844.
577 1881 *History of Saline County, Missouri*, p. 258.
578 *Ibid.*
579 Kennedy, *Arrow Rock News Commerce & Comments*, p. 18.
580 1881 *History of Saline County, Missouri*, p. 262.
581 *Ibid.*, p. 259.
582 *Ibid.*, p. 263.
583 *Ibid.*, p. 262.
584 Kennedy, *Arrow Rock News Commerce & Comments*, Marshall *Weekly Democrat*, July 22, 1859.
585 1881 *History of Saline County, Missouri*, p. 265.
586 *Ibid.*, p. 266.
587 *Ibid.*
588 Kennedy, *Arrow Rock News Commerce & Comments*, Marshall *Weekly Democrat*, Dec. 21, 1859.
589 *Ibid.*, *Weekly Democrat*, December 2, 1859.
590 *The Messages and Proclamations of the Governors of Missouri, Vol. II*, State Historical Society of Missouri, Columbia, 1926, John Sappington Marmaduke by C.H. McClure.
591 *Ibid.*
592 Arrow Rock SHS Manuscript Collection.
593 Bartels.
594 Rainey, p. 55.
595 *Ibid.*
596 Barnhill, p. 17.
597 United States War Department, Series I, Vol. 3, p. 173.
598 *Ibid.*
599 *Ibid.*, p. 177.
600 Burge.
601 United States War Department, Series I, Vol. 8, p. 400.
602 *Ibid.*, p. 35.
603 Arrow Rock, Missouri, Post Office Records.
604 Rainey, p. 60.
605 Hardeman, *Wilderness Calling*, p. 247.
606 Hardeman, "Bushwhacker Activity on the Western Border," p. 269.
607 United States War Department, Series I, Vol. 13, pp. 316–317.
608 Hamilton, Records of the Town of Arrow Rock.
609 1881 *History of Saline County, Missouri*, p. 312.

610 Barnhill, p. 17.
611 Hamilton, Records of the Town of Arrow Rock.
612 Date on tombstone at Sappington Cemetery SHS.
613 1881 *History of Saline County, Missouri*, p. 320.
614 *Ibid.*
615 United States War Department Series I, Vol. 34, Part IV, p. 471.
616 *Ibid.*, p. 52.
617 Rainey, p. 33.
618 United States War Department, Series I, Vol. 41, Part II, p. 336.
619 1881 *History of Saline County, Missouri*, p. 316.
620 Rainey, p. 33.
621 *Ibid.*
622 United States War Department, Series I, Vol. 41, Part 1, p. 220.
623 *Ibid.*
624 1881 *History of Saline County, Missouri*, p. 306.
625 *Ibid.*
626 *Ibid*, p. 307.
627 *Ibid.*
628 United States War Department, Series I, Vol. 41, Part 1, p. 220.
629 Pickard, Saline County MOGen Web Project.
630 Hardeman, "Bushwhacker Activity on the Missouri Border" pp. 270–271.
631 1881 *History of Saline County, Missouri*, pp. 306–307, 474.
632 Denny and Lay web sites.
633 United States War Department, United States War Dept., Series I, Vol. 48 Part II, p. 287.
634 Rainey, pp. 86–87.
635 Barnhill, p. 22.
636 Rainey, p. 62. Tableaux were "living pictures" in which a group would strike a pose in costume to represent historical, dramatic or classical events.
637 Rainey, p. 19.
638 Kremer, "Life in Post-Civil War Missouri."
639 1881 *History of Saline County, Missouri*, p. 376.
640 Rainey, p. 20.
641 *Ibid.*
642 *Ibid.* pp. 20–21.
643 1881 *History of Saline County, Missouri*, p. 376.
644 Hamilton, Records of the Town of Arrow Rock.
645 Rainey, pp. 33–34.
646 *Ibid.*, p. 34.
647 Hamilton, 1973, p. 3.
648 Rainey, p. 34.
649 Columbia, Missouri *Statesman*, SHSM.
650 Kennedy, *Arrow Rock, Missouri, and Thereabouts*, pp. 37–38.
651 *Ibid.*, p. 74.
652 1881 *History of Saline County, Missouri*, p. 383.
653 Kremer, "Life in Post-Civil War Missouri."
654 Kennedy, *Arrow Rock, Missouri, and Thereabouts*, p. 615.
655 *Ibid.*, p. 31. *Saline County Progress*, September 11, 1868.
656 Hamilton, Records of the Town of Arrow Rock.
657 *Ibid.*
658 van Ravenswaay, p. 20.
659 Boonville *Weekly Eagle*, January 3, 1873, Arrow Rock SHS transcript.
660 *Saline County Progress*, January 1, 1873, Arrow Rock SHS transcript.
661 *Ibid.*

662   *Ibid.*, "Sack" may have been "Zack" referring to Zack Bush.
663   *Ibid.*
664   Boonville *Weekly Eagle*, January 31, 1873, ARSHS transcript.
665   *Ibid.*
666   *Ibid.*
667   *Ibid.*
668   Jefferson City *The Peoples Tribune*, February 12, 1873, ARSHS transcript.
669   Hamilton, Records of the Town of Arrow Rock.
670   Rainey, pp. 83–84.
671   Kremer, "Life in Post-Civil War Missouri."
672   Kremer and Hoaglin, pp. 4–5.
673   Pennytown Historical Marker.
674   *Ibid.*
675   Noble.
676   *Ibid.*
677   Kennedy, *Arrow Rock, Missouri, and Thereabouts*, pp. 14–15.
678   Kremer and Hoaglin, p. 14.
679   *Ibid.*
680   van Ravenswaay, p. 20.
681   *Ibid*, p. 21
682   Arrow Rock *Statesman*, August, 23, 1912, Arrow Rock SHS.
683   *Ibid.*
684   Report of the Board of Managers of Arrow Rock Tavern, October 5, 1937, Arrow Rock SHS file copy.
685   *Ibid.*
686   Friends of Arrow Rock, Inc., 40th Anniversary Celebration Program, 1999.
687   *Ibid.*
688   *Ibid.*

Archival Sources

Arrow Rock State Historic Site, Arrow Rock, Missouri. (ARSHS)

Friends of Arrow Rock, Inc., Arrow Rock, Missouri. (FAR)

Joint Collections, State Historical Society of Missouri and Western Historical Manuscript Collection, Columbia, Missouri. (SHSM — WHMC)

Missouri Historical Society, St. Louis, Missouri. (MHS)

Bibliography

A

American Indian History From Prehistory to the Nineteenth Century Relating to Regional St. Louis (Missouri and Illinois). Http://www.usgennet.org/usa/mo/- county/stlouis/native/indian.html.

"Arrow Rock Ferry Account 1852–1853." Missouri History Not Found in Textbooks. *Missouri Historical Review* (MHR) 42:99 (October, 1947).

Arrow Rock State Historic Site Museum Exhibits Plan. 1993.

Atherton, Lewis. *The Frontier Merchant in Mid-America*. Columbia: University of Missouri Press, 1971.

B

Babcock, Rufus, ed. *Forty Years of Pioneer Life: Memoir of John Mason Peck D.D.* Carbondale and Edwardsville: Southern Illinois University Press, 1965.

Barnhill, Frank Clifton. *History of Freemasonry in Saline County*. Missouri Lodge of Research, 1956.

Barry, Louise. *The Beginning of the West*. Topeka: Kansas State Historical Society, 1972.

Bartels, Carolyn M. *Missouri Civil War Engagements*. Lexington, Missouri: Two Trails Publishing, 2000.

Baumann, Timothy E. "'Because That's Where My Roots Are:' Searching for Patterns of African-American Ethnicity in Arrow Rock, Missouri." Ph.D. diss. University of Tennessee-Knoxville, 2001.

Baumann, Timothy E., Ph.D. and Brett Rogers and J. Alex Miller. "Oak Grove: A Plantation Study in Missouri's Little Dixie." Paper presented at the Midwest Archaeological Conference in Milwaukee, Wisconsin, October 17–19, 2003.

Beachum, Larry M. *William Becknell: Father of the Santa Fe Trail*. University of Texas at El Paso: Texas Western Press, 1982.

Benson, Maxine, ed. *From Pittsburgh to the Rocky Mountains: Major Stephen Long's Expedition.* Golden, Colorado: Fulcrum, Inc., 1988.

Biggs, Paul. *The Most Historic Spot in Missouri: Old Tavern Built 1830.* Arrow Rock, 1927.

Blaine, Martha Royce. *The Ioway Indians.* Norman: University of Oklahoma Press, 1979.

Bloch, E. Maurice. *The Paintings of George Caleb Bingham: A Catalogue Raisonné.* Columbia: University of Missouri Press, 1986.

Bowen, Elbert R. "The Circus in Early Rural Missouri." *Missouri Historical Review* (MHR) 42 :1–17.

Bradbury, John. *Travels in the Interior of America in the Years 1809, 1810, and 1811.* London: Sherwood, Neely and Jones, 1819. Library of the Fur Trade Historical Source Documents. http://www.xmission.com/~drudy/mtman/html/bradbury.html.

Breckenridge, Henry Marie. *Views of Louisiana, Together with a Journal of a Voyage Up the Missouri River, 1811.* Pittsburgh: Cramer, Spear and Eichbaum, 1814. Alexander Street Press in collaboration with the University of Chicago. http://www.alexanderstreet2.com/EENALive/eena.toc.sources.html.

Bryan, William S., and Robert Rose. *A History of the Pioneer Families of Missouri.* St. Louis: Bryan, Brand and Co., 1876.

Burge, Mary. "Notes on Arrow Rock Churches taken 1970-1999." Friends of Arrow Rock, Inc. (unpublished)

Burns, Louis. *Osage Indian Bands and Clans.* Fallbrook, California: Ciga Press, 1984.

Burns, Louis. *Osage Indian Customs and Myths.* Fallbrook, California: Ciga Press, 1984.

Burns, Louis. *The History of the Osage People.* Fallbrook, California: Ciga Press, 1989.

C

Caldwell, Dorothy J. *Missouri's National Historic Landmarks: Village of Arrow Rock and George Caleb Bingham Home.* Reprint by Friends of Arrow Rock, Inc., 1968.

Christ-Janer, Albert. *George Caleb Bingham of Missouri, The Story of an Artist.* New York: Dodd, Mead & Company, 1940.

Christensen, Lawrence O., William E. Foley, Gary R. Kremer, and Kenneth Winn, eds. *Dictionary of Missouri Biography.* Columbia: University of Missouri Press, 1999.

Clokey, Richard. *William H. Ashley, Enterprise and Politics in the Trans-Mississippi West.* Norman: University of Oklahoma Press, 1990.

Coues, Elliott, ed. *History of the Expedition under the Command of Lewis and Clark.* 4 vols. 1893. Reprint. New York: Dover Publications, 1964.

Coyner, David H. *The Lost Trappers; A Collection of Interesting Scenes and Events in the Rocky Mountains; Together With a Short Description of California: Also Some Account of the Fur Trade.* Cincinnati: E.D. Truman, Publisher, 1850.

Crighton, John C. *Stephens, A Story of Educational Innovation*. Columbia, Missouri: American Press, 1970.

D

David Rumsey Map Collection, www.rumsey.com.

Denny, James. "The Battle of Glasgow Missouri." Missouri Civil War Roundtable. http://www.mmcwrt.org/2000/default0009.htm.

Dickey, Michael. "The Osage Trading House at the Arrow Rock." A paper presented at the War of 1812 in the West Symposium, Arrow Rock State Historic Site, 1998.

Dickey, Michael. "George Caleb Bingham, A Synopsis." Arrow Rock State Historic Site Interpretive Files, 2000.

Dickey, Michael. "Specie, Sweat and Survival: the Economic Impact of the Santa Fe Trade on Missouri." A paper presented at the National Santa Fe Trail Symposium, Kansas City, Missouri, 2003.

Duffus, R.L. The Santa Fe Trail. New York: Tudor Publishing, 1943.

Dyer, Robert. "A Brief History of Steamboating on the Missouri River with an Emphasis on the Boonslick Region." Boonslick Heritage 5 (June 1997), pp.4–13. http://members.tripod.com/~Write4801/docs/moboats.html.

E

Eastham, Harry A. "Arrow Rock Cemetery Records." Compiled for Saline County Genealogy. www.rootsweb.com/~mosaline/5tombstones/arrowrock.html.

"Expedition Against Indians of Western Missouri in 1814." Missouri History Not Found in Textbooks. *Missouri Historical Review* (MHR) 32: pp.122–123 (October, 1937).

F

Foley, William. *A History of Missouri, 1673–1820*. Columbia: University of Missouri Press, 1971.

Forry, Richard R. "Arrow Rock Chronology." 1976.

Forry, Richard R. "Arrow Rock State Historic Site Conceptual Development Plan 1984." Arrow Rock: Division of State Parks, 1984.

Forry, Richard R. "Sappington Cemetery State Historic Site Conceptual Development Plan." Arrow Rock: Division of State Parks, 1984.

Forry, Richard R. "Boone's Lick State Historic Site Conceptual Development Plan." Arrow Rock: Division of State Parks, 1985.

Forry, Richard R. "Joseph Huston Chronology." 1985.

Friends of Arrow Rock, Inc. "Excerpts From the Arrow Rock Enterprise." 1987.

Friends of Arrow Rock, Inc. "40th Anniversary Celebration Program." 1999.

Friends of Arrow Rock, Inc. "Sappington Negro Cemetery." 2001. (unpublished)

Fuenfhausen, Gary Gene. "The Cotton Culture of Missouri's Little Dixie." *Midwest Open Air Museums Magazine* 22 (2001).

Fun & Games of Long Ago. Scotia: *American Review*, 1973.

Furse, O.L. *Four Score Rural Years*. Austin, Texas: Eakin Publications, 1983.

G
_____

Garrard, Lewis H. *Wah-to-yah and the Taos Trail*. Norman: University of Oklahoma Press, 1979.

Gregg, Josiah. *The Commerce of the Prairies*. Norman: University of Oklahoma Press, 1954.

Gregg, Kate L., ed. *Westward With Dragoons: the Journal of William Clark on His Expedition to Establish Fort Osage, August 25 to September 22, 1808*. Fulton, Missouri: The Ovid Bell Press, 1937.

Gregg, Kate L. "The War of 1812 on the Missouri Frontier Parts I, II, and III." *Missouri Historical Review* (MHR) 33 (1938).

Gregg, Kate L. ed. *The Road to Santa Fe: The Journal and Diaries of George Champlin Sibley*. Albuquerque: University of New Mexico Press, 1952.

Greifenstein, Charles. "Benjamin Rush, Man of Many Parts." *We Proceeded On* (May, 2002).

Griffith, Cecil R. *The Missouri River: The River Rat's Guide to Missouri River History and Folklore*. Leawood, KS. 1974.

Guitar, Sarah and Floyd C. Shoemaker, eds. *The Messages and Proclamations of the Governors of the State of Missouri, Vol. VII*. Columbia: State Historical Society of Missouri, 1926.

H
_____

Hafen, LeRoy R. ed. *The Mountain Men and the Fur Trade of the Far West*. Glendale, California: Arthur Clark Co., 1969.

Hagin, William T. *The Sac and Fox Indians*. Norman: University of Oklahoma Press, 1958.

Hall, Thomas B., Jr. "Two Missouri Gunsmiths of the Boonslick Area." *Muzzle Blasts*, magazine of the National Muzzle Loading Rifle Association, July, 1969.

Hall, Thomas B., Jr., M.D. and Thomas B. Hall III, M.D. *Dr. John Sappington of Saline County, Missouri 1776–1856*. The Friends of Arrow Rock, Inc., second edition, 1986.

Hall, Thomas B., Jr., M.D. and Thomas B. Hall III, M.D. *Medicine on the Santa Fe Trail*. Friends of Arrow Rock, Inc., second edition, 1987.

Hall, Thomas B. III. "Complete Descriptions of the Historic Weapons in the Christopher Collection of Early Missouri Firearms." Friends of Arrow Rock, Inc., May, 1990.

Hall, Thomas B. III. "Wallace Gusler on the Development of the American Long Rifle: A Summary." Friends of Arrow Rock, Inc., September, 2000.

Hamilton, Jean Tyree. "Records of the Town of Arrow Rock, 1840–1875." Transcribed 1960, Arrow Rock State Historic Site Library.

Hamilton, Jean Tyree. *Arrow Rock: Where Wheels Started West.* Friends of Arrow Rock, Inc., 1963.

Hamilton, Jean Tyree. Missouri Archeological Society newsletter No. 274, October, 1973.

Hardeman, Nicholas P. "Bushwhacker Activity on the Missouri Border." *Missouri Historical Review* (MHR) 58: 265–277 (April, 1964).

Hardeman, Nicholas P. *Wilderness Calling: The Hardeman Family in the American Westward Movement 1750–1900.* Knoxville: University of Tennessee Press, 1977.

Harper, Linda and Richard R. Forry. "Multiple Resource Nomination, National Register of Historic Places." Arrow Rock, Missouri, 1976.

History of Howard & Cooper Counties. St. Louis: National Historical Publishing Company, 1883.

History of Saline County, Missouri. St Louis: Missouri Historical Publishing Company, 1881.

Hurt, Douglas R. "Seeking Fortune in the Promised Land: Settling the Boon's Lick Country, 1808–1825." *Gateway Heritage* (Summer, 1992).

Huston, John Percy. "The Old Tavern at Arrow Rock." An address by J. P. Huston, Marshall, 1914.

I
_____

Illustrated Atlas Map of Saline County, MO. St. Louis: Missouri Publishing Company, 1876.

J
_____

Jones, Landon Y. "Iron Will." *Smithsonian Magazine* (August, 2002).

K
_____

Kennedy, Catherine Waters. *Arrow Rock News Commerce & Comments* as excerpted from the *Weekly Democrat*, Marshall, Missouri, January 15, 1858 to July 31, 1861. Arrow Rock State Historic Site Library. (unpublished)

Kennedy, Catherine Waters. *Arrow Rock, Missouri, and Thereabouts*, selected items published by the *Saline County Progress* Newspaper, January 3, 1868 to December 30, 1870. Arrow Rock State Historic Site Library. (unpublished)

Kennedy, Catherine Waters. Glasgow Missouri, Items from the Glasgow *Weekly Times*, October 5, 1848 to December 25, 1851. Arrow Rock State Historic Site Library. (unpublished)

Kochan, James L. *Men at Arms, The United States Army 1812–1815.* Oxford, England: Osprey Military, 2000.

Kremer, Gary R. *James Milton Turner and the Promise of America: the Public Life of a Post-Civil War Black Leader.* Columbia: University of Missouri Press, 1991.

Kremer, Gary R. and Antonio F. Holland. *Missouri's Black Heritage.* Columbia: University of Missouri Press, 1993.

Kremer, Gary R. and Amber M. Hoaglin. "Arrow Rock's African-American History: Giving Voice to an Unheard Past." William Woods University, Fulton, Missouri, 1998.

Kremer, Gary R. "Life in Post-Civil War Missouri." A paper presented to the Friends of Arrow Rock, Inc., September, 2000.

L
_____

Lay, William. *Early Boone's Lick Indian Events.* Transcribed from the Lyman Copeland Draper Manuscripts, Rolls 6-S, 30-C and S. Wisconsin Historical Society, Madison, Wisconsin. Arrow Rock State Historic Site Library. (unpublished)

Lay, William. *Notes on Missouri River Steam Boats from the Missouri Intelligencer and Boonslick Advertiser.* Arrow Rock State Historic Site Library. (unpublished)

Lay, William. *Notes on the Santa Fe Trail from the Missouri Intelligencer.* Arrow Rock State Historic Site Library. (unpublished)

Lay, William. Additional Notes on the Battle of Glasgow. Missouri Civil War Roundtable. http://www.mmcwrt.org/2000/default0009.htm.

Leopard, Buell and Floyd Shoemaker, eds. *The Messages and Proclamations of the Governors of Missouri, Vols. I., II & III.* Columbia: State Historical Society of Missouri, 1922.

"Letter of Agreement; Marmaduke, Sappington & McMahan Oct. 30, 1827." Western Historical Manuscript Collection-State Historical Society of Missouri, Columbia, Missouri. (SHSM-WHMC)

"Letter of Mathias Bingham to Amanda (Bingham) Barnes, January 2, 1858." Bingham Family papers, Collection 998. (SHSM-WHMC)

"Letter of Mrs. Walter Raleigh Lenoir, 1835." Missouri State Historical Society-Western Manuscript Collection, St. Louis, Missouri. (MSHS-WMC) Transcript in Arrow Rock SHS Library.

"Letter of W.A. Beeding to Norman Lackland, June 1, 1847." (MHS)

Lottinville, Savoie, ed., and W. Robert Nitke, translator. *Duke Paul of Wurttemburg, Travels in North America 1822–1824.* Norman: University of Oklahoma Pres, 1973.

M
_____

Magoffin, Susan Shelby. *Down the Santa Fe Trail and Into Mexico.* New Haven: Yale University Press, 1962.

"Manuel Alvarez Papers, New Mexico State Records Center and Archives, Santa Fe, New Mexico." http://elibrary.unm.edu/oanm/NmAr/nmar%231960-001/nmar%231960-001_m8.html.

March, David. *History of Missouri Vol. I and Vol. II.* New York: Lewis Historical Publishing, 1967.

Mathews, John Joseph. *The Osage, Children of the Middle Waters.* Norman: University of Oklahoma Press, 1961.

McCandless, Perry. *A History of Missouri, Vol. II, 1820–1860.* Columbia: University of Missouri Press, 1971.

McDaniel, Lynn, ed. *Boonslick Sketches.* Boonville, Missouri: Boonslick Historical Society, 1976.

McDermott, John Francis. *George Caleb Bingham, River Portraitist*. Norman: University of Oklahoma Press, 1959.

"Memorial of the State of Missouri in Relation to Indian Depredations Upon the Citizens of That State, Washington, D.C., 1825." Missouri Historical Society, St. Louis, Missouri.

Missouri Society, Daughters of the American Revolution. "Chapter House-Former Home of Dr. Matthew Walton Hall, Pioneer Physician of Arrow Rock, Missouri." 1963.

Missouri State Archives, Saline County web site. www.sos.mo.gov/archives/resources/county/croll1.asp.

Mitchell, Beth and Lester Turley, et al. "Turley Family Records." Turley Family Historical Research Association, 1981.

Monaghan, Jay. *Civil War on the Western Border 1854–1865*. Lincoln: University of Nebraska Press, 1955.

Moulton, Gary E. ed. *The Journals of the Lewis & Clark Expedition August 30, 1803–August 24, 1804, Vol. 2*. Lincoln: University of Nebraska Press, 1986.

N

Napton, W. B. [Jr.]. *Over the Santa Fé Trail in 1857*. Kansas City, MO: Franklin Hudson Publishing Co., 1905. Reprint by the Friends of Arrow Rock, Inc., 1991; Jean Tyree Hamilton, editor.

Napton, William Barclay, Jr. *Past and Present of Saline County Missouri*. Indianapolis and Chicago: B. F. Bowen & Company, 1910.

National Historic Landmarks Program. "George Caleb Bingham House." National Parks Service web site.; http://tps.cr.nps.gov/nhl/detail.cfm?ResourceId=294&ResourceType=Building.

"New Light on Dates of Arrow Rock Buildings." Missouri History Not Found in Textbooks. *Missouri Historical Review* (MHR) 33: 464 (April, 1939).

Noble, David W. *The Progressive Mind, 1890–1917*. Chicago: Rand McNally & Company.

Norall, Frank. *Bourgmont, Explorer of the Missouri 1698–1725*. Lincoln: University of Nebraska Press, 1988.

"Notes/Letters Written by J. Locke Hardeman, Arrow Rock, to Nathaniel B. Tucker, Williamsburg, Virginia, December 15, 1845." (WHMC-SHSM)

P

Parkman, Francis, Jr. *The Oregon Trail*. New York: Caxton House, 1847.

Parsons, Pam and Habernal, Teresa. "A History of Brown's Chapel Free Will Baptist Church." Friends of Arrow Rock, Inc., 1999.

Phillips, Christopher. *Missouri's Confederate, Claiborne Fox Jackson and the Creation of Southern Identity in the Border West*. Columbia: University of Missouri Press, 2000.

Pickard, Kevin. Saline County MOGen Web Project. http://www.rootsweb.com/~mosaline/familyhistories/piper.html.

R
_____

RPH Laboratory Medicine. 1998–2002. http://www.rph.wa.gov.au/labs/haem/malaria/history.html.

Rainey, Thomas C. *Along the Old Trail, Pioneer Sketches of Arrow Rock and Vicinity.* Reprint of 1914 edition by the Friends of Arrow Rock, Inc., 1971.

Rathbone, Perry T., ed. *Westward the Way.* City Art Museum of St. Louis, Von Hoffman Press, Inc., 1954.

Read, Allan Walker. "Attitude Towards Missouri Speech." *Missouri Historical Review* (MHR) 19: 269.

"Report of the Board of Managers of Arrow Rock Tavern October 5, 1937." Arrow Rock SHS file copy.

Riley, Eula Gladys. "John Sappington, Doctor and Philanthropist." Submitted in partial fulfillment of the requirements for the degree of Master of Arts, University of Missouri, Columbia, 1942.

Rusk, Fern Helen. *George Caleb Bingham the Missouri Artist.* Jefferson City, Missouri: Hugh Stephens Co., 1917.

S
_____

Sappington, Dr. John. *The Theory and Treatment of Fevers, Revised and Corrected by Ferdinando Stith, M.D.* Arrow Rock, 1844. Reprint by the Friends of Arrow Rock, Inc., 1971.

Shapiro, Michael Edward. *George Caleb Bingham.* National Museum of American Art, Smithsonian Institution, New York: Harry N. Abrams Inc., 1993.

"Sibley, George C. to William Clark, November 28, 1813." Territorial Papers XIV: 713–714. (photographic copy in Arrow Rock SHS files)

Spaulding, George F., ed. *On the Western Tour With Washington Irving, The Journals and Letter of Count de Pourtales.* Norman: University of Oklahoma Press, 1968.

Stubbs, Sue. "The Life and Times of John Sites." Excerpts from a talk delivered to the Friends of Arrow Rock, Inc., 2000.

Sunder, John E. "The Early Telegraph in Rural Missouri, 1847–1859." *Missouri Historical Review* (MHR) 51: pp. 42–43.

T
_____

Thorp, Judge Joseph. *Early Days in the West, Along the Missouri One Hundred Years Ago.* Liberty, Missouri, 1924. Transcribed by William Lay.

Thwaites, Reuben Gold, ed. Maximilian, Prince Zu Wied-Nuewied, Alexander Philipp. *Early Western Travels, Vol. 22*: Part I of Maximilian, Prince of Wied's Travels in the Interior of North America, 1832–1834. Cleveland: A.H. Clark Co., 1906. Alexander Street Press in collaboration with the University of Chicago. http://www.alexanderstreet2.com/EENALive/eena.toc.sources.html.

U

United States War Department. *The War of the Rebellion: a Compilation of the Official Records of the Union and Confederate Armies.* Washington, D.C., 1880–1901. Cornell University, Making of America. http://cdl.library.cornell.edu/moa/browse.monographs/waro.html.

V

van Ravenswaay, Charles. *Arrow Rock: The Story of a Town, Its People and Its Tavern.* Bulletin of the Missouri Historical Society, April, 1959.

von Sachsen-Altenburg, Hans and Robert L. Dyer. *Duke Paul of Wuerttemberg on the Missouri Frontier 1823, 1830 and 1851.* Boonville, Missouri: Pekitanoui Publications, 1998.

W

Weatherford, Hardin. *A Treatise on Cholera.* Louisville, Kentucky, 1833. American Memory, The Library of Congress. http://memory.loc.gov/ammem/ammemhome.html.

William Ashley Burial Ground. www.rootsweb.com/~mocooper/Cemeteries/WILLIAM_ASHLEY-BURIAL_GROUND.

Wilson, Michael R. "Laws of the State of Missouri Revised and Digested by Authority of the General Assembly, 21 February 1825, The Missouri Militia 1821–1832." Transcribed November 19, 1999.

Windell, Marie George. "Westward Along the Boone's Lick Trail in 1826. The Diary of Colonel John Glover." *Missouri Historical Review* (MHR) 39: pp. 184–199.

Index

Photographs and illustrations are noted in **boldface**.

Photographs and illustrations are noted in **boldface**.

Photographs and illustrations are noted in **boldface**.

Photographs and illustrations are noted in **boldface**.

Photographs and illustrations are noted in **boldface**.

Photographs and illustrations are noted in **boldface**.